BIBLICAL ANATOLIA
FROM GENESIS TO THE COUNCILS

This publication was made possible through
the support provided by the İstanbul Chamber of Commerce
to commemorate the role played by Anatolia in the development of Christianity.

BIBLICAL ANATOLIA

FROM GENESIS TO THE COUNCILS

Fatih Cimok

A TURİZM YAYINLARI

FRONT COVER
Mt Ararat. Looking east.

BACK COVER
Noah's ark. Manuscript painting. Detail. Late sixteenth century. *Zübdetü't Tevarih,* the 'Legendary Chronicle of the Prophets' Lives'. Museum of Turkish and Islamic Arts. İstanbul.

TITLE PAGE
Cross and biblical inscription from the rock-cut eastern entrance of Anazarbus (Anavarza). Sixth century CE. In Greek it is the beginning of the Psalm 46: 'God is our refuge and our strength, an ever-present help in distress.'

EDITOR
Takeko Harada

PICTURES
Archives of A Turizm Yayınları

First printing June 2000

ISBN 975-7199-25-7

Copyright © A Turizm Yayınları

PUBLISHERS
A Turizm Yayınları Ltd Şti
Şifa Hamamı Sokak 18,
Sultanahmet, İstanbul 34400, Turkey
Tel: (0212) 516 24 97 Fax: (0212) 516 41 65
e-mail: aturizm @ superonline.com

CONTENTS

'Lord, receive the offering of those whose names Thou knowest.'
Dedicatory inscription in Greek from the mosaic floor of a church from Antioch on the Orontes.
First half of the sixth century CE. Hatay Archaeological Museum. Antakya.

Preface

This book is intended to serve as a companion to the general reader, before, during or after his visit to Turkey. To achieve this objective effort has been spent to construct each chapter as a compact reading piece, almost independent of the other sections and as if the reader has almost no or little information about the subject. Thus some repetitions become indispensable. Similar effort has been spent to keep the texts as unacademic as possible.

The protohistorical narrative of the Bible begins in about the first half of the second millennium with Abraham's journey from Ur of the Chaldeans to Canaan through Haran and ends with the penetration of the Israelites into the Promised Land in the twelfth century BCE and the subsequent establishment of the United Monarchy. The historical section covers the divided monarchies of north (Israel) and south (Judah) and ends with the establishment of the independent Hasmonean kingdom in the middle of the second century BCE. The New Testament begins with the coming of Christianity and terminates at the end of the first century CE with the Revelation of the Apostle John at Patmos. A large number of the nations, empires, events and places encountered in this long narrative of about two millennia, no matter if they are just folktales or actual events, also concern Anatolia. In this book, in addition to these, in order to give to the reader a more complete picture of the role Anatolia played in the formation of present-day Christianity, some topics which are not mentioned in the Bible, such as Edessa (Urfa) or the Ecumenical Councils, are also included.

In dealing with the Old Testament narrative a flexible plan of key references and a brief history of the subject in relation to Anatolia and Palestine has been followed. For the sites mentioned in the New Testament, only their early Christian history has been dealt with.

The dates used in the book are often approximate and this approximation increases for the earlier periods. In the spelling of ancient names their most popular forms among non-academics, without any attempt at consistency between their Greek or Latinized forms, have been used. Also, instead of Asia Minor, Anatolia, the name of the region which derives from the Greek noun *anatole*, in the sense of the East or Orient, the place where the sun rises, has been preferred.

HISTORICAL INTRODUCTION

Palestine, which was in the past called the land of Canaan, is a small piece of soil squeezed between Anatolia, Syria and Mesopotamia and Egypt. Its history from about the middle of the second millennium BCE to the Common Era coincides not only with the events told in the Bible but also with great social and economic changes such as the discovery of the alphabetic script, the replacement of bronze with iron, the invention of coinage, the rise and death of Greek *polis,* and suchlike: innovations or achievements which played important roles in man's attainment to the present-day culture.

The traditional view holds that the Patriarchal era, which covers the lives of Abraham, Isaac, Jacob and Joseph came to an end in about the middle of the fifteenth century BCE. About this time Egypt was ruled by pharaohs of the New Kingdom, Syria and northern Mesopotamia by Mitanni, precariously situated at the centre, and Anatolia by the Hittites. Assyrians beyond the Euphrates displayed their power sporadically but had not yet become the war machine of the Near East as the Neo-Assyrian empire. Babylonia after the fall of the Old Babylonian empire suffered a temporary set-back during which the Kassite kings of Babylon did not have any territorial ambitions. It was to rise again towards the end of the seventh century BCE as the Neo-Babylonian empire. Beyond the Aegean was Ahhiyawa, or the Mycenaeans, whose king was regarded by the Great King of Hittites as his equal. As a result of the cuneiform tablets and other archaeological material, which is constantly brought to light by excavations, our information about the ancient history of these countries grows every day. These empires are known to have made more wars to subdue the small states in and around their realms than with each other. When they were not sure of each other's strength they seem to have preferred to establish lasting commercial and diplomatic relations from which they would mutually benefit. The archives which kept the records of their diplomatic relations tell us that they signed agreements, formed coalitions, married each other's daughters, exchanged ambassadors, physicians (magicians), gifts and letters. Although they spoke different tongues they corresponded in the same international language and writing: the Akkadian cuneiform. This was a system of signs which showed syllables and was applied by a sharpened reed on a flattened clay piece which was later baked. Each ruler kept an archive with Akkadian-speaking scribes who translated his letters dictated in the native tongue into Akkadian and did the same for the answers received. The Hattusa archives and Amarna Letters are regarded among the finest of these records.

During the latter part of the Late Bronze Age from 1500 to 1200 BCE Palestine was within the political sphere of the Egyptians who looked at it as their own soil.

(opposite) Dedication stone of the church of the Apostles. Anazarbus (Anavarza). First half of the sixth century CE. The wreath encloses a cross with Alpha and Omega, the first and last letters of the Greek alphabet signifying God's eternity and infinitude (Rv 1:8; 21:6) or Christ's (Rv 22:13).

Relief with musicians. End of the eighth century BCE. Karatepe (Azitiwataya). Four musicians are seen playing the most popular instruments in the ancient Near East: a frame drum, harp, lyre and a double-pipe. These instruments are frequently referred to in the Bible for example when Samuel (1 Sm 10:5) tells Saul to look for a particular sign of his divine election as the first king of Israel as he entered the garrison of the Philistines he says he 'will meet a band of prophets, in a prophetic state, coming down from the high place preceded by lyres, tambourines, flutes and harps.'

After the Kadesh treaty Rameses II invited Hattusili III to visit his country saying 'I will go (ahead) into Canaan, to meet my Brother.' It was split among a number of petty kingdoms each controlling a hinterland which was usually settled by pastoral nomads. Its population, referred to as Canaanites, was predominantly Amorite[1] and created a fairly homogeneous culture throughout the Levant. Canaan's size and geography did not allow its city-states to unite and create a single strong kingdom which could stand against Egypt. The Egyptian garrisons planted among the Canaanite settlements were responsible for the collection of taxes and tributes. Throughout their early history, unless they formed a temporary loose confederation, jealous and suspicious of each other these Canaanite cities either coveted one or the other of the main powers around them or fought among themselves and thus were led by the events outside Palestine.

During the invasion of the Sea Peoples around 1190 BCE both Anatolia and Palestine suffered the same fate. However, in Anatolia, while the downfall of the Hittites was followed by a 400-year set-back known as the Dark Ages, in Palestine the disappearance of Egyptian hegemony prepared the conditions for the Israelites to infiltrate the Promised Land and to found the polity which was later called the

[1] Akkadian *amurru*, or 'western'. Semitic-speaking tribes who began migrating in all directions from their home in north Arabia and the Syrian desert towards the end of the third millennium.

Gezer Calendar. 925 BCE. İstanbul Archaeological Museum. It consists of a small flat piece of limestone, incised with a concordance table harmonizing the twelve lunations with the periods of the agricultural year and thought to have been a school exercise, to be learnt by heart. The inscription is regarded as one of the most ancient samples of surviving Hebrew writing dating back to the end of the United Monarchy.

United Monarchy. After the fall of the Hittite empire in Anatolia, its material culture survived in the architecture and writing of the principalities of the southeastern highlands. Carchemish, Milid (Malatya), Gurgum-Marqasi (Maraş), Samal (Zincirli) and Azitiwataya (Karatepe) were the most important of these Neo-Hittite kingdoms. Despite the existence of some Hittite characteristics these city-kingdoms were dominated by the Aramaic culture which was later supplemented by some Assyrian elements. In Canaan this period coincides with the rise of Phoenicia (Byblos, Sidon and Tyre) and with the reigns of Saul, David and Solomon. Before long, additional powers such as Urartu, the Lydians and Phrygians, Tabal to the north of the Taurus and Que (Cilician plain) would emerge in the rest of Anatolia and fill the political gap created by the absence of the Hittites. In northern Mesopotamia and Syria, Mitanni was replaced by Assyria. In southern Mesopotamia Babylonia waited to re-emerge. Ultimately Assyria would outlive all of these powers and even capture Egypt. The arrival of the Cimmerians (the biblical Gomer) and the Scythians (the biblical Ashkenaz) from the north of the Caucasus made the picture of the Near East in the eighth to seventh century BCE more complicated. Almost all of these kingdoms or nations are mentioned in the Bible and connected with the ethno-geographical history of Anatolia.

After the sixth century BCE the history of Anatolia and Palestine is easier to follow because they shared the same fate: both countries became a part of the Medio-Persian empire for about two centuries and both of them felt the political and cultural impact of the conquest of Alexander the Great and the rule of the successor Hellenistic monarchies, the Ptolemies and the Seleucids, for about another two hundred years. The ascendancy of the Aramaic language and script, which had replaced the Akkadian cuneiform by the eighth century BCE, lasted until the establishment of these Hellenistic kingdoms. In the third century Greek began gradually to take the place of both Aramaic and the local tongues as the common language, an event which would serve the spread of the gospel in the Gentile world. The roots of the Imperial cult which would later become the stumbling block for Christianity and cause persecutions were also planted in the Hellenistic era.

In the second century BCE the Romans penetrated into Anatolia and shortly afterwards Palestine. Consequently during the last epoch of biblical history Anatolia and Palestine again found themselves under the hegemony of the same power. The direct impact of the Roman existence in Anatolia and Palestine would however, not be seen in the Old Testament but the New Testament. Although it was born in the tiny world of Judea, Christianity would win its fight against both paganism and Judaism to a large extent in the Greco-Roman world of Anatolia from the Tigris to the Aegean Sea and become ultimately first the official and later on the exclusive religion of the later Roman empire by the end of the fourth century CE.

RIVERS OF EDEN

The name of the third river is the Tigris; it is the one that flows east of Asshur. The fourth river is the Euphrates (Gn 2:14).

In Genesis (2:14) the Tigris and the Euphrates are two[1] of the branches of the river which flows through the Garden of Eden. To the Israelites the Euphrates was known as *Perath* (Akkadian *Purattu*). The Hittites called it *Mala* or *Purana*. In the Bible it is often referred to just as 'the River' or 'the Great River' (Gn 15:18) to indicate the eastern boundary of the civilized world and the border of the Promised Land on this side. The river's present-day name is derived by the Greeks from *Ufratu,* its name in Old Persian.

In Hittite annals the Tigris was known as the *Aranzah* which is originally a Hurrian name. The river's name in Hebrew was *Hiddeqel* (AV) derived from the Akkadian *Idiglat*. In the Bible it is also referred to just as 'the River'. Its present-day name comes from the Old Persian *Tigra*.

Both of the rivers rise in eastern Anatolia, fed by the snow of its mountains, and in antiquity reached the Persian Gulf separately. Their branches penetrate into the mountains like a net, with ancient fortresses built where their deep gorges are fordable. The Euphrates is about 2800 km and the Tigris 2000. Although narrower than its sister the Tigris carries more water. Flowing south-wards as soon as it rises the Euphrates makes large curves across the country. This physical difference is remarked by Isaiah (27:1) when he says 'Leviathan the fleeing serpent, Leviathan the coiled serpent'. In the Sumerian creation myth the two rivers sprung from the eyes of the primeval Sumerian goddess Tiamat when she was killed by the god Marduk; 'the Tigris is her right eye, the Euphrates is her left eye.' Later Enki, the god of wisdom, filled the rivers with fish and appointed a deity

Personification of the river Tigris. Mosaic from Seleucia Pieria (Çevlik). First half of the second century CE. The Detroit Institute of Art. Detroit. Michigan.

[1] The other two branches, the Pishon and Gihon cannot be identified.

over each of them. Negligence of sacrifices before crossing the rivers would anger their gods and result in divine punishment.

Once they came out of the mountains into the north Syrian and Mesopotamian plains the rivers became the major water sources available for the armies or caravans which moved through the desert as well as the settled population. They have been the driving force in the creation of the Mesopotamian civilizations. In fact Mesopotamia[2] came into existence by the silt brought down by them and was the most fertile piece of land between the Indus and the Nile. Herodotus writing in the late fifth century BCE claims that the soil of Mesopotamia was more fertile[3] than that of Egypt. The functioning of these rivers as arteries of transportation and trade between north and south, enabled some of the desert settlements to become important trade centres with riverside wharfs, custom houses and harbour masters, guards and checkpoints. Although the northern highlands were settled earlier the people in the south, by managing the control of the water of the rivers and their branches, created an irrigation economy. The entrepots of such cities contained all of what Mesopotamia produced locally: wool, hides, cereals, textiles and bitumen and what it imported: gold, silver, tin, bronze and other metals, timber, ivory, lapis lazuli, perfumes and spices, oil and wine. In addition to rafts carrying armies or merchandise, Sumerian literature mentions rafts of logs from the 'cedar mountain' (the Amanus) floated down on the Euphrates like 'giant snakes.' To facilitate transportation and to make better use of the water the rivers were connected by irrigation canals. The earliest of the civilizations came into existence in the southernmost part of Mesopotamia where the Euphrates and Tigris join each other some 200 km from the Persian Gulf. Some of the most important cities of these civilizations were founded on these highways of water or their tributaries: Ur of the Chaldeans, Uruk (the biblical Erech), Babylon, Mari and Carchemish on the Euphrates, Nineveh, Nimrud (the biblical Calah) and Asshur on the Tigris.

Ancient literature and records contain fragmentary but interesting references to both rivers. As early as the third millennium the transportation upon them was mostly done by boats with a framework of branches with woven reeds and covered with animal hide. These vessels were known as 'turnips' and were rowed from bank to bank. Herodotus says that the boats which sailed down the Euphrates

---

[2] Greek *Mesopotamia*, or 'between the two rivers', is derived from either the Hebrew 'Aram Naharaim', or 'Syria of the rivers', or the term's Aramaic or Arabic equivalents.

[3] Although not to yield two- or three-hundredfold corn as Herodotus and Strabo claim.

were circular in shape and made of hide, each paddled by two men, and the biggest with a capacity of some fourteen tons. Every boat carried a live donkey — the larger ones several — and when they reached Babylon and the cargoes had been offered for sale, the boats were broken up, the frames and straw sold and the hides loaded on the donkeys' backs for the return journey. There was no wind to waft them upriver and it was not worth pulling empty rafts by animals or men. In the mid-nineteenth century Henry Austen Layard constructed two of the largest of such rafts known until then, each made of 600 inflated goat and sheepskins, for a 1,000 km journey from Nimrud to the mouth of the Tigris to carry a colossal statue of a bull and a lion, now in the British Museum. Lawrence of Arabia is also said to have made use of the current of the Euphrates to float down the reliefs he had dug up in Carchemish. In the third millennium BCE Sargon of Akkad, as a child, was cast into the current of the Euphrates by his mother. Hattusili I (1650-1620 BCE) boasted that he and his army crossed the river on foot. Egyptian annals mention that the pharaoh Tuthmosis III[4] (1479-1425 BCE) after raiding Palestine invaded Syria as far as Alalah (Tell Açana) and crossed the Euphrates. On reaching the bank of the river, the Egyptians, who were used the Nile's flowing 'upstream' from the south, were suprised to see that this river was flowing 'upstream' from the north. It is also from these annals that one for the first time hears the existence of elephants in the region. One of these animals broke loose near Carchemish and menaced the pharaoh. A soldier, however, saved him by slashing off the beast's trunk with his sword. A few hundred years later, the Assyrian king Tiglath-pileser I (1114-1076 BCE) boasted that he killed ten male elephants in the district of Haran and took their tusks and hides to his capital together with four more elephants which he had caught alive. In an inscription he left on the cliffs to the northeast of Diyarbakır he says 'I went to the source of the Tigris. I washed the weapon of Asshur there, where the water comes out.' The later shortage of ivory in Assyria at the end of the eighth century BCE is interpreted as a sign of the extinction of elephants in the region. The same king claims that he had to cross the Euphrates twenty-eight times in pursuit of the Aramean marauders, getting his soldiers across the river on inflated goatskin rafts, known today as 'kelek' (Akkadian *kalakku*). Ashurnasirpal (883-859 BCE) is another Assyrian potentate who has left us the

(opposite) Ancient Tigris-crossing at Eğil (Assyrian *Ingıla*) near Diyarbakır. To the left by the water is the remains of the rock to which the cables of an ancient suspension bridge were tied. On the right bank further away by the water is an Assyrian rock-cut tomb complex.

---

[4] The Egyptian hieroglyphic inscription on the obelisk in İstanbul, which came from Karnak, partly commemorates this expedition. The other three surviving obelisks of Tuthmosis III are in Rome, London and New York.

records of his hunts of wild boars and lions in the region of the upper Euphrates. The existence of lions in the beds of rushes by these rivers was recorded as late as the fourth century CE. His successor Shalmaneser III(858-824 BCE) decorated the gates of his palace at Balawat with bronze reliefs which showed his sacrifice and the carving of his image at the source of the Tigris where the originals have survived. The inscription of king Sarduri II (764-734 BCE) of Urartu in which he claims that he crossed the Euphrates when the river was calm, is now left in the water of the Karakaya dam.

The streams frequently flooded their banks by changing their courses and one of such disaster may have inspired the Mesopotamian flood epic. Although excavations have brought to light flood silt layers from various ancient sites in Mesopotamia, each one dates from a different period and there is as yet no evidence about a universal flood.

The fame of rivers in ancient human minds is echoed in the biblical narrative. The Judaistic and Christian interpretation of the Euphrates as the frontier between the earth and nether world is inspired by Babylonian mythology. When Isaiah (11:15) says 'The LORD[5] shall...wave his hand over the Euphrates in his fierce anger and shatter it into seven streamlets' so that the remnant of Israel in Assyria would return, he uses the word in this ancient sense. In Revelation (16:12) John says that the Euphrates' water is 'dried up to prepare the way for the kings of the East,' the rulers of the nether world before the final battle of God and Satan at Armageddon. In Revelation (9:14) the river is mentioned as the boundary between the world of the living and the realm of the dead. God commands the release of the four angels of death 'who are bound at the banks of the great river Euphrates.' Also when Daniel was 'on the bank of the great river, the Tigris' he looked up and saw the vision of the archangel (Dn 10:4).

After the Roman conquest and the establishment of *pax Romana,* or 'Roman peace', in the reign of Augustus (27 BCE-14 CE) the Euphrates served as the frontier between Rome and its eastern neighbours; first the Parthians and then the Sassanians. The river's function as a boundary, in the physical sense, is also extended to the divided Western and Eastern Churches.

[5] Because of its sanctity *Yhwh,* or 'Yahweh' is often substituted by the Hebrew *adonas,* or 'my Lord,' written by most modern Bibles in small capitals.

MOUNT ARARAT

The ark came to rest on the mountains of Ararat (Gn 8:4).

The most celebrated location which is mentioned in the Bible related to Anatolia is Ararat. Genesis (8:4) informs us that at the end of the Flood the Ark came to rest on the mountains of Ararat. The Semitic languages have a three-letter root from which almost all nouns, verbs and adjectives derive by insertion of consonants or suffixes. Ararat, spelt *rrt* in the Bible probably should have been vocalized as Urartu, the name by which the region was known in the Iron Age. The Israelites may have heard of the legendary height of the mountains of Urartu before or during the Babylonian captivity. However, since Genesis does not give the exact location of the spot where the Ark was grounded but just says 'the mountains', more than one tradition about this mountain's location was born. The Israelites and Christians have regarded this as being Mt Ararat in eastern Anatolia, an extinct volcano with two tops known as the Greater Ararat ('Büyük Ağrı', 5165 m) and the Lesser Ararat ('Küçük Ağrı', 3846 m). Its majestic view rising uninterrupted from a large plain and mysterious top hidden in snow and clouds makes this mountain the most appropriate location for the rebirth of mankind. The people who lived in the region

Noah's Ark inscribed *kibotos*. Mosaic. Detail. End of the fourth-beginning of the fifth centuries CE. Misis Mosaic Museum. It belonged to the floor of the nave of a building which was a church or synagogue. The shape of the vessel must have been inspired by Hebrew word used for the Ark in the Bible *teba,* or 'chest' which was translated into Greek as *kibotos,* or 'box'. The Ark of the Covenant was used to keep the two stone tablets of the Law that Moses received from God on Mt Horeb (Sinai) and some other relics. In one of the corners of the panel a sixth-century CE restoration shows the figures of Noah, Shem and Japheth as they come out of the vessel to prepare a sacrifice have survived (Gn 8:18).

however, did not use the word 'Ararat' to refer to this mountain. For the Persians it has been the 'mountain of Noah'. The Armenians have called it 'Masis' which just means 'Mountain'. The Koran (11.44) says that the Ark came to rest upon 'Al-Judi' which means 'the heights', without mentioning either a region or a mountain. Local Moslem traditions, also the Nestorians, have generally regarded 'the mountain' or 'the heights' as the highest spot they knew where they lived, such as Mt Cudi[1] (2114 m) in southeastern Anatolia. Mt Demavand in Iran and Mt Nisir[2] in Iraq are among the popular traditional 'heights' where the Ark was supposed to have come to rest.

The story of the Deluge is the most universal folktale of which over 500 variations have been encountered. The flood legends of Anatolia and Palestine — also of Greece — are all thought to have come from Mesopotamia where several versions existed. Otherwise these countries of arid geography neither receive too much rain nor are short of drainage-beds and consequently are not expected to have experienced floods. The penetration of the story of the Deluge into Hebrew literature may have been either through Abraham who perhaps heard it when he was at Ur of the Chaldeans and brought it to Palestine, or through the authors of the Bible who may have heard of it during their Babylonian captivity and recorded it after they returned to the Promised Land. The main elements of the biblical flood story are thought to have been borrowed from a source written in Hurrian in which the hero's name *Nahmizuli,* bears the Hebrew word for Noah, *nhm,* in its first three letters. Although some flood stories existed in ancient Egyptian literature, in this country the seasonal inundation of the Nile was a source of life rather a disaster, and the possibility of Moses carrying an Egyptian story home during the Exodus is regarded as weak.

In Anatolia the existence of several flood stories has been known since the Phrygian era. The one told by the first-century CE Roman writer Ovid in *Metamorphoses* is thought to have been based on such a Phrygian or earlier Anatolian story and may have reached Anatolia from Mesopotamia directly, because it bears no resemblance to the flood story in Genesis inasmuch as here, the cause of inundation is not rain but subterranean waters, the Ark is absent and the heroes, Philemon and his wife Baucis after they entertained Jupiter (Zeus) and Mercury (Hermes), who visited their house disguised as mortals, escape from being drowned by climbing up a hill. At the end of this story, the earth is repeopled when Prometheus and Athena

(opposite) Noah's Ark. Manuscript painting. Late sixteenth century. *Zübdetü't Tevarih,* the 'Legendary Chronicle of the Prophets' Lives'. Museum of Turkish and Islamic Arts. İstanbul. The Koran (11.38) does not elaborate on the animals taken into the Ark: 'a pair from every species,' and also Noah's tribe, 'your tribe (except those already doomed), and all the true believers'.

[1] Mt Nippur of the Assyrians.

[2] Mt Nimush of the Babylonian flood story on which the Ark lands.

shaped *eikons,* or 'images' of mud at Zeus' order. Ikonion or Iconium (Konya) was said to have been named after these images.[3] Deucalion's flood story again told by Ovid may have reached Greece by way of Anatolia or Phoenicia. In this story the ark lands at the summit of Mt Parnassus and Deucalion and his wife Pyrrha again throw pieces of rocks over their shoulders which take human shapes and becoming either men or women populate the world. The conception of transformation of rocks into people is thought to have been of Hurrian origin and may have reached Greece by way of Anatolia (p 33). Deucalion's grandchildren Dorus, Xuthus and Aelus became the progenitors of major Greek tribes, the Dorians, Ionians and Aeolians.

In the course of time the Phrygian flood story was probably adapted to the geography of the region so that in a flood story at Apamea (Dinar) an abyss full of water opens in the earth and begins engulfing people in their homes. An oracle tells the local king that unless his most valued possessions are thrown into it the abyss will not close. When everything fails the king's son jumps in it and saves the world. The story may have been inspired by the nature of the Lycus valley where earthquakes were frequent and the appearance of underground rivers and lakes was known. Such a natural phenomenon may have inspired the story of miracle at the church of St Michael of Chonai near Colossae (p 161). When the Mesopotamian Jews were settled in western Anatolia by the Seleucid king Antiochus III at the end of the third century BCE they may have found several flood stories but all different from their own. It is not known whether the existence of such stories or their efforts to set up a history for their new home caused the Jewish population at Apamea, despite the absence of a high mountain at their city, to associate it with Noah's Flood as depicted on some Apamean coins from the second-third centuries CE.

The location, shape and size of the Ark seem to have occupied man's mind from early times. The 'gopherwood' (Gn 6:14) of which the Ark was made is not mentioned elsewhere in the Bible and its substance is not known. The fact that it was covered 'inside and out with pitch' has led some present-day scholars to regard 'gopherwood' as reeds cemented with bitumen and made waterproof and to take some petrified formations on Ararat as the Ark's remains. The most popular of these is known as the Devil's Rock ('Şeytan Kayası'). Some writers from antiquity such as the first-century CE Jewish historian Josephus claim that the people who climbed the mountain and reached the surviving part of the Ark scraped off its bitumen to use for amulets. Jacob (James) of Nisibis is also said to have climbed

---

[3] Konya may have been the Hittite *Ikkuwaniye/Ikuna.*

the Ararat to look for the Ark. Marco Polo, who is said to have travelled through the region, remarks only that the mountain on which the Ark is said to have stood is 'always in snow and that no one can ascend it'. Among the contemporary visitors a few even claimed to have climbed to the top of the Ark.

Belief in the Ark from time to time was taken as a matter of faith. In the fourth century John Chrysostom asked his audience 'Let us therefore ask they who do not believe: Have you heard of the Flood — of that universal destruction? That was not just a threat, was it? Did it not really come to pass — was not this mighty work carried out? And are not the remains of the Ark preserved there to this very day for our admonition?'

Formation which looks like a ship near Mah-şer village some 20 km to the southeast of Mt Ararat.

TABLE OF THE NATIONS

These are the descendants of Noah's sons, Shem, Ham and Japheth...The descendants of Japheth: Gomer, Magog, Madai, Javan, Tubal, Meshech...The descendants of Ham:...Heth...the Hivites...Togarmah...The descendants of Shem:...Asshur... Lud and Aram (Gn 10; 1 Chr 1).

Yahweh decided to destroy all life on earth by means of a flood to punish the human race for its corruptness. But Noah, of the tenth generation after Adam had led a blameless life. He was saved from the Flood by being allowed to set out upon its waters in a ship, or ark, he had constructed. His wife and three sons, Shem, Ham and Japheth and their wives accompanied him, and so did every sort of living creature. After the Ark had come to rest on the mountains of Ararat (Urartu) they all re-emerged on dry land and began repopulating the world.

This chapter of Old Testament known as Table of the Nations or 'descendants of Noah's sons' (Gn 10; 1 Chr 1) presents a classification of the various peoples known to the ancient Israelites during the later part of the Iron Age with the three sons of Noah as their eponymous ancestors, without giving any exact location except in a few cases. Scholars believe that the chart was drawn when the Babylonian captives freed by Cyrus the Great returned home in 538 BCE and the authors or editors put this view into writing basing it on their pre-exilic recollections or what they learned during their captivity. In its general outlines Japheth's seven sons, the Indo-Europeans, populated the area to the north of Canaan from the Taurus westwards, including Greece and northwards as far as the Caucasus. The children of Ham occupied the lands extending from Lebanon and the Mediterranean to the Indian Ocean, Egypt and the lands beyond. This group also included some Mesopotamian cities which are associated with the progeny of Ham because of their connection with Nimrod. Shem's five sons, the ancestors of the Semites, spread in and around Mesopotamia. Scholars have spotted many mistakes and anachronisms in this list, especially between the tabular and the narrative genealogies.

While some of the locations or people mentioned in this list, especially those who are included in Japheth's progeny such as Tubal or Meshech, may be regarded as being indigenous to Anatolia, some, such as Aram or Asshur, are closely related with Anatolia's ancient history.

Table of the Nations. Paintings of Noah and his sons are from *Sabhat al-akhbar*, the 'Rosary of the Times'. Seventeenth century. National Library. Vienna. In addition to his halo Noah is identified with the Ark in the background.

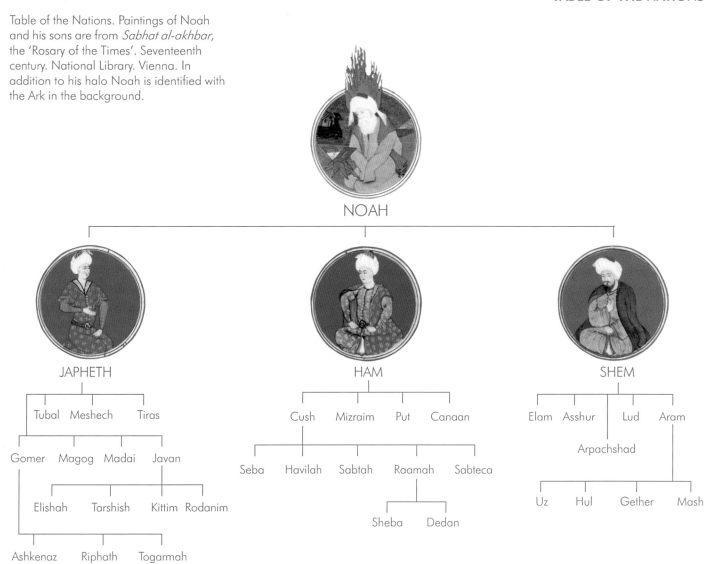

NOAH

JAPHETH

Tubal   Meshech   Tiras

Gomer   Magog   Madai   Javan

Elishah   Tarshish   Kittim   Rodanim

Ashkenaz   Riphath   Togarmah

HAM

Cush   Mizraim   Put   Canaan

Seba   Havilah   Sabtah   Raamah   Sabteca

Sheba   Dedan

SHEM

Elam   Asshur   Lud   Aram

Arpachshad

Uz   Hul   Gether   Mash

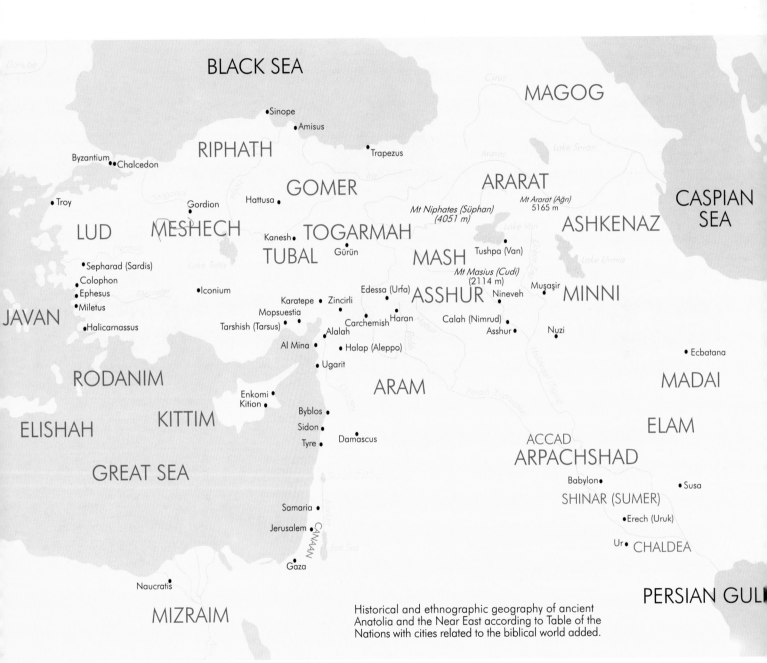

BLACK SEA

MAGOG

- Sinope
- Amisus
- Trapezus

RIPHATH

ARARAT

CASPIAN SEA

Byzantium
- Chalcedon

GOMER

Mt Niphates (Süphan)
(4051 m)

Mt Ararat (Ağrı)
5165 m

- Troy

LUD

MESHECH

- Gordion

Hattusa

- Kanesh

TOGARMAH

TUBAL

- Gürün

ASHKENAZ

Tushpa (Van)

MASH

Mt Masius (Cudi)
(2114 m)

- Sepharad (Sardis)
- Colophon
- Ephesus
- Miletus

- Iconium

Edessa (Urfa)

ASSHUR

- Muşaşir

MINNI

- Karatepe
- Zincirli
- Nineveh

JAVAN

- Halicarnassus

Mopsuestia

- Carchemish
- Haran

Calah (Nimrud)

- Asshur

- Nuzi

Tarshish (Tarsus)

- Alalah

- Ecbatana

RODANIM

- Al Mina

- Halap (Aleppo)

MADAI

- Ugarit

ARAM

- Enkomi
- Kition

KITTIM

- Byblos

ELISHAH

- Sidon
- Tyre

- Damascus

ELAM

ACCAD

ARPACHSHAD

GREAT SEA

- Babylon

- Susa

SHINAR (SUMER)

- Samaria

- Erech (Uruk)

- Jerusalem

CANAAN

Ur • CHALDEA

- Gaza

- Naucratis

PERSIAN GULF

MIZRAIM

Historical and ethnographic geography of ancient
Anatolia and the Near East according to Table of the
Nations with cities related to the biblical world added.

HARAN

Terah took his son Abram, his grandson Lot, son of Haran, and his daughter-in-law Sarai, the wife of his son Abram, and brought them out of Ur of the Chaldeans, to go to the land of Canaan. But when they reached Haran, they settled there (Gn 11:31).

Haran (Harran), in the Bible spelt *hrn,* was founded at a spot where the main west-east communication route from the Mediterranean by way of Alalah and Aleppo to Mardin, Nisibis and the Tigris valley into Mesopotamia, crossed the north-south route from inland Anatolia to the Euphrates valley, on the river Balih (Greek *Belikos,* Assyrian *Balikhu*), a branch of the Euphrates. Its meaning is thought to have been 'crossroads' (Akkadian *Harran,* 'track, road, path'). In Genesis (11:31) when Terah came to Haran with his family it was probably one of the flourishing settlements on the Fertile Crescent,[1] established at a point where the highlands of Anatolia and the Mesopotamian lowlands met. The town was probably inhabited by the Amorites and Hurrians. The latter at that time was the most common ethnic group in north Mesopotamia and their dispersion played a big role in the diffusion of Sumerian culture throughout the ancient Near East, Egypt and Anatolia. In the course of time Haran's population would be supplanted by Aramean immigrants from the Syrian desert. In addition to local handicrafts the caravans of donkeys which made refreshing stops here supplied its bazaars with goods of distant lands. It may have had a population of around 10,000 and for miles was the only place where the semi-nomads of the neighbouring countryside could exchange their produce of wool and hides, cheese or meat for the merchandise of settled life: pottery, jewellery, woven cloth and the like. In his prophecies against the foreign nations Ezekiel, speaking about Tyre (Ez 27:23-24), mentions Haran as one of the cities which traded with it in 'rich garments, violet mantles, embroidered cloth, varicolored carpets, and firmly woven cords'. Although the individual merchandise mentioned here may not be more than an epic cliché it nevertheless shows Haran as a prosperous trading centre. The existence of an important shrine of the moon-god Sin, known as *Ehulhul* ('House of the great Joy') attracted visitors of all sorts, poor and rich alike, especially during his festivals and Haran benefited from this lucrative pilgrim trade.

To reach the land of Canaan from Ur of the Chaldeans situated at the head of the Persian Gulf, Terah and his family, first journeyed up the course of Euphrates until

---

[1] The stretch of cultivable land extending along the mountain chains which connect Egypt by way of the Mediterranean shore to southeastern Anatolia and Mesopotamia.

they arrived at Haran. As most of the herding nomads liked to do when they found a suitable populated settlement, Terah and his tribe pitched their tents here. After his father's death at Haran, Abraham together with his wife Sarah and nephew Lot 'and the persons they had acquired in Haran went to Canaan' because in Haran God spoke to him — for the first time — and commanded him to go to the land of Canaan (Gn 12:1-5). Later when Abraham decided to introduce Sarah in Egypt and Gerar as his 'sister' to protect her (Gn 12:13; 20:1-2) he may have picked up the custom from the Hurrians at Haran who could adopt a wife as a sister to give her a higher status.

When Abraham did not want his son Isaac to take a Canaanite bride he sent his servant to Paddan-aram[2] to find a wife for him among his kinsmen who had been left behind. This is repeated in the marriage of Isaac's son Jacob. Among the spots traditionally associated with these biblical weddings the most celebrated is a well some two kilometres outside Haran's city wall which has come to be known as Jacob's Well[3] or 'Bir Yakub' to which Rebekah went to draw water for Abraham's servant and his camels[4] (Gn 24), and from which Jacob helped Rachel to roll the stone to water 'his uncle's sheep' (Gn 29). Later tradition also associated the well with the one at which Moses met the 'seven daughters of a priest of Midian' (Ex 2:15), an event which must have happened several centuries later, with the one at Haran. Haran's water was supplied by wells which were fed by underground rivers that ended up in 'Ayn-al-Arus', the source of the Balih (Cülap) river. The name of this water source means 'the spring of the betrothed' and is traditionally associated with the stories of the betrothal of Rebekah and Rachel. Except for Benjamin, the other eleven sons of Jacob were born in Haran.

The ancient fame of Haran came from its temple of the Mesopotamian moon-god Nanna, called by the Semites Sin. It was invoked as early as the 2000s BCE to ratify political treaties, and respected by all the empires which ruled in the region at different times.[5] One of these belongs to an agreement made by Suppiluliuma

(opposite) Abraham's senior servant, (Gn 15:2) meets Rebekah, the future bride of Isaac. Manuscript painting. Sixth century CE. Vienna Genesis. National Library. Vienna. To the upper right is the city of Nahor near Haran. Rebekah has left the city and walks along a colonnaded street carrying a jar on her shoulder. The water flowing out of the jar as a spring, which is personified as a nude nymph, fills a basin. Behind Abraham's servant, who is seen drinking from Rebekah's jar, are the ten of his master's dromedaries.

[2] 'Field' or 'tableland of Aram'. The term was used until medieval times for a locality near Haran.

[3] Not to be confused with Jacob's well at Sychar (Shechem) in Samaria (Jn 4:5-6).

[4] Historically camels were not used as beasts of burden until the Persian period.

[5] Sinai, the traditional name of the mountain where Yahweh made his covenant with Moses and the stretch of wilderness where the Israelites sojourned for forty years may also have come from the god Sin.

I (1370-1330 BCE) of the Hittites and king Shattiwaza after the latter was restored to the Mitannian throne. Although excavations at the tumulus of Haran show traces of settlement as early as the Chalcolithic Age these come to an end about 2000 BCE. On the other hand the limited research on the ruins of Haran has not yet brought to light traces older than of the thirteenth century BCE when the Assyrians held the city in high regard and on some occasions gave it privileges, perhaps because of the existence of the temple of Sin. Consequently, archaeologically, the history of Late Bronze Age — the biblical — Haran is still in darkness. In its later history the city, being situated on the Hittite-Assyrian frontier, changed hands frequently and was incorporated in the latter kingdom. When king Sennacherib wrote to king Hezekiah of Judah to surrender Jerusalem to his forces Haran is mentioned among the cities which in the past had rebelled against Assyria and suffered punishment from Sennacherib's ancestors (2 Kgs 19:11-12; Is 37:12).

Abraham. Wall painting. Mid-eleventh century CE. Karanlık (Dark) church. Göreme Outdoor Museum. Cappadocia.

After their capital Nineveh was invaded by the Medes in 612 BCE the Assyrians fled to Haran and tried to raise a new front under their new king Ashur-uballit (611-610 BCE). Nevertheless, both Haran and the temple of Sin are known to have been reduced to ruins two years later by the Babylonians and their allies the Medes. The mother of the future Neo-Babylonian king Nabonidus may have been enslaved in this event and carried to south Mesopotamia. She is thought to have been from a prominent family in Haran and even a priestess at the temple of Sin.

Texts which came both from Babylon and Haran inform us about the rebuilding of the temple by Nabonidus (555-539 BCE). His work was probably the last and most extensive building activity that the temple of Sin underwent. In the Haran inscription Sin himself appears to the king and orders the rebuilding of the temple. The text also mentions the north Arabian expedition of Nabonidus and his ten-year sojourn (p 58). Towards the end of his reign, to the discontent of the other temples in Babylonia, the king moved Sin to the head of the Babylonian pantheon, in Marduk's seat.

In its later history Haran, known then as Carrhae, witnessed the defeat of the Roman general Crassus by the Parthians (55 BCE) where the Roman legions for the first time in their history abandoned their standards, the Roman 'eagles.' Writing at about this period the elder Pliny in *Natural History* mentions Carrhae as the market town of the region where various sorts of incense gums especially the 'stobrus tree', used for the purpose of fumigation, were available.

The Byzantine emperor Julian is known to have visited the shrine of a moon deity (Luna) in Haran in 363 CE. The worship of moon-cult seems to have been included in the Sabian pantheon during the second half of the first millennium CE. Ancient writers and limited archaeological research have identified several moon temples[6] and one of them may be the location of the most ancient temple of Sin.[7] The Sabians are known to have practiced in Haran a pagan religion which believed in the existence of spiritual beings between men and a supreme deity. These spiritual things inhabited the planets and their motion created the material world. Rejecting

[6] One at 'Ayn-al-Arus,' dedicated to Sin; a second at Aşağı Yarımca some eight km outside in the direction of Urfa, dedicated to Selene; and a third in the core of the castle at Haran. The mound at the centre of the site might also have contained the core of the earliest temple of Sin.

[7] In the Sumerian pantheon the moon was the chief astral deity, male and represented by a god, Sin. Later his seat was replaced by the sun, who was below him, and in classical mythology became female to be represented by a goddess.

the function of a prophet the Sabians directed their prayers to these intermediatery spiritual beings. The existence of Sabians in Haran continued until the eleventh century CE.

There is no information about the introduction of Christianity to the city. Although ancient literature mentions the 'strangers of the lands of Nisibis and Haran' attending the preaching of the legendary Thaddeus (Syriac Addai) who is said to have converted Edessa (p182) Haran stayed pagan until the sixth century CE.

Among the north Mesapotamian locations encountered in ancient records and which are associated with Shem's son Arpachshad's descendants Serug, Assyrian *Serugi*, (the district in which stood Batnae — the classical Anthemusia — to the south of Haran) still survives as Suruç.

Ruins of the Ulu Cami (Great Mosque). Haran. First built in the Umayyad period (660-750 CE).

HORITES (HURRIANS)

and the Horites in the hill country of Seir (Gn 14:6).

The Horites of the Old Testament are thought to have been the Hurrians. They are mentioned as the people who lived in the highlands or land of Seir (Petra) before the Edomites, and referred to as 'the descendants of Seir the Horite' in Genesis (14:6). The Horites or Hurrians are the most convincing of the pre-Israelite nations because they had existed in the region since the beginning of the protohistorical biblical narrative inasmuch as the mid-fifteenth century Egyptian sources refer to the north Canaan and other Asiatic lands as the land of Hurru. To the general reader, however, although they played a very important cultural role in the ancient Near East, the Hurrians are not as well known as the Babylonians or Assyrians.

The Hivites are another ethnic group mentioned in Table of the Nations (Gn 10:17; 1 Chr 1:15) among the progeny of Ham by Canaan living in Palestine when the Israelites began to penetrate into the region. Scholars think that the authors of the Bible have used the term 'Hivites' indiscriminately to refer, in some cases, to the Horites (Hurrians) and in other cases to other kinds of non-Semitic populations in Palestine.

The original home of the Hurrians is thought to have been the foothills of the Zagros mountains where their existence was recorded towards the end of the third

Entrance of the palace building of king Niqmepa during whose reign the Hurrians constituted the majority of city's population. Fifteenth century BCE. Tell Açana (Alalah). The doorway was flanked by a pair of single wooden columns supported by polished basalt bases. Niqmepa's treaty with Ir-Teshup of the city of Tunip for the return of runaways recalls 1 Kings 2:39 where Shimei is permitted to enter Philistine territory to search for his runaway slaves and implies the existence of similar agreements between Solomon and neighbouring cities. The return of runaway slaves is also encountered in the New Testament (Phlm; Col 4:9).

millennium in the annals of Sargon of Akkad. Their language which was non-Semitic and non-Indo-European is not yet well understood. In any case, they migrated and by the middle of the second millennium became the largest ethnic group in the Fertile Crescent. Research has shown that the Hurrians were the major factor in the diffusion of Sumerian culture, along with their own pantheon, in this vast region. In Anatolia their existence is recorded at Alalah (Tell Açana) near Antakya as early as the first half of the second millennium BCE. The Hittite destruction of the small states of Syria and Babylonia around 1600 BCE gave the Hurrians a chance to extend their power in the direction of Cilicia where they founded the kingdom of Kizzuwatna, from which their influence reached Hattusa. In Palestine traces of their infiltration come from Tell Taanach and Shechem (Nablus). Most of the rulers of Canaanite city-states of this period carry Hurrian names. The frequent appearance of Indo-aryan names among the Hurrian rulers implies the existence of a soldier-caste called the *Maryannu*.

The town of Gasur (Nuzi) in the middle Tigris region was a predominantly Hurrian settlement in the fifteenth and fourteenth centuries BCE. The cuneiform tablets uncovered here bear interesting folkloric information recalling the narrative of the Patriarchal age. Similar information comes from the cuneiform texts discovered at Alalah. We learn that the rulers at Alalah exchanged villages, as Solomon and Hiram (I) of Tyre did (1 Kgs 9:11) or named one of their sons as heir against the other sons to prevent rivalry, as done by the aged David (1 Kgs 1). A text which dates from the late thirteenth century BCE — several hundred years after king Idrimi's reign — informs us that after an unexplained event in Halap (Aleppo), his ancestral home, Idrimi was forced to flee to his mother's relatives at Emar, recalling David's escape to Moab (1 Sm 22:3) or Absalom's (2 Sm 13:37) to his maternal grandfather. Here winning support, Idrimi was divinely guided, recalling David's story (2 Sm 2:1-4; 5:1, 3). After a seven-year exile just as in the story of Joseph (Gn 11:1) Idrimi crossed by boat from Canaan to the foot of Mt Hazzi where the Orontes river flows into the sea and recovered his kingdom of Mukish, whose capital was Alalah, just as in the story of David. Later Idrimi was reconciled with his overlord Parrattarna, king of Mitanni, which was the most important of the Hurrian states at the time.

Mitanni, also called Hurri or Hanigalbat was established between the Euphrates and its branch the Balih. Its capital Washukkanni has not yet been located, but was probably to the west of Mardin. Mitanni challenged both the Hittites and Egypt for the hegemony of Syria. Hattusili I remarks that 'the enemy from Hanigalbat forced his way into my country, and all the lands fell from me. Only the town of Hattusa

Mt Hazzi; Mt Cassius, or 'Kel dağ' (1760 m). View from the ancient port of Seleucia Pieria (Çevlik). For the Phoenicians it was Mt *Sapan* (Semitic *Zaphon*), abode of the god Baal. In Israel it is identified with *Zion*, abode of the Jewish God.

Presentation in the Temple. Icon. Detail. Nineteenth century. Antalya Archaeological Museum. Joseph is represented holding a plate with two fowls, 'a pair of turtledoves or two young pigeons' for purification (Lk 2:22-24). The Hurrian customs and religion bear other similarities with the information obtained from the Bible. Although it is not known whether it existed in Palestine before their arrival, purification ritual by bird sacrifice prescribed in Leviticus (14, 15) had its parallel among the Hurrians.

alone remained'. In the early sixteenth century the Hittite king Mursili I crossed the Taurus and destroying Alalah invaded Syria. After the destruction of Halap (Aleppo), the capital of kingdom of Yamhad, which was the strongest Hurrian vassal to the west of Euphrates, 'all the towns of the Hurrians' fell to him. The most important campaign of the pharaoh Tuthmosis III (1479-1425) was directed against Mitanni. After its capital was captured and its lands were devastated by Suppiluliuma I sometime around 1350 BCE it survived as a second-class power and was annexed to Assyria by Shalmaneser I (1274-1245 BCE).

The Hurrian epic of 'Song of Ullikummi' seems to have inspired the Jewish eschatological legend of Armillus, the Antimessiah. The subject of this Hurrian myth is the attempt of the storm (weather) god Kumarbi to dethrone his son Teshup who had displaced him from his throne. Kumarbi impregnated a 'great mountain peak' which gave birth to Ullikummi, a blind and deaf monster made of diorite. Teshup climbed to the peak of his mountain Hazzi at the mouth of the Orontes river to see this stone monster growing out of the sea, today's Gulf of İskenderun. At the end of the story the gods waged war on the monster and seem to have destroyed it. This theme of the birth from stone may have been brought by the Hurrians from their home in northeastern Mesopotamia. The idea was familiar to western Semites, who revered animated stones that could be regarded as symbolic mothers of human beings, as encountered in Jeremiah's reproach (2:27) to his country-fellows for going after the strangers 'who say to a piece of wood, "You are my father," and to a stone, "You gave me birth." ' The concept is encountered several times in the Bible such as when in Isaiah (51:1-2) Abraham and Sarah are likened to rocks who gave birth to the people of Israel: 'Look to the rock from which you were hewn...Look to Abraham, your father, and Sarah, who gave you birth.' The imagery is also encountered in Matthew (3:9) when John the Baptist says 'For I tell you, God can raise up children [Hebrew *banim*] to Abraham from these stones [Hebrew *abanim*]', repeated in Luke (3:8). According to the legend of Armillus

there is in Rome a stone of marble, and it has the shape of a beautiful girl. She was created in the six days of the Beginning. And worthless people from the nations come and lie with her, and she becomes pregnant, and at the end of nine months she bursts open, and a male child emerges, in the shape of a man whose height is twelve cubits and whose breadth is two cubits. His eyes are red and crooked, the hair of his head is red like gold, and the steps of his feet are green, and he has two skulls. They call him Armillus.

The concept of transformation of stones into people at the end of both Anatolian and Greek flood stories (p 20) may have originated from this Hurrian conception.

HETH (HITTITES)

When the news reached the kings west of the Jordan, in the mountain regions and in the foothills, and all along the coast of the Great Sea as far as Lebanon: Hittites, Amorites, Canaanites, Perizzites, Hivites and Jebusites, they all formed an alliance to launch a common attack against Joshua and Israel (Jos 9:1).

According to the narrative genealogy of Table of the Nations (Gn 10:15; 1 Chr 1:13) *ht*, voiced *Heth* (Hittites) is a son of Canaan, thus a grandson of Ham. Although the name is mentioned in the Old Testament over twenty times the Hittites of Hattusa and the Hebrews did not know each other because the first group had disappeared from the political arena a few decades before the entrance of the Israelites into the Promised Land.[1] Also, if the biblical *Heth* referred to the Hittites of Hattusa it would have probably been included among the sons of Japheth who is the ancestor of most of the Indo-European nations according to Table of the Nations.

The classical Hittites are thought to have penetrated Anatolia in the closing centuries of the third millennium and, mixing with the local people created one of the strongest empires of the Late Bronze Age from about 1800 until the 1190s BCE. It is not known if they came across the straits or the Black Sea or the Caucasus. It has also been claimed that they may have been some of the indigenous people of Anatolia. Their language is known as the oldest Indo-European tongue (like Sanskrit, Greek, Latin or English) of which written records survive. They called themselves 'people of the Land of Hatti' after the region in which they were centred.

For the Hittites Palestine was a part of Egypt and outside their political orbit. Enigmatic information about the actual movement of the Hittites into Egyptian territory comes from the text of the Kurustama treaty found at Hattusa. Here we are informed that some Hittite subjects from the city of Kurustama to the northeast were moved and settled in the Syrian territories subject to Egypt. Scholars believe that this single example cannot be taken as the sign of other Hittite emigrations from Anatolia into the domain of Egypt. Even if there were Hittite enclaves established in Canaan in the Late Bronze Age in the course of time they must have been absorbed by larger ethnic groups such as the Amorites and the way that they were

[1] The most memorable of these mentions is the purchase of the cave of Machpelah a burial place for Sarah around Hebron from the Hittite Ephron by Abraham (Gn 23:8-9).

Re-used slab with Hittite hieroglyphs and Christian crosses from the vicinity of Kayseri (Caesarea). İstanbul Archaeologial Museum. The stone originally was a Hittite monument which still bears some of its hieroglyphic inscription. It was redecorated in the Christian era with a large cross on an incised hill of Golgotha flanked by two pairs of smaller crosses, and used as a gravestone. The pair of rosettes and zigzags encircling it may have belonged to its original decoration.

Altar base with a hole at the top from Hattusa. Stone. Fourteenth century BCE. Museum of Ancient Oriental Arts (İstanbul Archaeological Museum). It is decorated with a man praying in front of a vertical stone altar set up in such a base.

introduced in the Bible as one of the aboriginal tribes living there (Jos 9:1) is unhistorical. The Hittites rarely penetrated as far south as today's Lebanon and when they did this the objective was just to check the Egyptian offensive against Syria, not to settle there. The Kadesh agreement (1280 BCE) signed between these two great empires brought peace to Palestine until the arrival of the Sea Peoples in about 1190 BCE when both the Hittites and the petty kingdoms in Canaan crumbled against them.

It has been suggested that the Palestinian cities may have learned the art of building posterns from the Hittites, of which the finest sample has survived to the present day at Hattusa (Boğazkale). In the Book of Judges (1:25) a man of Bethel (ancient Luz) shows the Israelites such 'a way into the city', probably a postern, by which they enter and capture it. Despite the absence of any direct contact between the Hittites of Hattusa and the Israelites, scholars have pointed to some interesting resemblances between their rituals. Even if the Hittite culture may have reached Palestine by way of Ugarit, most of such religious similarities are not unique to these two nations but encountered in the other cultures of the Near Eastern civilizations, with differences in details. They have, however, survived best in Hittite texts.

One of the most evident common practices was the use of obelisks of up to about three metres in height placed on carved bases and set up either in the temples or rural shrines, where they stood together with trees. Such stones, of which samples have been recovered by excavations in both Anatolia and Israel, are thought to have been set up for libations in some cult of the dead or as monuments of the presence of a deity as recounted in Genesis (28:16-22) where Jacob when he woke up in the morning took the stone which he had used as pillow and set it as a memorial, for he regarded the site as sacred as an 'abode of God'. Other references to such sacred pillars placed in groves are found in Exodus (34:13), Deuteronomy (12:3) and 2 Kings (17:10). In Hittite records this was called the *huwasi* stone and in Hebrew *masseba* which is translated in the Bible as 'pillar' or 'sacred pillar' standing at the 'high places' or 'hill shrines'. In the course of time some of these stones were probably sculpted into idols and their usage would later be prohibited as in 2 Kings (18:4) when Hezekiah, the king of Judah 'removed the high places, shattered the pillars, and cut down the sacred poles' or in 2 Kings (23:14) when Josiah 'broke to pieces the pillars'.

The idea that a living carrier may take the evil away from the community is encountered among the Hurrians, Hittites, Israelites and other peoples of the ancient Near East. The underlying belief of this ritual is that as it was possible to shift a material weight from one person's back to another's, it was also possible to shift the psychological burdens or sins to other people, who would suffer them in their place. According to Hittite records this may have been an animal such as a cow, sheep, goat, donkey, or even a mouse or bird or also a human. It is referred to as *nakkassi* (from the Hurrian *nakkuse*, 'the one who has been released'). In a similar manner in Leviticus (16:10), on the Day of Atonement Aaron is instructed to take two goats and to cast lots. One of the animals is a sin offering to the Lord and the other on which the lot falls 'for Azazel,' who may have been a desert demon. Aaron lays his hands on the head of the goat, confesses over it all the sins of the children of Israel, loading its head and sends it away into the wilderness. Azazel (from *azazum*) which also means a cathartic sacrifice is a Semitic loan-word from the Hurrian. It is sometimes translated as the 'escaping goat' which has given us the English word 'scapegoat'.

The form of the biblical covenants such as the one signed between Yahweh and Abraham in Genesis (17) follows the traditional Mesopotamian structure, which has again best survived to the present among Hittite cuneiform texts. A typical Hittite treaty of this kind begins with an introduction of the name of the Hittite king and his titles as the author of the treaty, followed by the favours conferred on the second party, stipulating the latter's obligations (such as in Abraham's case circumcision), witnessing deities and finally curses upon those who should break it.

Also both nations had the practice of killing an animal to sanctify a treaty as observed in Exodus (24:5-8) where Moses says 'This is the blood of the covenant which the LORD has made with you in accordance with all these words of his' as he sprinkled sacrificial blood on the attendants. The practice of offering the entrails to the gods while the participants consume the rest of the meat is another feature which was practiced both among the Hittites and Israelites.

Another religious similarity which the Hittites and Israelites share is a particular sort of ritual of purification. After suffering a defeat the Hittite soldiers walked through the cut pieces of a sacrifice of an animal such as a goat, puppy, a little pig or even a man. This ritual took place by a river where the participants also sprinkled water on themselves for cleansing. Jeremiah (34:18) mentions the existence of a similar ritual among the Hebrews: 'The men who violated my covenant...I will make like the calf which they cut in two, between whose parts they passed.' The idea was to invoke a similar fate to that of the cut beast if they should foreswear. In the covenant made between Abraham and God (Gn 15) Abraham upon God's command brings a heifer, a she-goat and a ram and splits them into two. After this a smoking brazier and a blazing torch (God's presence) pass between the pieces. Although it is not mentioned in the text Abraham is also assumed to have walked between the split carcasses. In Numbers (31:22-23), after slaughtering the Midianite women and children the Israelite soldiers purify all objects of metal with fire and others which cannot stand fire 'with lustral water'.

After the collapse of the Hittite empire some Neo-Hittite states rose to power in southeastern Anatolia and northern Syria between the eleventh and eighth centuries BCE. Azitiwataya (Karatepe), Samal (Zincirli), Carchemish, Gurgum-Marqasi (Maraş) or Milid (Malatya) were

Neo-Hittite grave stele from Maraş. Bazalt. Eighth century BCE. Hatay Archaeological Museum. Antakya.

among the most important of these. In about 1000 BCE north Syria was already settled by Aramean nomads who gained political ascendancy in some of these Neo-Hittite kingdoms. These Aramean settlers were also called Hittites by the Assyrians. If the Israelites exported chariots bought from Egypt to sell to 'the Hittite and Aramean kings' at the time of Solomon (1 Kgs 10:29, 2 Chr 1:17) the buyers must have been the rulers of these Neo-Hittite states. The ethno-geographical usage of 'Land of Hatti', which had once been used to refer to Anatolia proper, for these kingdoms, Syria or even for Palestine lasted well through the seventh-sixth centuries BCE in the Near East, and is even encountered as late as the Seleucid period. Thus when the scribes of the Bible made the army of Ben-hadad (II), king of Damascus (the biblical Hadad-ezer) say 'The king of Israel has hired the kings of the Hittites' to fight with them (2 Kgs 7:6) they were referring to either Neo-Hittite principalities or any other force in the so-called 'Land of Hatti'.

The Old Testament mentions various marriages between the Israelites and the Hittites. It is very probable that in such instances the scribes used the term 'Hittite' as a substitution for 'native'. Also, except for David's guard Uriah[2] all the other so-called Hittites, such as the brides married by Esau or Solomon, bear Semitic names; having a Hittite name does not necessarily imply an ethnic origin. An event which is mentioned in the reign of David again brings to mind the Hittite belief of affording to the blind and the lame magical properties. Here, when David besieged Jerusalem, the Jebusites who lived in the city put such people on the walls believing 'the blind and the lame will drive you away' (2 Sm 5:6).

At the time that the Old Testament was recorded the Greeks knew much less — or nothing — than the Israelite scribes about the Hittites. When Herodotus saw the Hittite relief at Karabel near İzmir he thought that it showed the Egyptian king Sesostris and that the accompanying Hittite hieroglyphs were 'Egyptian sacred script'.

[2] Whose wife Bathsheba David saw bathing and then ordered Uriah to be put in the most dangerous place in the battle, against the walls of a besieged city. After he was killed, David married her who gave him Solomon (2 Sm 11; 12:1-25).

SEA PEOPLES

The catastrophe which is known as the immigration of the Sea Peoples is the most important event in the ancient history of the Aegean world, Anatolia and the eastern Mediterranean. This disaster seems to have begun in the second half of the thirteenth century BCE and when it came to an end, before the middle of the twelfth century the social and political structure of Greece, Anatolia and the Levant had become unrecognizable.

Towards the closing decades of the thirteenth century BCE the quiet world of the Aegean and eastern Mediterranean changed. A series of disturbances began and spread to Greece, the Aegean islands, Anatolia and the Levant; they even extended almost as far as the banks of the Euphrates and hit the Nile delta, where they subsided. Scholars, although unable to name or discover a single important cause (famine, epidemic, seismic tremor or another sort of natural disaster) which began this commotion, have given up looking for some mysterious group of invaders from northern Europe who all of a sudden fell upon these countries like birds of prey. The upheavals were not the cause but the result of the disintegration of the great powers of the time, the Mycenaeans and the Hittites, whose structures were more fragile than they seemed to be and had carried signs of disintegration since their rise.

The unrest may have begun in any part of the Aegean world. The internal feud among the royal houses which formed the Mycenaean aristocracy may have encouraged other Greeks to emigrate into the southern periphery. Although, having felt themselves insecure, cities like Mycenae, Tiryns and Corinth had reinforced their fortifications a few decades earlier, in the closing years of the thirteenth century a violent destruction overtook all of them. What is known about Hittite history

Sea Peoples. Transcript of the relief from the wall of the mortuary temple of Rameses III at Medinet Habu. Men, women and children are on the move in heavy ox-wagons, with two solid wheels and with solid or wicker sides. Both types are seen in Anatolia where the normal yoke however is two oxen. The extra pair in the drawing may have been hitched in order to keep with the others. The scene brings to mind Judges (18:21) where after their hero Samson's death his tribe, the Danites — alleged kinsmen of the Denyen among the Sea Peoples — 'placed their little ones, their livestock, and their goods at the head of the column' and moved to a new settlement.

shows how much they suffered from the existence of a widespread royal line which led to permanent internal power struggles. The collapse of central powers must have triggered different forces which contributed to the havoc and made it more extensive and complex. Smaller or larger groups of different or related groups with the advantage of their long swords, helmets and body armour, which they are thought to have produced locally imitating prototypes from the Balkans, had been set into motion. This was not an organized military movement but an immigration of many loosely-coordinated insecure tribes who moved wherever events took them, some looking far a new homeland and some driven by the objective of war spoils — mostly gold and women — and destroyed anything that stood against them. Tribes from western, southwestern and southern Anatolia which included Cretan colonists may have constituted the core of the movement. Hittite texts show how unstable the political structure of western Anatolia was in this period. Once started, they probably set other people into motion and their easy success may have encouraged some semi-civilized people like the Kaskas in the Pontic region to attack their former rulers, the Hittites.

The wanderings of Aegean or Anatolian hordes and their employment as mercenaries was not an unknown thing in the Late Bronze Age. The Amarna Letters show that some groups of people called Lukka raided the coasts of Alasiya (Cyprus) and Egypt as early as the 1370s BCE. The Sherden, who would later show up among the Sea Peoples, had first raided Egypt at the time of Amenophis III and served as mercenaries in the army of Rameses II. When the latter faced Muwatalli III at Kadesh (1296 BCE) some groups who would later be shown by Homer fighting in the Trojan War as Troy's allies, such as the Masa, Karkisa, Lukka and the Derden, or Dardanians (*Dardanoi* of Homer), that is the Trojans themselves, fought on the Hittite side, some of them probably as mercenaries.

The earliest reports of unrest are not found in the Aegean world but come from the other side of the Mediterranean. Shortly before the major upheavals, a minor wave of immigrants seems to have found its way to North Africa by sea. Inscriptions from the reign of Merneptah's (1213-1204 BCE) mention the existence of mercenaries such as the Sherden, Shekelesh, Ekwesh, Lukka and Teresh who fought along with the Libyans and their neighbour the Meshwesh.[1] These invaders, however, managed to enter the Nile delta and settled there to be later recruited by pharaoh's army.

---

[1] Writing some seven hundred years after these events in his account of the Libyan tribes Herodotus describes the Maxyes (Meshwesh) as 'a people who grow their hair on the right sides of their heads and shave it off on the left. They stain their bodies red and claim to be descended from men of Troy.' He probably alludes to the Greek tradition which held that in the generation preceding the Trojan War certain Greek heroes went to North Africa.

Shortly after this isolated raid, the upheavals in the Aegean and Anatolia began. The most powerful cities of the Mycenaean kingdom such as Mycenae, Tiryns, Pylos and Corinth were sacked one after the other. In Anatolia, Troy,[2] Sardis, Miletus, Hattusa, Alacahöyük, Tarsus (Gözlükule) and Alalah (Tell Açana) were some of the settlements which were destroyed and burned or abandoned. It is, however, difficult to find direct evidence which would connect the destructions in Greece with the ones in Anatolia. Some of these cities never recovered and fell into oblivion. The invasion extended to Enkomi and Kition (Larnaca) in Alasiya (Cyprus) and Kadesh, Aleppo and Emar by the Euphrates. Along the Phoenician coast Ugarit (Ras Shamra) was destroyed. The cuneiform tablets found among the ruins of some of these cities were all of a sudden filled with desperate cries for help stating that they could not hold back the enemy. Byblos, Sidon and Tyre may have saved themselves by either collaborating with the invaders or paying them tribute.

At the time that the catastrophe began in the Aegean world, Palestine was still enjoying the relatively long peace and prosperity that the Kadesh agreement (1280 BCE) had brought to the region. The disaster swept through Canaan and struck Egypt in the reign of Rameses III (1184-1155 BCE). The pharaoh knew about the unrest. Earlier in his reign he had recruited some Sea Peoples that he had met as allies of the Libyans and settled them, specifically the Sherden, in his garrisons at Canaan and probably made use of their knowledge of metalworking. He did not wait for the invaders to reach his frontiers but confronted them outside the Egyptian soil. The battle fought in the southern coastal plains of Canaan seemed to halt the advance of the marauders but did not prevent them from reaching Egypt's frontiers. Having failed to enter Egypt in their second attempt, which they made by sea and where they were defeated, the loose coalition of the invaders disintegrated. The Medinet Habu inscriptions of Rameses III inform us that

'The foreign countries [Sea Peoples] made a conspiracy in their islands. All at once the lands were removed and scattered in the fray. No land could stand before their arms, from Hatti, Kode [Cilicia], Carchemish, Arzawa, and Alasiya [Cyprus] on, being cut off at [one time]. A camp [was set up] in one place in Amor [Amurru]. They desolated its people, and its land was like that which has never come into being. Their confederation was the Peleset, Tjekker, Shekelesh, Denyen, and Weshesh.'

The Egyptian victory, however, was far from being complete because some of the invaders could not be prevented from settling in Canaan. The pharaoh recruited

[2] In the Greek literature only the sack of Troy has been dealt with as a separate episode.

Relief of David and the Philistine hero Goliath from the former church of the Holy Cross at Akdamar island near Van. 915-21 CE. 1 Samuel (5-7) describes Goliath's armory as a bronze helmet, a bronze corselet of scale armour, bronze greaves and a bronze scimitar and a javelin with iron head. The description fits the gear of the Aegean warriors of the Late Bronze Age as later described by Homer in detail. The inscriptions in Armenian read: 'The prophet David' and 'Goliath the Philistine'.

these and employed them in his garrisons. At the end of the nineteenth century scholars began to use the term 'Peoples of the Sea' to refer to this movement although most of the invaders were probably not 'Sea' but 'Land' Peoples.

After the last battle some of the ethnic groups mentioned in the Egyptian sources disappeared. They may have sailed away to Cyprus, Sardinia, Sicily or other places, settled there, mixed with local people, even named the country after themselves. Ancient literature informs us that the three major groups which settled along the coast of Palestine were the Tjekker, the Sherden and the Peleset, who were later called 'Philistines' and gave the country its name, 'Palestine'. Table of the Nations shows an enigmatic group called Caphtorim, among the sons of Mizraim (Egypt) (Gn 10:14; 1 Chr 1:12) as the progeny of the Philistines, a fact which may indicate their arrival from the south after their defeat by Rameses III. In other cases (Jer 47:4; Am 9:7)[3] the Philistines are said to have come from the coasts of Caphtor which is thought to have been Crete. The Peleset are also suggested to have travelled from Crete to Anatolia and joining other groups on the move continued to the Levant by land. The Denyen of Rameses III's inscriptions may also have settled in Palestine to later become the Danites, the 'tribe of Dan'. The seafaring remark about the tribe of Dan (Jgs 5:17) that 'Dan spend his time in ships' but does not participate in the war against the Philistines is peculiar for an Israelite tribe. In Genesis (49:16) when Jacob prophesies about the twelve tribes of Israel he says 'Dan will be just for his people like any other tribe of Israel', and he may imply that until then Dan was not regarded 'like' a tribe of Israel. The fact that the invaders had come by that route and Denyen may have been connected with the Danuna of Cilicia (p 92) has led some scholars to regard Caphtor as the mountainous section of Cilicia. After all the Greek translation of the Old Testament (the Septuagint) uses the word Cappadocia instead of 'Caphtor', (Cilicia Tracheia) and the southern frontier of this region is known to have included in antiquity rugged Cilicia, reaching the Mediterranean. Egyptian sources show the Tjekker settled around Dor, south of Mt Carmel. This group may have been connected with Teucri in the Troad or with the Greek hero Teucer who is said to have founded Salamis in Cyprus. The tribe of Asher, which according to Joshua (19:24) was settled in the coastal territory to the north, is sometimes associated with the Sherden.

Shortly after the death of Rameses III, the Egyptian hegemony over Canaan came to an end and the settlements of Sea Peoples became free of foreign tutelage. In

[3] Earlier biblical references to the Philistines such as in Genesis (21) or Exodus (13) are anachronisms.

the latter part of the twelfth century the Philistines seem to have absorbed the other groups who had settled in the area and enlarged their territory.

The entrance of the Israelites into the Promised Land coincides with this period. As the vacuum created by the disappearance of Egyptian authority enabled the Philistines to consolidate their power it also gave a chance to the semi-nomadic Israelite tribes who found the coastal strip settled by the enemy (Gn 26; Ex 13; 23) to invade and occupy the barren hill country. It was perhaps the threat of the Philistines which brought the Israelite tribes together into a nation. David's foreign bodyguard (2 Sm 8:18; 20:23) included groups such as the Cherethites and Pelethites. While the latter is a different name used for the Philistines, scholars suggest that the Cherethites who occupied a part of Negev (1 Sm 30:14), probably a piece of land close to Gaza, may have been Cretans.

The arrival of the Philistines is regarded as the end of the Late Bronze Age in Canaan and the beginning of the Iron Age. The monopoly of these new settlers on metalworking (mostly bronze) is remarked in 1 Samuel (13:19-22): 'All Israel, therefore, had to go down to the Philistines to sharpen their plowshares, mattocks, axes, and sickles...And so on the day of battle neither sword nor spear could be found in the possession of any of the soldiers with Saul and Jonathan.' This region seems to have continued to function as a major centre of metalworking because when Solomon brought the bronze-worker Hiram from Tyre (1 Kgs 7:13-14) for the fittings of the Jerusalem Temple, the bronzes were 'cast in the neighbourhood of the Jordan, in the clayey ground between Succoth and Zarethan' (1 Kgs 7:46), the central Jordan valley.

The immigration of the Sea Peoples must have made a deep impact on the Greek mind that survived for many generations in the oral tradition. Greek legends, when written down some six or seven hundred years after this period, personalized these invasions as the wanderings of heroes such as Odysseus, Menelaus, Nestor, Amphilochus, Teucer or Mopsus and others. In Greek legends following the Trojan War these heroes wander around the Aegean and the Mediterranean world sacking cities, sailing away with rich war spoils or founding cities. Scholars have pointed out the phonetic resemblances between the names such as Priam and Piram (Jos 10:3), Anchises and Achish (1 Sm 27:2) and Paris and Perez (Gn 38:29). Some of these ventures such as those of Mopsus of Colophon, who is said in the years following the Trojan War to have led the peoples from the Ionian coast across the Taurus mountains into Pamphylia and Cilicia and further to the south, may have been more than stories. Traditionally, he is the founder of Greek colonies such as Aspendos, Phaselis, Mopsuestia, Mopsucrene and Mallus in Cilicia and even Hierapolis in Phrygia, whose history does not go further than the Hellenistic period.

His name also occurs at Perge, Sillyum and in the bilingual inscription at Karatepe, where the city's late eighth-century king Azitiwatas refers to himself as being from the house of Muksas ('Mopsus'), king of Adaniya by the name that the region was known to the Hittites (p 90).

The migration of the Sea Peoples brought radical social, political and economic changes to the Aegean world, western and central Anatolia and the eastern Mediterranean. The collapse of the major powers of the Late Bronze Age created a vacuum which could not be filled until about the ninth-eighth centuries BCE. This long period about which almost no pictorial or written evidence has been found, is referred to as the Dark Ages. If it not had been for the archaeological material which comes from the Neo-Hittite and the Near Eastern kingdoms our information for these couple of hundred years in Anatolia would have been blank. During the Dark Ages the people of these countries seem to have returned to nomadic or semi-nomadic life. On the ruins of the cities destroyed by the Sea Peoples hastily built slum settlements rose. The fine baked clay pottery of the previous period disappeared. The Dark Ages lasted until the birth of the city civilizations such as Athens and Corinth, Samos, Miletus, Ephesus and Priene and the appearance of various Anatolian kingdoms such as the Lydians, Phrygians and Urartu. After a few hundred years when the fog began to thin new people such as the Mysians, Carians or Lycians, whose names bring to mind the Masa, Karkisa or Lukka of the Late Bronze Age, appeared. However, it is impossible to know if these people were connected with those of the past centuries or if they only occupied the same lands.[4]

A distant echo of the commotion also comes from the Assyrian king Tiglath-pileser I (1115-1076 BCE). Assyrian texts inform us that at the beginning of his reign '20,000 *Muski* with their five kings' emigrated and settled to the northwest of his lands and that he had to fight and defeat them in the upper Tigris region. It is, however, difficult to guess if these were the ancestors of the later Phrygians who moved from the west or another group which penetrated Anatolia from the north of the Caucasus after the fall of Hattusa and which would later be integrated with the Phrygians. Tiglath-pileser I also claims that the Kaska people, whose home was known to have been the Pontus region and who were known as the most formidable enemies of the Hittites, also appeared at the northern frontiers of his kingdom. The height of the Taurus chain, the Euphrates and the strong Assyrian army may have halted the advance of the immigrants in the direction of Mesopotamia.

[4] Except for the Lycians who are known to have descended from the Lukka people. The Luwian language survived in the region as late as the Hellenistic period.

(opposite) Samson destroying the temple of Dagon. Manuscript painting. Detail. Late sixteenth century. *Zübdetü't Tevarih,* the 'Legendary Chronicle of the Prophets' Lives'. Museum of Turkish and Islamic Arts. İstanbul.

ARAM (ARAMEANS)

The LORD had caused the army of the Arameans to hear the sound of chariots and horses, the din of a large army, and they had reasoned among themselves, 'The king of Israel has hired the kings of the Hittites and the kings of the borderlands to fight us' (2 Kgs 7:6).

According to Table of the Nations Aram, the grandson of Noah by Shem, is the progenitor of the Arameans (Gn 10:22; 1 Chr 1:17). Although Genesis (22:21) mentions Kemuel, a son of Nahor, as the father of a junior Aram, he is not regarded as an eponymous ancestor for he is referred to as 'the Aramean' (Gn 25:20; 28:5). Among the sons of Aram, Mash (Gn 10:23; 1 Chr 1:17) is tentatively associated with the ancient Mt Masius (Tur Abdin[1]) above Nisibis (Nusaybin).

The region that the Arameans lived in is referred to in the Old Testament as *Aram Naharaim*, or 'Syria of the rivers', a term which is also used to refer to the whole of Mesopotamia. The Arameans were nomadic people who occupied the central steppes of Syria. Towards the end of the second millennium they began to move from their traditional home in almost all directions into the settled world of the Near East. Their migration may have resulted both from the worsening climatic conditions in the desert and the gap of authority created by the disappearance of powerful kingdoms around Syria. In the territories to which they moved some of these tribes continued their semi-nomadic existence but some mixed with the local population and beginning in the eleventh century BCE founded a number of Aramean city-kingdoms of different sizes centred on cities such as Aleppo, Damascus and Hamath.

The biblical narrative is the major source of information about relations between the Aramean kingdoms established on the borders of Palestine and frontiers of Israelite kingdoms. Nevertheless, the earliest references to the Arameans outside the Bible date from probably several centuries after the time of Jacob and thus calling his uncle Laban an 'Aramean' (Gn 25:20) and having him speak Aramaic would seem to be an anachronism.

The Old Testament informs us that Saul, David and Solomon had to fight against Aramean kingdoms such as Aram-Zobah (1 Sm 14; 2 Sm 10), Aram-Beth-rehob (1 Sm 14; 2 Sm 8), Aram-maacah (1 Chr 19:6), Geshur (2 Sm 13;15), Damascus and Hamath of Zobah, established on their frontiers or beyond. The most important

---

[1] Literally 'mountain for the servants [of] God; Tur derives from 'Taurus'.

Column base with lions from the time of
Tiglath-pileser III (744-727 BCE) from Tell
Tainat on the Orontes river. Hatay
Archaeological Museum. Antakya.

among them however, was Damascus, the United Monarchy's most dangerous enemy, which later continually interfered with the politics of the divided monarchies of Israel and Judah. The relations however were not always unfriendly. In the ninth century (1 Kgs 20:34) Ben-hadad (I) of Damascus, having lost the battle, addresses king Ahab of Israel[2] thus: 'I will rest on the cities which my father took from your father, and you may make yourself bazaars in Damascus as my father did in Samaria.'

When Shalmaneser III of Assyria invaded Syria, Ahab and the Phoenician cities — with Arabic and Egyptian reinforcements — took their place in the Aramean coalition led by Ben-hadad (II) of Damascus at the battle of Karkar (853 BCE) on the lower Orontes. Although the Assyrian king claimed victory the indecisive battle had forced the Assyrians to return home. Nevertheless, immediately after the battle Israel and Judah broke with Damascus and during the ensuing war king Ahab was killed. The feud between the divided kingdoms gave a chance to Hazael of Damascus to subdue Jehu and his successor Jehoahaz (814-798) and Israel became a vassal of Damascus.

In the first half of the eighth century Assyria was pre-occupied with Urartu and Palestine took a brief respite. Jeroboam II (782-753 BCE) of Israel even captured Damascus. In 2 Kings (16:5), when the kings of Damascus and Samaria forced the neighbouring kingdoms into alliance against Assyria and laid siege to Jerusalem, Ahaz of Judah asked Tiglath-pileser III (the biblical Pul) for help, which ended with the conquest of Damascus by the Assyrians (733 BCE). Israel was also overrun and devastated and inhabitants were exiled to Assyria. Ahaz was forced to pay a very heavy tribute.

At the same time as their settlement along the northern and eastern frontiers of Palestine, the Arameans penetrated north Syria and the skirts of the Taurus and became the predominant population in the already existing cities. Among the kingdoms that they founded on the fringes of the Anatolian highlands the strongest were Bit-Zamani[3] on the Tigris near Diyarbakır and Bit-Adini referred to as 'the Edenites' (2 Kgs 19:12; Is 37: 12) or as 'Beth-eden' (Am 1:5) or as 'Eden' (Ez 27:23) between the the Euphrates and its branch the Balih. Its capital was Til-

---

[2] Better remembered for his Phoenician wife Jezebel.

[3] Aramean kingdoms were often named with the word *bit* (Arabaic *beit*; Hebrew *beth*), or 'household' or 'dynasty', followed by the name of the ancestor.

Barsip (Tell Ahmar). The reliefs which came from the ruins of the Neo-Hittite kingdom of Samal (Zincirli), founded at the crossing point from the mountains into Cilicia, are also regarded as the finest surviving examples of Aramaic culture. Here in spite of the employment of Hittite hieroglyphs for some inscriptions, in the language and alphabet, names and gods, dress and ornaments and the style of carving Aramaic and Assyrian styles prevail.

To their east the Arameans also migrated towards Assyria and Babylonia. Jeremiah (35:11) informs us that when he invaded Judah and captured Jerusalem in 586 Nebuchadnezzar's army included Arameans. The type of tribute that the Aramean states paid to the Assyrians gives us an idea about the sources of the Arameans' wealth. In addition to textiles and iron which probably came from Cilician metals like gold, silver, bronze and tin, implying intensive commercial relations with the rest of Anatolia, it included incense which brings to mind the control of the trade routes to Saba (the biblical Sheba; Yemen) and South Arabia.

The Arameans spoke a Semitic language not very different from Hebrew or Phoenician. Although they were unable to create a single large kingdom, the dispersion of Aramean settlements of smaller or larger sizes and their interest in trade made Aramaic the most popular spoken language, replacing Akkadian. By this period the Phoenicians had began to use a more streamlined script of only twenty-two letters, which could easily be inscribed on materials such as papyrus, leather or wood. The Arameans borrowed this simple Phoenician alphabet of shapes representing consonant sounds and simplified it. By the end of the ninth century BCE this new script had began replacing the Akkadian cuneiform writing. This new alphabet would soon become popular and adopted by all of the states in the Near East including the Assyrians and their successors the Medes and Persians. The popularity of Aramaic for diplomatic exchanges is mentioned in the Bible. During Sennacherib's siege of Jerusalem in 701 BCE Hezekiah's officials plead with an Assyrian official not to speak 'in Judean within the earshot of the people who are on the wall' (the Assyrian wanted ordinary people to understand his call to surrender) but in Aramaic because they understand it (2 Kgs 18:26-27). Nehemiah (13:24) in the fifth century BCE informs us that half of the Jewish children in Jerusalem could not speak Hebrew but knew only 'Ashdodite', the language spoken at Ashdod, likely Aramaic. Parts of books of Daniel and Ezra were recorded in Aramaic. Although Greek was widelly spoken, especially in the cities, by the beginning of Christianity the common language of Palestine, and the language Christ himself spoke, was Aramaic and it was used predominantly.

ASSHUR (ASSYRIANS)

Meanwhile, Ahaz sent messengers to Tiglath-pileser, king of Assyria, with the plea: 'I am your servant and your son. Come up and rescue me from the clutches of the king of Aram and the king of Israel, who are attacking me' (2 Kgs 16:7).

According to Table of the Nations Asshur, a grandson of Noah by Shem, gave his name to the Assyrians (Gn 10:22; 1 Chr 1:17). The word appears frequently in the Bible referring to the Akkadian land, its people or its capital on the middle Tigris. To the general reader the name Assyrians brings to mind a ruthless nation who created havoc among its neighbours and destroying Jerusalem took the 'Ten Tribes'[1] into captivity.

In Genesis the founder of Assyria is identified as Nimrod (Gn 10:8), 'a mighty hunter by the grace of the LORD', a great grandson of Noah by Ham. He was famed as a builder. After founding cities like Babylon, Erech and Akkad in Shinar (Sumer) Nimrod went to Assyria and founded Nineveh (Gn 10:10-11) a remark which suggests the colonization of Assyria from Babylonia. In Micah (5:5) 'The land of Assyria' is mentioned as 'the land of Nimrod'. Later Christian and Moslem traditions regard Nimrod also as the king of Edessa (Urfa) and associate him with Abraham. Nimrod's name was attached to the monuments whose construction were thought to have been beyond man's power. In ancient extrabiblical narratives he is identified as Ninus son of Belus, the eponymous founder of Nineveh, the later Assyrian capital.

The word Asshur, which may also be transcribed as 'Assur' or 'Ashur', was used for the country, city and their principal god, from which the Greeks derived the word Assyria. The Assyrians played an important role in the history of both Anatolia and Palestine. Their first penetration into Anatolia however, outdates that of Palestine by over a millennium. Excavations at Kanesh (Kültepe) near Kayseri and other sites have shown that as early as about 1950 BCE the Assyrians had established trade colonies in Anatolia. The caravans of black donkeys, after covering a track of about 1,000 km (a journey of about two months), arrived here, paid duty to the native ruler who lived in the city and continued to the actual Assyrian colony, the *karum* which stood outside the walls. Here the merchandise, mostly tin which Anatolia lacked and was indispensable for the production of bronze and quality-textiles, was unloaded, checked and stored to be traded with silver, gold and copper in the future. The latter may also have been traded for the first two metals which would be carried home.

[1] Northern tribes of Israel, except those of Judah and Benjamin who lived in the southern monarchy of Judah.

The cuneiform tablets discovered in this settlement gave scholars invaluable information about the world of the Middle Bronze Age in this region. Some Akkadian stories dealing with the deeds of Sargon of Akkad and his grandson Naram-Sin with which the Hittite kings later compared their own achievements may have reached Anatolia by way of these colonies. With the disappearance of political stability, which kept these long trade routes open, in the beginning of the eighteenth century the Assyrian traders seem to have returned home.

After an ascendancy during the first half of the second millennium Assyria suffered a set-back and their reappearance had to wait for the weakening of the kingdom of Mitanni in the 1350s BCE by the Hittites. Thus at the beginning of the history of the Israelites, replacing Mitanni, Assyria again emerged as a powerful empire from beyond the Euphrates. In the following century Tukulti-Ninurta I (1244-1208 BCE) would defeat Tudhaliya IV (1239-1209 BCE) at Surra (Savur) north of Tur Abdin and engulf what was left of the crippled Mitanni.

Assyria did not suffer the calamity created by the Sea Peoples in the 1190s. Having a strong army and its location beyond the Euphrates may have played a

Ruins of *karum* (literally 'quay, port, trading station, harbour') where the Assyrian merchants lived. 1950-1800 BCE. Looking south towards the mound of Kanesh (Kültepe).

ASSHUR (ASSYRIANS)

part in this. Nevertheless, some of the immigrants seem to have marched inland towards Mesopotamia because Tiglath-pileser I (1114-1076 BCE) mentions his victory against 20,000 *Muski* people who had seized one of his northern provinces for fifty years and against the Kaska people, whose home was the Black Sea region, but who had then migrated to his frontiers.

Beginning in the middle of the ninth century and until the fall of their capital Nineveh to the Medes in 612 BCE, politics in the Near East would be shaped by Assyria. The only power which challenged the Assyrian offensive in this long period was Urartu. If the Assyrian army suffered any defeat this was in its wars against the latter. Nevertheless, even Urartu became an Assyrian vassal during the later part of its history and paid the latter tribute.

The Neo-Hittite kingdoms which were established along the southeastern fringe of Anatolia bore special attraction for Assyria because they were situated on the trade route from Mesopotamia to the Mediterranean and Anatolia, which meant slaves, horses, metals and timber for the Assyrians. Although Assyrian kings carried out isolated campaigns against Anatolia or Syria and Palestine, the classical cycle of an Assyrian campaign included northern Syria where they subdued Aramean states such as Bit-Adini (the Beth-eden in Amos 1:5) on the Euphrates, or one or more of the Neo-Hittite kingdoms such as Milid (Malatya), Carchemish or Samal (Zincirli) from where they reached Que (Coa or Cilician plain) which in the ninth century became an Assyrian province. A permanent Assyrian existence in the region is displayed by the number of Assyrian reliefs on rock surfaces near Adana and Antakya. Following the Mediterranean coastline, Assyrian armies marched to Phoenicia (Byblos, Sidon and Tyre) whose forests were their major source of timber. The richness of Tyre is mentioned in Ezekiel (27) and the decoration on the bronze gates of the Assyrian palace at Balawat includes boats loaded with tribute from this Phoenician city. To the south the Philistine cities which occupied the narrow coastal strip, the divided monarchies of Israel and Judah and the Aramean states, of which the strongest was Damascus, were in permanent conflict and coveted Assyria's friendship amongst each other. If they ever forgot their local problems and raised an allied front against Assyria this was at Karkar on the Orontes river in 853 BCE where Ben-hadad (II), king of Damascus (the biblical Hadad-ezer), leading the Arameans and Ahab of Israel, fought together and prevented Shalmaneser III (858-824 BCE) from entering their lands. In 841 Shalmaneser returned and both Damascus and Israel became Assyrian vassals.

The rivalry and animosity of the kingdoms in Syria and Palestine towards each other gave Assyria an excuse for invading their territory frequently. Among the most

Assyrian relief at Karabur near Antakya. Ninth-seventh centuries BCE. To the left a god stands with his right hand raised in blessing. His other hand holds a lotus flower. He wears a helmet with three horns.

The lack of beard of the person opposite him may indicate his being eunuch and imply his position as a royal official. Between the figures there are six symbols belonging to different deities.

ASSHUR (ASSYRIANS)

important campaigns which are mentioned in the Bible, one belongs to Tiglath-pileser III (744-727 BCE) (the biblical Pul) who after sacking Damascus did not invade only Israel, where he put Hoshea on the throne, but also Judah which had asked for his protection (2 Kgs 16:7). Israel had to pay a heavy tribute and many of its inhabitants were deported. When Hoshea, the puppet king of Israel, rebelled after Tiglath-pileser's death, it was invaded by Sargon II (721-705 BCE) and its capital Samaria was sacked (721 BCE) following a three-year siege. Its inhabitants were deported to Assyria and Media (2 Kgs 17:6) and colonists were brought in their place from various parts of Mesopotamia. Jewish literature referred to the exiles of these invasions as the 'Lost Ten Tribes'. If a single state was allowed to stay independent in the region, this was Judah of king Hezekiah (715-687) to whom the Bible (2 Kgs 20:20; 2 Chr 32:30) ascribes the building of the tunnel in Jerusalem from the spring of Gihon to the pool of Siloam to access its water in the time of siege.

During the latter part of the reign of Sargon II the war front of Assyria moved north against its enemies in Anatolia: Urartu, Tabal and Mita of Mushki (Midas of Phrygia) and defeated them one after the other. The last time Sargon II is mentioned in Assyrian sources is when he was fighting against the Cimmerians (the biblical Gomer) in central Anatolia.

Hezekiah, however, after Sargon's death, joined a coalition against Assyria as told in Isaiah (39) and in 701 Judah was invaded by Sennacherib. Lachish was captured and Jerusalem was besieged but not taken. Before the city fell, the Assyrians broke the siege and went home as told in Isaiah (37) and 2 Kings (19):

'That night the angel of the LORD went forth and struck down one hundred and eighty-five thousand men in the Assyrian camp. Early the next morning, there they were, all the corpses

(previous page) Assyrian war chariot. Wall painting. Til Barsip (northern Syria). Seventh century BCE (after A. Parrot's 'The Arts of Assyria').

The Angel Smiting the Assyrians before Jerusalem (2 Kgs 19; Is 37). Fresco. 1315-21. Kariye Museum (former church of the monastery of St Saviour in Chora). İstanbul.

of the dead. So Sennacherib, the king of Assyria, broke camp, and went back home to Nineveh.'

More probably the Assyrian supply lines may have been threatened by the Egyptians. Herodotus also narrates a related event in which 'thousands of field-mice (suggestive of plague-carrying rodents) swarmed' Sennacherib's, or Sanacharibos' army in Egypt 'during the night, and ate their quivers, their bowstrings, and the leather handles of their shields, so that on the following day, having no arms to fight with, they abandoned their position.' The Bible informs us about the end of this king that he was killed by his two sons who after the murder fled to Ararat (Urartu) (2 Kgs 19; Tb 1; Is 37).

Towards the end of the eighth century several new powers entered on the historical stage in north Mesopotamia. These were the Cimmerians (the biblical Gomer), their kin the Scythians (the biblical Ashkenaz), the Medes (the biblical Madai) and to the south the Neo-Babylonian empire. According to Assyrian records, under the pressure of the Cimmerians the Lydian king Gugu (Gyges) sent envoys to ally himself with their king Ashurbanipal II (668-627 BCE). However, once the Cimmerian threat moved on, Gyges did not hesitate to send assistance to Psammetichus II of Egypt who had rebelled against Assyria (p 77).

In 612 a coalition of the forces of the Medes, Scythians and Babylonians attacked the Assyrian capital Nineveh and capturing it brought an end to the Assyrian empire. Although Herodotus at the beginning his book tells us that he will relate the city's fall in another place, he does not fulfill his promise.[2] It has been suggested that when the prophet Nahum (1:8) says 'when the flood rages; He makes an end of his opponents, and his enemies he pursues with darkness' he refers to an event where a tributary of the Tigris river washed away a part of Nineveh's defences and caused its fall, an anecdote also mentioned by the Greek historians Diodorus and Xenophon. The Assyrian court fled to Haran and Carchemish and made a last stand here. Haran fell in 610 and the battle of Carchemish (605 BCE) ended with the defeat of the Assyrians and their allies the Egyptians by Nebuchadnezzar II.

Later tradition claims that in Anatolia Aphrodisias was founded and called Ninoe after Ninus, the mythical king of Assyria. The Assyrians from Nineveh may have settled in Aphrodisias in the seventh century BCE and established a cult of the goddess Ishtar there. The tradition of the cult of Zeus Nineudius, which is thought to have been connected with Nineveh, is recorded in the inscriptions from the city's Roman history.

[2] Probably lost.

ARPACHSHAD (BABYLON)

At that time, when Merodach-baladan, son of Baladan, king of Babylon, heard that Hezekiah had been ill, he sent letters and gifts to him (2 Kgs 20:12).

Arpachshad of Table of the Nations (Gn 10:22; 1 Chr 17), a son of Shem, is generally accepted as Babylon which is listed together with Erech (Uruk) and Accad (Akkad) as one of the chief cities of the kingdom of Nimrod. In the Bible the term refers both to the city and the kingdom established here. Among Arpachshad's descendants Serug, Nahor and Terah are encountered as place names in the region of Haran. For the general reader the name Babylon immediately brings to mind the Exile.

According to Genesis (11:2) descendants of Noah 'came upon a valley in the land of Shinar and settled there.' In Shinar, with bricks hardened with fire they created a city with a tower (the tower of Babel) whose top reached the sky. Genesis (10:10) identifies Shinar (Sumer) as the land where Babel (Babylon), Erech (Uruk) and Accad (Akkad) stood; the alluvial basin of the lower Tigris and Euphrates.

The cities of Babylonia are known to have been the creators of the earliest civilizations. The script they invented, known as the Akkadian cuneiform, became the

Calf relief from the Ishtar Gate at Babylon. Glazed tile. Reign of Nebuchadnezzar II (605-562 BCE). İstanbul Archaeological Museum. In the Mesopotamian pantheon the bull represented the weather god, the Akkadian Adad.

international language of trade and diplomacy until it was replaced by Aramaic language and writing towards the end of the ninth century BCE. The history of relations between Anatolia and lower Mesopotamia goes back to this period. It is said that in the reign of Sargon of Akkad (2340-2284 BCE) the empire's frontiers extended from beyond the Persian Gulf to the 'cedar mountain' (the Amanus) and the 'silver mountain' (the Taurus). An epic Sumerian poem known as 'King of the Battle' describes Sargon campaigning in Cappadocia to support the oppressed merchants against the native king of Burushattum (Hittite Purushanda, probably Acemhöyük near Aksaray). The story, if not written to edify Sargon, may imply the existence of Akkadian trade colonies in the region before those of the Assyrians. Sargon's story of a childhood in which he was put in a basket of rushes and thrown into the Euphrates is the oldest of similar tales based on the motif of the exposed children such as Moses (Ex 2:1-10), Krishna, Romulus and Remus and some other great men.

An inscription which comes from the Diyarbakır region names a conquered town in central Anatolia and shows that his grandson, king Naram-Sin (2260-2223 BCE), also travelled as far north as that. Another story which was probably made up to edify him associates him with a campaign like that of Sargon of Akkad to Burushattum in Anatolia.

Sometime around 1600 BCE king Mursili I of the Hittites campaigned to Syria and after conquering Halap (Aleppo) marched for about 800 km down the Euphrates as far as Babylon and capturing the city brought about the end of the First Dynasty, whose most famous king was Hammurabi (1792-1750 BCE).

After this period Babylon was ruled by a new dynasty known as the Kassites who were not involved in Near Eastern international politics. However the appearance of Babylon in the biblical world as the Neo-Babylonian empire (626-539 BCE) — albeit later — would play a very important part in the formation of the Jewish religion and culture as known today. The first mention of a Neo-Babylonian empire in the Bible is when king Hezekiah was won over by its king Merodach-baladan (2 Kgs 20; 2 Chr 32; Is 39) and rebelled against Assyria. Hezekiah's venture ended with Sennacherib's invasion of Judah in 701 BCE. In 612 BCE, in the reign of Nabopolassar, the Babylonians, as allies of the Medes, captured the Assyrian capital Nineveh. Nabopolassar's son Nebuchadnezzar II defeated the forces of the last Assyrian king Ashur-uballit and his ally Necho II of Egypt, whose army included Greek mercenaries, at the battle of Carchemish in 605. To the general reader Nebuchadnezzar II is better remembered by the 'Hanging Gardens', which he is said to have built for a Median wife of his who missed the wooded mountains of her native country and which would later be known as one of the Seven Wonders of the World.

ARPACHSHAD (BABYLON)

Following the fall of Nineveh the Babylonians became the natural sovereigns of Palestine. Hoping for support from Egypt, Judah under Jehoiakim (609-598 BCE) rebelled against the Babylonians, an event which ultimately led Nebuchadnezzar II to march and capture Jerusalem in 597, after a few months' siege. He ordered the king, the royal family, all the important military and civilian population and those who would be useful in case of another revolt, to be exiled to Babylonia where they would sit and weep and 'remember Zion' by its rivers (Ps 137:1). Jehoiakim's uncle Mattaniah was put on the throne, with his name changed to Zedekiah (2 Kgs 24:15-17).

A second attempt to throw off the Neo-Babylonian yoke also ended in disaster. Nebuchadnezzar II captured Jerusalem in 586 after a two-year siege. The fortifications of the city were demolished, the palace and the temple were looted and destroyed and a large part of what was left of its population, including Zedekiah, who was blinded, were led into exile to Babylon which would last for about fifty years. Nabonidus, the last Babylonian king, was a zealous believer of the moon-god Sin of Haran and is known to have restored the god's temple there. According to Herodotus Nabonidus (Greek Labynetus) was one of the two diplomats (the other was Syennesis of Cilicia) who handled the details of the peace treaty signed between the Lydians and the Medes after the battle of 585 BCE fought in Cappadocia. At the beginning of his reign the king undertook a campaign to Cilicia, with such success that he was able to dedicate nearly 3,000 prisoners of war as temple slaves. In the third year of his reign Nabonidus took his army for a ten-year campaign to north Arabia. Babylon of this period is used as the setting for the Book of Daniel, which is known to have been written towards the end of the second century BCE. The story of the seven-year madness of king Nebuchadnezzar in Daniel (4) is thought to have been inspired by this long sojourn of Nabonidus. Belshazzar, his son and regent in Babylon during his absence is introduced in the story as the actual king (Dn 5).

In 539 BC Cyrus the Great of Persia, who had by this date replaced the Median dynasty, captured Babylon and freeing the Judean captives made himself memorable for Hebrew literature (p 85). The city's final important appearance in history was on the death of Alexander the Great here in 323 BCE.

By the beginning of the Christian era the name of Babylon had become a synonym for wickedness as the Apostle John remarked: 'On her forehead was written a name, which is a mystery, "Babylon the great, the mother of harlots and of the abominations of the earth" ' (Rv 17:5), comparing the city in a coded attack upon the iniquities of Roman empire (also 1 Pt 5:13).

URARTU

Summon against her the kingdoms, Ararat, Minni, and Ashkenaz...the king of Media (Jer 51:27-28).

Votive plaque. Bronze. Eighth-seventh centuries BCE. Van Museum. It is decorated with the god Haldi, head of the Urartian pantheon, standing on a lion and holding a standard in his left hand. His other hand is raised in blessing. He carries crossed wing-like quivers. Opposite him under the hieroglyphs is his wife, the goddess Aurabaini. Between the couple is a sacrificial goat.

The spelling of Urartu encountered in the Old Testament is *rrt*, mistakenly vocalized as Ararat. In the Bible it is mentioned as the mountainous district where the Ark came to rest. It is also mentioned as the enemy kingdom to which the two sons of the Assyrian king Sennacherib (704-681 BCE) escaped after assassinating their father (2 Kgs 19:37; Tb 10:21; Is 37:38). What is referred to as Ararat in the Bible was popularly known in the past as Urartu, its name among its arch-enemies, the Assyrians.

The tribes which occupied the heights of southeastern Anatolia were ethnically Hurrian and in the middle of the second millennium they were incorporated in the kingdom of Mitanni. With the disappearance of Mitanni these people seem to have returned to their nomadic state and survived as independent tribes.[1] The campaigns of the Assyrian king Shalmaneser III (858-824 BCE) to Urartu imply that by his reign the Hurrian tribes had consolidated their power around a single chief, Sarduri I (844-832 BCE) probably to stand against the growing Assyrian pressure. Thus in the middle of the ninth century BCE the 400-year tribal history of the region was replaced by that of a powerful kingdom. The archaeological evidence shows that after this period for two and half centuries Urartu was the only kingdom among Assyria's neighbours which stood against it and ultimately outlived it. Assyrian records show that Urartu's irrigation systems, technological achievements and strong garrisons even won the praise of its enemies.

The kingdom's heart was the Van basin. Its capital was Tushpa (citadel of Van) on a defensible rock outcrop by the shore of lake Van. Today its former territory extends into Turkey's eastern neighbours. In the past its neighbours were the Neo-Hittite states such as Milid (Malatya), Gurgum-Marqasi (Maraş) and Kummuh (later Greco-Roman Commagene; Adıyaman) to the west, Qulha (Greek Colchis) towards the Black Sea, and cities situated in the great bend of the Euphrates and the lands of

---

[1] Urartian is not a later continuation of Hurrian, but both languages are independent branches of a common 'root-language', a proto-Hurrian-Urartian, branches of which had grown apart as early as the third millennium.

Manneans (the biblical Minni) to the southeast of lake Urmia. Subduing all of these isolated independent powers, the Urartian kings tried to raise a common front against the Assyrian threat.

In the middle of the eighth century internal problems in Assyria enabled Urartu to expand and control the trade route from Mesopotamia to Anatolia and even gain temporary access to the Mediterranean. The setback of Assyrian power lasted until Tiglath-pileser III (744-727 BCE) (the biblical Pul) sat on the throne. Re-establishing the Assyrian hegemony over the Neo-Hittite states and other allies of Urartu, this king secured the Assyrian trade routes to Anatolia and the Mediterranean. Campaigns of both Tiglath-pileser III and his successor Sargon II (721-705) devastated Urartu. The war spoils that they brought Assyria included even 'cypress beams from the roof' of palaces. Against such formidable Assyrian campaigns Urartu often retreated to distant mountain pockets and by avoiding a pitched battle saved its army.

An important event of Sargon II's campaign of 714 BCE was his sack of Muşaşir. This holy city was situated between Urartu and Assyria and housed the most important seat of god the Haldi and was also held sacred by all the nations. The shrine may be compared to Delphi of the Classical era and its destruction shocked the ancient world including the Assyrians themselves. The spoil obtained from the temple of Haldi is known as the richest of its kind in the ancient Near East.

Already in the beginning of the eighth century BCE Urartu was threatened by the Cimmerians but until it was crippled by the last attack of Sargon II it held the enemy at its frontiers. However, in the closing decade of the century it was invaded by the Cimmerians.

Urartu was unable to recover from the Cimmerian invasion and in the last hundred years of its history became Assyria's vassal. Before long the Cimmerian threat was replaced by that of the Scythians. Towards the end of the seventh century politics in the region began to be shaped by the Medes, who captured Nineveh in 612 BCE and brought an end to the Assyrian kingdom. The last biblical reference to Urartu belongs to the fourth year of king Zedekiah's reign (594 BCE), when Jeremiah (51:27-28) prophesies that Babylon will fall at the hands of foreign nations; that is Ararat (Urartians), the Minni (Manneans), the Ashkenaz (Scythians) and the Medes. However, historically, the fortune of the first three foreign nations mentioned was in decline by this date and the stage was left to the Medes. The end of Urartu may have been brought about either by the Scythians or king Cyaxares of Medes when he marched in 585 BCE against king Alyattes of Lydia through eastern Anatolia.

Warpalawas (738-710 BCE), king of Tabal before the god Tarkhunzas. Rock relief at İvriz near Ereğli (Hibushna), Konya. The king wears an embroidered robe and a long shawl-like fringed coat fastened on the chest with a semicircular fibula. His hands are raised in a gesture of prayer. He is deliberately shown smaller than the god opposite him. Both the bossed fibula and the design of swastikas on his robe are of Phrygian type. In contrast his hair, beard and face are worked in Aramean-Assyrian style. The artist who carved it may have been a local sculptor influenced from the East. Warpalawas was known to have established peaceful relations with Mita of Mushki (Midas of Phrygia). Tarkhunzas, the god of storm (weather) and crops wears a headdress with two horns, a short-sleeved shirt with a v-neck, a short skirt curving in volutes at each edge and ending above the knee, and a broad belt. In his left hand he grasps heads of wheat still growing from the ground, and in his right bunches of grapes. On his feet are slippers curling up at the toe.

TUBAL (TABAL)

Javan, Tubal, and Meshech were also traders with you, exchanging slaves and articles of bronze for your goods (Ez 27:13).

In Table of the Nations Tubal (Akkadian *Tabalu*) is shown as a son of Japheth (Gn 10:2; 1 Chr 1:5) and in the biblical narrative is frequently accompanied by Meshech, another son of Japheth (Ez 27; 32; 38; 39). Assyrian records also refer to the two groups together as *Tabali Muski,* occupying the region which would later be known as Cappadocia, and describe these nations as neighbours of Que (Cilician plain). The region was known to the Hittites as the Lower Land and corresponds to today's Kayseri.

The allusion in Ezekiel (27:13) that Tabal (together with Meshech) supplied Tyre with 'slaves and articles of bronze' is thought to have been inspired by the social and economic world of the Levant in the tenth-ninth centuries, during which the interests of the Phoenician city of Tyre were directed to north Syria and Cilicia, territories which had relations with Tabal beyond the Taurus.

With its metal resources and especially the silver of the Taurus, which was known as the 'silver mountain' as early as the third millennium BCE, Tabal was a vital part of the Assyrian economic periphery. The list of war spoils that the Assyrians took from Muşaşir when they sacked it in 714 BCE includes objects of silver referred to as being from Tabal. The name appears for the first time in a document related to a campaign of the Assyrian king Shalmaneser III (858-824 BCE) which informs us that he fought against a force of over twenty-four kings of Tabal. This information implies that Tabal was probably ruled by a number of small principalities which may have from time to time consolidated their forces under a single king, who referred to himself as the 'Great King' in Hittite hieroglyphs in the reliefs on prominent rock surfaces in central Anatolia. In the eighth century the region was united under the dynasty of Burutas whose best known king was probably Warpalawas (738-710 BCE) also known to the Assyrians as Urbala of Tukhana (Tuwana, later Tyana; Kemerhisar). The principalities of Tabal survived under the hegemony of Assyria and tried to shake off its yoke by forming alliances with the Phrygians and Urartu. Tabal was raided by the Cimmerians from the north in the beginning of the seventh century, who according to Herodotus had set up their base in the Sinop region.

MINNI (MANNEANS)

Summon against her the kingdoms, Ararat, Minni, and Ashkenaz...the king of Media (Jer 51:27-28).

The Minni of the Bible are thought to be the Manneans who lived in the northeastern Mesopotamian highlands to the south of lake Urmia. Jeremiah's prophecy (51:27-28) shows them as an enemy of Babylon. Their name is encountered frequently in Urartian and Assyrian records from the ninth to the seventh century BCE.

The general impression given by these records is that *Mana*, the land of *Mannai* was divided among a number of independent principalities who either fought among themselves or allied themselves with one or more stronger kingdoms in the region. In the eighth to seventh centuries the interests of the Urartians and Assyrians conflicted in *Mana* and the Manneans suffered between their two powerful neighbours. The word 'Armenia,' or 'Ar-Minni' is thought to have meant the 'high land of Manneans'.

Bossed Phrygian fibula. Bronze. Seventh-sixth centuries BCE. İstanbul Archaeological Museum.

MESHECH (PHRYGIANS)

There are Meshech and Tubal and all their throng about her grave, all of them uncircumcised, slain by the sword, for they spread their terror in the land of the living (Ez 32:26).

In Table of the Nations Meshech is the third son of Japheth (Gen 10:2; 1 Chr 1:5) and elsewhere coupled with Tubal (Tabal). This coupling is also true for their geographical location and the chronology of the two kingdoms and their trade in copper vessels (Ez 27; 32; 38; 39). Meshech is thought to be the name of the Phrygians who appeared on the Anatolian plateau in about the middle of the eighth century BCE, some four hundred years after the fall of the Hittites. Although the Phrygian hegemony was not comparable with that of the vastness of the Hittite empire, archaeological evidence shows that by this date most of the former Hittite strongholds such as Hattusa, Alacahöyük, Alişar and Pazarlı were settled by Phrygians. Homer says that the Phrygians were already in Anatolia when the Trojan War was fought. Strabo and other Greek writers bring them from Europe at a later date. Excavations, however, have not yet brought to light any convincing evidence about their origins. While they may have invaded Anatolia before or during the upheavals created by the Sea Peoples, they may have at that time already been living there under the Hittite hegemony.

MESHECH (PHRYGIANS)

The earliest reference to the Phrygians comes from the annals of Tiglath-pileser I (1114-1077 BCE) in which they are referred to as *Muski*. The king claims that at the beginning of his reign he fought and defeated 20,000 Mushki under five kings who came and seized one of his provinces in the northeast. It seems that a group of people had marched as far as the bend of the upper Tigris during the commotion created by the Sea Peoples. This group however may have invaded Anatolia across the Caucasus but later been incorporated in the kingdom of Midas. An Assyrian text from the eighth century BCE seems to mention a Gordias who installed a vassal as far east as Tegarama (the biblical Togarmah) on the upper Euphrates. Gordias may have been the king who founded Gordion and was said to have dedicated a chariot, binding the yoke to the pole with the Gordion knot, which was later to be cut by Alexander the Great in 334.

In the second half of the eighth century Assyrian texts frequently mention a kingdom of Mushki — even though this term may have comprised other ethnic groups than the Phrygians — and its ambitious ruler Mita (Midas). The latter seems to have tried to expand his frontiers and captured towns in Cilicia, the Assyrian province of Que, threatening Assyria's north Syrian frontiers, and formed a coalition with Carchemish against the Assyrians. At the beginning of the seventh century the Cimmerians, after routing Urartu, invaded Anatolia and sacking Gordion (696 BCE) brought an end to the Phrygian kingdom, with the legendary Midas committing suicide by drinking ox-blood.[1] In antiquity ox-blood was thought poisonous because of its magical power. In Exodus (24:8) Moses consecrates his people by sprinkling on them the blood of sacrificed bulls.

Mushki and Tabal and their association were also known by the Greeks because Herodotus places their remnants side by side when he says that the Pontic Moschoi and Tibarenoi paid tribute to the Persians and supplied their army with soldiers.

The story of Midas of the golden touch, a legendary hero inspired by the historical Midas, has a set of tales which take place in various countries including Anatolia. Having captured the besotted old satyr Silenus, Midas returned him to Dionysus and was rewarded with his fondest wish — the golden touch. When the starving Midas discovered that even his food and drink turned to gold on touch, he repented his folly to the god and was instructed to wash himself in the river Pactolus (Sart çayı).

[1] The elder Pliny records that 'bull's blood coagulates and hardens very quickly, and is therefore considered poisonous to drink fresh.' A mode of committing suicide that is said to have been also chosen by Athenian statesman Themistocles in the 460s BCE at Magnesia on the Meander (Menderes Manisası), drinking the blood of the bull he sacrificed at the temple of Artemis here.

'Kırık Aslantaş' ('Broken Lion-stone') from the Phrygian valley near Afyon. 540-530 BCE. Originally it was one of the pair which flanked the entrance of a rock-cut tomb.

MESHECH (PHRYGIANS)

Rock-cut altar at Midas City near Eskişehir. Seventh-early sixth century BCE. A seated statue of the goddess Cybele was probably placed on it during ceremonies. To the left it bears an inscription in Phrygian which reads from left to right.

This river which seems to have been a major source of the riches of Midas later provided the economic foundation for that other symbol of wealth, Croesus of Lydia. The use of thumb and first finger for what is called the Phrygian blessing in the past is also related to Phrygia's legendary period and the gesture may have inspired the Latin blessing.

What has been brought to light from the Phrygian sites shows that their culture was related to certain earlier Anatolian cultures. The Phrygian capital was Gordion, situated at the point where later the Persian Royal Road crossed the Sangarius (Sakarya) river. The land route from the Near Eastern civilizations to Greece ran through the Phrygian plateau and the city must have been an important trade centre via which some objects and art forms of the East reached Greece. The rich finds from Great Tumulus (Gordion) show that the Midas' wealth was not purely legend but had some truth about it.[2]

The Phrygians are known as one of the earliest people who used alphabetic writing. Scholars, although they accept that this writing is almost identical with the Greek alphabet, differ about its origins. Some of them think that the Phrygians may

[2] Research has shown that the construction of this tomb predates Midas' death and it probably belonged to his father Gordias.

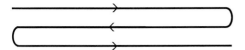

Boustrophedon writing

Argos wearing a Phrygian cap. Detail. Mosaic of the Red Pavement from Daphne. Second century CE. Hatay Archaeological Museum. Antakya.

have borrowed it from the Neo-Hittite states of southeast Anatolia where Phoenician was spoken and written along with Hittite hieroglyphic script or Aramaic languages. Some scholars even suggest that in addition to the sea route, the Phoenician system of writing may have been first introduced to Greece by the Phrygians. The inscriptions which have survived mostly on Phrygian vessels and relatively longer ones on the monuments, especially those at Midas City near Eskişehir, show that the Phrygian language belonged to the Indo-European family; but though legible, it cannot be understood completely. It could be written both from left to right or right to left or in a regularly alternating sequence known as *boustrophedon,* or 'ox-plowing'.

The information in Acts (2:10) that the Phrygians in Jerusalem were surprised to see that the Apostles were speaking their language, among many others, and said 'We are...inhabitants of...Phrygia' is probably no more than an allusion to a strange tongue. It may also point out that the Jewish communities in Phrygia did not lose their connection with the Holy Land and went on pilgrimages. Otherwise, except for some Phrygian grave inscriptions against tomb plundering, their language was forgotten by the first century BCE. A certain Philip, 'a Phrygian by birth' is also mentioned among the governors who Antiochus IV Epiphanes left in Jerusalem after his pillage of the Temple and city (2 Mac 5:22; 6:11).

According to Herodotus, the Egyptian king Psammetichus I (663-609 BCE) wanted to discover the identity of the most ancient of mankind and tried a linguistic experiment. Two new-born children of poor parents were given to a shepherd to be raised by his flock with no human speech. The king behaved like this to hear the first words the children would utter and thus learn the language which men naturally speak. The children were isolated for two years until one day the shepherd entered the room carrying bread. The children cried *bekos*, which the writer says was the Phrygian word for bread. Thus, the king discovered that it was not the Egyptians but the Phrygians who were the most ancient race of the world.

The history of the so-called Phrygian cap goes back to the pointed tiara which was the headdress of the Hittite weather god, but gradually evolved into a curving, horn-shaped cap, worn low on the forehead and curling forward at the tip. It was to become the most popular type of head-gear and was worn by people and gods alike in the Mediterranean world. Some two thousand five hundred years later it was revived as the liberty cap, or *bonnet rouge* or Jacobin cap, worn as a symbol during the French Revolution. The Greeks, not knowing anything about the Hittites and their gods, could not account for this strange headdress and invented the tale of Midas' ass-ears where he uses this cap to hide them. The term 'Phrygian' had a bad connotation among Greeks.

GOMER (CIMMERIANS)

Gomer with all its troops (Ez 38:6).

In Table of the Nations Gomer is placed at the head of Japhet's seven sons (Gn 10:1 Chr 1:5). He is the eponymous ancestor of the Cimmerians. In the records of kings of Urartu and Assyria, they are called *Gimirrai*. The original home of these semi-nomadic Indo-European hordes is thought to have been southeast Russia where they lived in the fourth and early third millennium BCE together with their kin the Scythians. They were probably the people who domesticated the horse first. Later they began to migrate westwards and southwards. Utilizing the advanced metallurgy of the Caucasus and with the weapons obtained from here they raided the Pontic steppe to the east of Dnieper at the turn of the first millennium BCE. From the last quarter of the eighth century their attention, partly owing to the rivalry

Ancient track in central Anatolia. The deep ruts have been worn by the wheels of carriages.

Arrowhead from Gordion. Bronze. Seventh century BCE. İstanbul Archaeological Museum. Such triangular types were mostly used by the Cimmerians and Scythians, though not peculiar to them. These horsemen may have picked the type from the Caucasus and introduced it to the Near East and Anatolia.

between Urartu and Assyria, partly from the pressure of the Scythians, turned to the south of the Caucasus. Their entry from the west of the Caucasus chain led them also to be known as the West Scythians. In the closing years of the eighth century BCE they broke through the northern heights into the interior of today's Iran and from here turning west routed the Manneans and Urartu, which were trying to recover from the recent invasion of Tiglath-pileser III (744-727 BCE) of Assyria.

When their return route was cut off by the Scythians they turned northwest, marching along the the Black Sea shore, and set up a base in the vicinity of Sinope from where they moved southwards towards Tabal. It was against this invasion that Mita of Mushki (Midas of Phrygia) forgot his hostility to Assyria and tried to establish an alliance with it. This pact, however, failed to check the Cimmerian push into central Anatolia. In 705 BCE, the Assyrian forces, perhaps including their allies the Phrygians and Tabal, were defeated in central Anatolia and the Assyrian king Sargon II is thought to have been killed on the battlefield. After this point Mita also disappears from ancient records. He might have retreated to his capital Gordion to prepare his capital for the anticipated Cimmerian invasion. The latter raided the lands of Tabal and Phrygia and sacked Gordion in 696 BCE causing Midas to commit suicide. In about 646 BCE they swept over Lydia under their king Dugdamme (Greek Lygdamis), sacked Sardis and killed king Gyges. Ephesus and Magnesia on the Meander (Menderes Manisası) suffered the same fate. After this period their decline was rapid. When they tried to penetrate into Syria by way of Cilicia they were stopped at the Cilician Gates and probably annihilated by Ashurbanipal II. By the beginning of the sixth century BCE they abandoned the Near Eastern stage, returning home beyond the Caucasus with the war spoils they had accumulated, and their place in the east was taken by the Scythians. Scholars put the Cimmerians in the group of nomadic hordes such as the Scythians, Huns and Tartars who did not contribute much to the civilized world. Their name survives in Crim Tartary and Crimea and in the adventures of the popular hero Conan the Cimmerian.

Some of the Cimmerians may have participated in Ashurbanipal II's conquest of Egypt in 661 BCE. Nevertheless four years later they would be expelled from here by Psammetichus I together with the Assyrian garrison.

ASHKENAZ (SCYTHIANS)

Summon against her the kingdoms, Ararat, Minni, and Ashkenaz...the king of Media (Jer 51:27-28).

In Table of the Nations Ashkenaz' descent from Japheth (Gn 10:3; 1 Chr 1:6) through Gomer (Cimmerians) confirms the historical fact of the succession of the Cimmerians by the Scythians in ancient Near Eastern politics. In the Assyrian texts they are called *Askuzai*.

The home of the Scythians was in the Altai mountains from which they migrated to the European steppes. They were related to the Cimmerians, both being Indo-European nomadic warriors speaking an Iranian language. Perhaps the only difference between them was that the first wave (Cimmerian) entered the Near East from the west side of the Caucasus and operated mostly in Anatolia, whereas the second wave (Scythian) came crossing the eastern part of the Caucasus and was active as far as Egypt. They were first mentioned in the annals of Urartu in the beginning of the eighth century BCE, as settled beyond the river Cyrus to the north.

The existence of Scythians beyond the Danube was known to the Greeks. In the *Iliad* Homer remarks that Zeus turned his shining eyes from the battlefield of Troy to the Scythian plain beyond the Danube. Herodotus says he 'was never to learn exactly what the population of Scythia is' and that they were 'the most uncivilized nations in the world.' He adds that the Scythians had neither cities nor fortifications but lived a nomadic life in wagons; all were mounted archers and they lived from their herds, not by agriculture. Herodotus ascribes many peculiarities to the Scythians such as that their warriors drank the blood of enemy, made mugs of skulls, cloaks of scalps and napkins of skins.

The Scythians routed the Cimmerians, who had sacked Urartu, and remained around lake Urmia until evicted by the Medes early in the sixth century. They were so powerful that to secure their alliance Esarhaddon, king of Assyria gave his daughter to their king Bartatua in 674 BCE. From their base they threatened all their neighbours and raided as far as the frontiers of Egypt. Psammetichus I (663-609 BCE) was able to buy off the Scythians who had reached frontiers of his country, who agreed to retreat, pillaging Ashkelon on their return, an act for which according to Herodotus they were 'punished by the goddess with the infliction of what is called the "female disease", namely homosexuality, and their descendants still suffer from it; a story which may have inspired the remark in 1 Samuel (5:6) that the Philistines at Ashdod were afflicted with hemorrhoids by God for the defiling

(opposite) Scythian slave sharpening his knife to flay Marsyas. Marble. Roman period. Manisa Archaeological Museum. Flaying alive was thought to have been a Scythian speciality. On the ground is the double-flute of Marsyas.

of the Ark of the Covenant. As allies of the Medes, who called them the *Saka*, they took part in the destruction of the Assyrian capital Nineveh in 612 BCE.

The Scythians, although Jeremiah's prophecy (51:27-28) shows them as Babylon's enemy, also accompanied the Neo-Babylonian crown prince Nebuchadnezzar II to Syria and Palestine after the battle of Carchemish, captured Ashkelon in 604 BCE and reached Egypt in 601 BCE. They may have been among the Babylonian forces during the capture of Jerusalem in about 597 and 586. Heredotus says that the Median king Cyaxares 'invited a greater number of them to a banquet at which they made them drunk and murdered them.' Thus the survivors fled, recrossing the Caucasus and probably joining other Scythians, and moved into the Pontic steppe. Here they were, mistakenly, welcomed by the Thracians as a relief from the Cimmerians. The Scythians continued to raid Persian lands over the Caucasus from the Pontic steppe and from beyond the Oxus river and Cyrus II the Great lost his life in battle against them. In 519 Darius I campaigned north and subdued the Asiatic Scythians. In 513 the king decided to attack the Scythians 'Beyond the Sea' and crossed Anatolia all the way to the north of the Danube. However since the Persian king was told the Scythians had no settlements or cultivated lands, but only their ancestors' graves to battle for, having failed to find anything to destroy in the country Darius returned home.

Scythians from the Gate of All Nations at Persepolis. Xerxes I (486-465 BCE). They are recognizable by their pointed hats and were one of the few vassal nations who were allowed to keep their weapons in the presence of the Persian kings.

ASHKENAZ (SCYTHIANS)

The Greeks knew the Scythians as barbarians, the way they were described by Herodotus and other Greek writers. The most evident reason for this was the Scythian habit of drinking wine neat rather than mixing it with water.[1] The Scythians continued to occupy the north of the Danube maintaining military control of the steppe, extorting payment in kind for granting a safe passage for profitable trade between the steppe and the Greek cities. They also supplied the Greeks with slaves, called 'Scythians' but more likely 'Thracians'. About 495 BCE a Scythian raid is said to have reached the shore of the Propontis (Sea of Marmara). In the course of time some of them probably mixed with the Thracians and became settled agriculturists. Their last king was killed during a battle in 339 by Philip II of Macedon and they evacuated the Danube region, moving further north towards Crimea. In Asia they are recorded fighting alongside the Persians against Alexander the Great when he tried to invade Sogdiana beyond the Aral Sea.

The name of the Scythians was equated with savagery. When the poor men whose crime was nothing more than to protest the theft of the gold vessels from the Temple were brought before Antiochus IV Epiphanes in 2 Maccabees (4:47) 'they would have been declared innocent even if they had pleaded their case before Scythians' but were sentenced to death. Beth-Shan of 1 Maccabees (5:52) is referred to elswhere (2 Mac 12:29 Jdt 3:10) as Scythopolis, its name in Greek.

In his Letter to the Colossians (3:11) Paul says the believers of the new faith are all equal: 'Here there is not Greek and Jew, circumcision and uncircumcision, barbarian, Scythian, slave, free; but Christ is all and in all' here he uses the word in the general Greek sense as 'barbarian'. Their land was allocated to St Andrew as his missionary field. Christian traditon has it that Scythia beyond the Danube was converted to Christianity by the Cappadocians, who were taken there as prisoners by the Gothic hordes who raided central Anatolia in the 250s and 260s.

The name has survived today in the *Ashkenazim*, one of the two main classes of Jews, those of German and Slavonic-speaking countries which were once populated by Scythians, as opposed to *Sephardim* (Spanish and Portuguese) deriving from the Rabbinical name for this country.

---

[1] The normal Greek manner was five parts of water mixed with two of wine.

RIPHATH

According to Table of the Nations (Gn 10:3; 1 Chr 1:6) Riphath is a descendant of Japheth by his son Gomer. In ancient literature, outside this remark the word is mentioned only once and by Josephus for the people living in Paphlagonia, in northwestern Anatolia. The land that the historian allotted to Riphath is suitable for a people related to the Gomer (Cimmerians) and the Ashkenaz (Scythians). It is also suggested that Riphath may have referred to Mt Niphates (Süphan dağı, 4051 m) to north of Van lake; but this does not explain why a mountain should be included in Table of the Nations.

TOGARMAH

Gürün (Togarmah?)

From Beth-togarmah horses, steeds, and mules were exchanged for your wares (Ez 27:14).

The *grm* in the Old Testament is vocalized as Togarmah. In Table of the Nations it is a descendant of Japheth and one of Gomer's sons (Gn 10:3; 1 Chr 1:6). Ezekiel (38:6) in the Gog-apocalypse mentions Togarmah side by side with Gomer as one of the nations which will pour upon Israel from the north. Beth-Togarmah (House of Togarmah) is also referred to in Ezekiel's prophecy (27:14) against Tyre, as supplying it with horses, bloodstock and mules.

The Hittite *Tegarama* and some other similar names encountered in the records of Assyria and Urartu are thought to refer to the same place as present-day Gürün situated in the Elbistan plain between Sivas and Malatya on a tributary (Tohma çayı) of the Euphrates. The city was situated in the Hittite territory but close to the restless southeastern frontier. Its inhabitants were later known in Cappadocia under the name of *Gamir* after *Gimirrai* (Gomer or Cimmerians). The region is still famous as it was once for its horses, mules and asses.

MAGOG

In Table of the Nations (Gn 10:2; 1 Chr 1:5) Magog is one of the sons of Japheth like Tubal and Meshech. When it is encountered elsewhere in the Old Testament (Ez 38; 39) the word also is coupled with the same nations and used with Gog interchangeably. Ezekiel, when he says turn towards the direction where Tubal, Meshech and Magog are located, probably had an actual nation in his mind in the same direction as Tubal and Meshech, that is northern Anatolia. His cryptic use of this name may have not prevented his readers of the time from guessing the real nationality of Magog. North, as remarked in Jeremiah (1:14-19) 'And from the north, said the LORD to me, evil will boil over upon all who dwell in the land' is the direction of the unknown quarters of the world from which unexpected dangers arrived; ie the Cimmerians or the Scythians from the southern steppes of Russia beyond the Caucasus.

Gog of Magog, however, is used as the single final enemy of God and Israel. It may to have been inspired by 'Gugu', the name of Gyges, famous king of Lydia, among Assyrians. However, since Gyges was killed by the Gomer (Cimmerians) his representation by Ezekiel as the 'chief prince' of Gomer cannot be true and may show that Ezekiel chose it just to refer to a mysterious mythological figure personifying the eschatological enemy and the darkness somewhere in the north, who did not have any actual connection with Palestine or the Israelites at all.

In Revelation (20:7-8) Gog and Magog are in the army of Satan before his final defeat. In early Christian writings Gog and Magog referred to the Romans and their emperor, the Antimessiah.

Yecüc Mecüc (Gog Magog). Manuscript painting. *Ahval-i Kıyamet,* the 'Events of Doomsday'. 1596. Staatsbibliothek. Berlin. In later Christian literature Alexander the Great, the 'Last World Emperor' builds a wall in the Caucasus mountains to prevent Gog and Magog from invading the world until the end of time, a story also adopted by the Koran (18) and other Islamic literature. They are said to live naked and be about one metre in height and have two long ears on one of which they sleep and the other use for a cover. They will invade on the Day of Judgement, drink up all the waters of the Tigris and Euphrates and massacre all the inhabitants of the earth. In painting they were often represented as Scythians, Tartars or Huns. In the picture the ones without mustaches are their women.

CARCHEMISH

Against the army of Pharaoh Neco, king of Egypt, which was defeated at Carchemish on the Euphrates by Nebuchadnezzar, king of Babylon, in the fourth year of Jehoiakim, son of Josiah, king of Judah (Jer 46:2).

Karkamis, 'quay of Kamish', took its name from the chief Moabite god Chemosh to whom Solomon built a high place in 1 Kings (11:7). Although the prophet Jeremiah had placed Carchemish 'on the Euphrates' (Jer 46:2), this river was about 2,800 km long and the city's discovery had to wait until 1876.

Carchemish (Karkamış) was founded on the west bank of an important crossing point of the Euphrates where it comes out of the mountain gorges but has not yet spread over the Syrian lowlands. The city's history extends to the beginning of the second millennium BCE and during the historical period it may have been originally ruled by an Amorite dynasty. The Hittite king Suppiluliuma I was besieging Carchemish in about 1354 BCE when he received a letter from the pharaoh's widow, who is just referred to as *Dahamunzu*, or 'the wife of the king' in the text and is claimed to have been Ankhesenpaaten (Ankhesenamun), a daughter of Akhenaten and widow of the famous Tutankhamun, informing the Hittite king that she wanted one of his sons as husband and king. The message made Suppiluliuma express his surprise, 'such a thing has never happened to me in my whole life'. Unfortunately Suppiluliuma's son Zananza never reached Egypt, for a Hittite text informs us that 'they killed him as they were conducting him to Egypt.' Carchemish fell to the Hittites after a siege of eight days. Suppiluliuma invaded Syria, captured Halap (Aleppo), subdued the kingdom of Mitanni and won Syria for the Hittites.[1] After this date Carchemish was governed by the princes from the Hittite royal family at Hattusa. It survived as the most important stronghold on the Euphrates and housed the religious seat of the goddess Kubaba (Cybebe/Cybele).

Cities in southeastern Anatolia may have been less affected by the catastrophe of the Sea Peoples and Carchemish, although its name is included by the scribes of Medinet Habu inscriptions as among those which were destroyed may have even been one of those which escaped destruction. After the fall of Hattusa the kings of

---

[1] The prisoners that the king carried home brought with them a plague which lasted for about twenty years killing one tenth of the population and probably also the king himself.

Carchemish began using the title 'Great King of Hatti' until the mid-tenth century BCE. The tribute of cedar logs exacted from the king of Carchemish by Tiglath-pileser I (1115-1076 BCE) shows that at this time the city's hegemony extended to the Amanus mountains which were the most important source of timber.[2] Its location dominating the north Syrian route from Mesopotamia to Anatolia and the Mediterranean made the city invaluable for the Assyrians and when joined to anti-Assyrian coalitions it was punished severely. The Assyrian support, however, protected it against the Aramean kingdoms of north Syria. This lasted until the 720s BCE when it became Assyrian soil.

Jeremiah's oracle about the battle of Carchemish relates to the latest period of the city's history when it became the last base of the fallen Assyrian kingdom. In 608 BCE Necho II of Egypt marched to Carchemish through Palestine to help the Assyrians and protect the status quo in Syria. He captured Gaza and Ashkelon, two of the cities of Philistines (Jer 47:5) and invaded Judah on his way to north (2 Kgs 23; 2 Chr 35). Details of the fierce battle fought at Carchemish in 605 BCE have been given in the Book of Jeremiah (46:2-12). The Babylonians were commanded by Nebuchadnezzar. The Egyptian forces, who included Lydian mercenaries ('Men of Lud') among their ranks, together with their Assyrian allies, were heavily defeated by the Neo-Babylonian army. The city was burned. At the heel of Necho II the victorius Nebuchadnezzar II entered Palestine. Judah submitted and among the prisoners taken to Babylon were Ezekiel and the fictional hero Daniel.

Like several other city states of this period Carchemish was situated at the crossing point of the Hittite and Aramaic and later Assyrian and Phoenician cultures. Its population may have included the descendants of those who had been living here for many centuries, some Hittite groups which were driven from the central plateau and the Arameans, originally nomads from the Syrian desert. The hybrid society is best reflected in the reliefs which once decorated the walls of some public buildings set by successive kings.

[2] Although the Cilician Taurus and Amanus ranges were two other major sources of timber (cedar, cypress, juniper or pine) for the Near Eastern civilizations the Bible refers only to the cedars of Lebanon. The forested heights of mount 'Amana' which is haunted by lions and leopards in the Song of Songs may refer to the Amanus (Sg 4:8).

Incense burner from İkiztepe tumulus near Uşak. Silver. About 500 BCE. Lydio-Persian. Uşak Archaeological Museum. The inscription on its base, which in Lydian reads *Artimas,* is its owner's name.

LUD (LYDIANS)

Forward, horses! Set out, warriors Cush and Put, bearing your shields, Men of Lud, stretching your bows! (Jer 46:9)

The Lud (Akkadian *Luddu*) mentioned in the tabular list of Table of the Nations as one of the sons of Shem (Gn 10:22; 1 Chr 1:17) refers to the Lydians. They were however, not Semites but Indo-Europeans and consequently should have been better listed among Japheth's descendants. The Lydian capital Sardis (Aramaic Sepharad) is mentioned in Obadiah (1:20). 'Lud' in Ezekiel (27:10) and (30:5) or Judith (2:23) does not refer to any definite country or nation but is used as a literary device.

The Lydian kingdom which was founded by Gyges (680-652 BCE) at Sardis ruled in western Anatolia and the central plateau. Ezekiel may have derived 'Gog' from 'Gugu', the name of this fabulous king, and used it as an epic cliché without having a specific person in mind (Ez 38; 39).

Gyges died fighting against the Cimmerians (the biblical Gomer) who, after sacking Urartu and destroying the Phrygian kingdom of Midas, had entered into his territory. Assyrian records inform us that all of a sudden an envoy showed up at the royal court in Nineveh and told Ashurbanipal II (668-627 BCE) of a dream that his king Gugu had seen. Gugu's country was invaded by the Cimmerians. In the dream the god Asshur told Gugu that if he submitted to Ashurbanipal he could defeat the enemy. Thus Gyges sent him an envoy with rich gifts and two Cimmerian captives. Ashurbanibal informs us that Gugu later forgot his promise to the god Asshur, probably when the Cimmerian pressure had eased, and sent troops to Psammethicus I of Egypt who had rebelled against Assyria. Ashurbanipal cursed Gyges and thus the latter lost the war and was killed by the Cimmerians. Although ancient literature identifies one of the large tumuli at Bintepe necropolis at Sardis as belonging to Gyges, scholars believe that this burial dates from a later period and the signs which were left on its walls and once thought to have meant *Gugu* are probably just mason's marks.

(opposite) Head from Aktepe tumulus. Wall painting. Detail. About 500 BCE. Uşak Archaeological Museum. The head belongs to a standing female figure. Her hair, which bears a red diadem decorated with an incised pattern, is painted in blue. Her ear is shown in dark red. The lips and skin are painted in tones of pink. The eyes and eyelashes are black.

Gyges is known to be the first king who sent Greek mercenaries — because the Lydians were not sailors, these were Ionian and Carian soldiers — to Egypt. Herodotus relates that an oracle predicted that the heir to Necho I, who was on the Egyptian throne, would receive help from bronze men who would come from the sea; and one day as he walked on the Mediterranean coast in his exile, he encountered a stranded boat bearing Ionian hoplites, blown off their course. With the help of these Psammetichus I sat on the throne. By the 630s he established a special inland town named Naucratis (Mistress of Ships) on the Nile for the Greek settlers in his country.

The Lydians ruled over Ionia and central Anatolia with the Halys river forming the frontier to the Median empire, which had replaced Assyria in the Near East. Herodotus says that king Alyattes (610-560 BCE) of Lydia allied himself with the Scythians, who were settled in the lands of Urartu, against the rising power of the Medes and the war which began thus between the two countries lasted for five years. During the last battle the 'day was suddenly turned into night'. This was the eclipse already foretold by Thales of Miletus. The soldiers broke off the fight and a peace agreement was made. It was sealed by a marriage between a daughter of Alyattes and a son of Cyaxares. The greed of its last Lydian king Croesus (560-546 BCE) for the lands beyond the Halys river brought him against king Cyrus II the Great (559-530 BCE). By this time the Median rule had been replaced by that of the Persians. Croesus lost the battle fought in Cappadocia and subsequently his capital Sardis was captured by Cyrus in 546 BCE.

The term Ludim, shown as the son of Mizraim (Egypt) in the narrative genealogy of Genesis (Gn 10:13; 1 Chr 1:11), is thought to refer to the Anatolian mercenaries whose existence in the army of Psammetichus II of Egypt was known. Despite this, the reason why a group of soldiers should be included in the world map cannot be explained and it may have been a later addition. This may be why Ezekiel associates the name with Cush and Put, two of Ham's sons. They are referred to at the battle

One of the graffiti from the legs of the colossal statues set up by Rameses II (1291-1224) at Abu Simbel in Egypt. 591 BCE. These inscriptions in Greek belong to the Greek mercenaries — Ionians, Carians and others — who served in the Egyptian army.

of Carchemish (605 BCE) fighting in the army of Necho II of Egypt, on the Assyrian side against the Babylonians. The biblical references introduce them as fierce fighters, a fact also remarked by Herodotus.

Ancient literature shows that dog sacrifice was a common ritual practiced in the ancient Near East and the Greco-Roman world. It was probably known by the Israelites when they were under Persian rule because Isaiah (66:3) uses the most apt expression 'like breaking a dog's neck' related to this ritual. Excavations in the Lydian market at Sardis have brought to light evidence that puppies were sacrificed for Hermes, locally called the 'Dog-Throttler'.

'Lydia' is mentioned in 1 Maccabees (8:8) as one of the regions that the Seleucid king Antiochus III had to give king Eumenes of Pergamum after his defeat by the Romans at the battle of Magnesia (190 BCE).

Baked clay vessels, skeletal remains of a immature canid and an iron knife belonging to ritual meals from the Lydian levels of ancient Sardis. Sixth century BCE. Manisa Archaeological Museum.

MADAI (MEDES)

Thus says Cyrus, king of Persia: 'All the kingdoms of the of earth the LORD, the God of heaven, has given to me, and he has also charged me to build him a house in Jerusalem, which is in Judah. Whoever, therefore, among you belongs to any part of his people, let him go up, and may his God be with him! Let everyone who has survived, in whatever place he may have dwelt, be assisted by the people of that place with silver, gold, goods, and cattle, together with free-will offerings for the house of God in Jerusalem' (Ezr 1:2-5).

In Table of the Nations Japheth's third son, Madai, is associated with the Medes (Gn 10:2; 1 Chr 10:5). The latter is the second among the four successive empires of the apocalyptic perspective of the Book of Daniel (2:36-45): the Babylonian (gold), the Median (silver), the Persian (bronze), and the Hellenistic (iron). In the Bible the word is used several times to refer to the Persians as well, as it is the case with classical writers such as Herodotus and Thucydides. In the biblical expressions such as 'a ram with two great horns, the one larger and newer than the other', while the two horns suggest the co-existence of both Medes and Persians, the last remark refers to the Persians taking over (Dn 8:3).

The original home of the Median tribes was the northern highlands of today's Iran, a region famous for its horses. Towards the end of the eighth century BCE the nomadic tribes living here began to move to the south. Among these, the Medes, brought together by Cyaxares (625-585) and making Ecbatana (Hamedan) their capital, extended their hegemony over the other tribes. In 612 BCE together with their allies the Babylonians and the Scythians they captured the Assyrian capital Nineveh. This event made the Medes a natural heir to the rest of the Assyrian territories. Both Anatolia and Palestine thus first became parts of the Median empire and later their kinsmen the Achaemenian Persians until the 330s BCE, the arrival of Alexander.

Although western Anatolia was located farther away than Syria and Palestine the Lydian push to the east of the Halys river (Kızılırmak) and their alliance with the Scythians compelled the Medes to turn in this direction. King Cyaxares' march against Lydia through eastern Anatolia was probably the end of Urartu as well. The war between the Medes and the Lydian king Alyattes lasted five years and ended up with a truce. Herodotus says that the last battle fought in 585 BCE was interrupted by an eclipse, which both sides regarded as divine interference and making peace strengthened it by a diplomatic marriage. The Halys river was accepted as a natural frontier between the two kingdoms.

MADAI (MEDES)

When the hegemony of the Medes was replaced with that of the Persians, the last Lydian king Croesus was busy expanding his lands to east of the Halys river. The Persian king Cyrus II the Great however, regarding himself as the natural owner of the Median territory, marched into Anatolia and at the battle fought in Cappadocia defeated Croesus. Without stopping here Cyrus continued to Lydia proper and captured Sardis (546 BCE) which they called 'Sparda' (the biblical Sepharad) in Old Persian. When the Bible says that God will give Cyrus 'treasures out of darkness, and riches that had been hidden away' (Is 45:3) it is thought that this was an allusion to the fabled treasures of Croesus which fell to the Persian king. However, his mind being on Babylon his southern neighbour, Cyrus did not stay long in Sardis but returned home. Because of its material resources and closeness to Greece, which would become the traditional enemy of Persia, Anatolia, especially its western region, witnessed a concentration of the Persian administration. After conquering the rest of the country, following their own administrative system, the Persians divided the peninsula into several satrapies (provinces) each to be ruled by a satrap (governor). The latter was often a relative of the Persian king and in some cases a noble personage from the local dynasty. In the Ionian cities they set up local tyrants who would rule in accordance with their system. As long as the satraps raised taxes and soldiers for the capital Susa, they were not very different from independent vassal kingdoms. The Lydians had invented and had been using coins and the western satrapies of the Persian administration were the few which paid their taxes not in kind but in money. This lenient rule was echoed in the administration of satrapies themselves. The ethnic or religious groups which constituted their population were allowed to retain their identity. Although it was interrupted by a few serious wars the literary evidence and archaeological findings show that the Persian rule was a long prosperous period in Anatolia's history. The Royal Road which connected Sardis to the Persian capital Susa was one of the most important amenities of the Persian rule. The worship of Ahura Mazda as well as the Persian and Aramaic languages and scripts encountered in Cappadocia are thought to have been introduced to the region by the Persian settlers of this period.

During this long period Anatolian satrapies bore the burden of the Persian expeditions to the west. The first of these was directed against the Scythians who were at the time living in the Pontic steppes. Darius I, a few years after his victorious campaign against the Asiatic Scythians beyond the Oxus river, turned against the European Scythians and marched into Anatolia. Crossing the Bosphorus by a floating bridge of boats in 512 BCE he invaded the Scythian territory beyond the Danube.

The expedition however, was without any result because the Scythian hordes had emptied their wooden towns and disappeared into the northern steppes.

Another event of Darius I's reign was the Ionian revolt (499-494 BCE). It began with the revolt of Miletus and spread to the other cities as far as Byzantium, the Aegean islands and Cyprus. It came to an end with the defeat of the allied fleet by the Persians before the island of Lade,[1] off Miletus and the capture of the city. If the Ionian cities had accomplished one thing at the end of it, this was the replacement of their tyrants with better ones and the lessening of taxes thay they paid to their Persian satraps.

The revolt, however, had been supported by Athens and Darius' successor Xerxes I wanted to punish the Greeks for this. In 481, marching from Susa, he wintered at Sardis. In the spring he continued to Troy where his thirsty soldiers are said to have dried up the Scamander (Karamenderes) river. Crossing the Dardanelles by two bridges of boats he had built Xerxes invaded Greece. He was, however, to suffer a defeat at Salamis (480 BCE) and having failed to conquer Greece, return to his country by way of Sardis.

In 539 BCE, immediately after coming home, Cyrus defeated the last Neo-Babylonian king Nabonidus and his son and co-regent Belshazzar, and captured

[1] Now a low hill in the plain of silt.

Relief of the Three Young Hebrews in the Fiery Furnace (Dn 3). Marble. Eighth-ninth centuries CE. İstanbul Archaeological Museum. The young men are represented frontally, their arms raised on both sides, hands open, in 'orant' pose. They are dressed in oriental costumes. The furnace is shown by six long undulating flames.

MADAI (MEDES)

Babylon. Thus he took over Judah and Israel automatically. Together with Syria, Palestine including *Yehud*, or Judea became a Persian satrapy called in Aramaic *Abarnahara*, 'Beyond the River (the Euphrates)'.

For the Persians Palestine was one of the most negligible pieces of land in their huge empire. Once in a while it served as a stopover for their armies marching to Egypt. With the traditional Median or Persian attitude towards minorities living under their rule, Cyrus allowed a group of the exiles in 538 BCE to return to Judah and ordered the reconstruction of the Temple (Ezr 1; 4). A certain Sheshbazzar was appointed as governor for Judah (Ezr 1:8), identified with Shenazzar, a son of Jeconiah (Jehoiakim) (1 Chr 3:17-18). These were some of the captives who had been deported to Babylon by Nebuchadnezzar after his conquests of Jerusalem in about 597 and 586. Thus Cyrus became the first biblical person for whom the title the Messiah — 'the Anointed One' (Is 45:1) — was given and was celebrated as 'the champion of justice' from the East and God's 'attendant' (Is 41:2). The Great

Parapet piece with Daniel in the Lions' Den (Dn 6) from the island of Thassos. Marble. Sixth century CE. İstanbul Archaeological Museum. In the corner the prophet Habakkuk held airborne 'by the crown of his head' by an angel brings him food from Judea (Dn 14:36).

King may also have had in mind his next objective, the conquest of Egypt when he treated the peoples of his new western province in such a lenient manner.

The captives released by Cyrus were once the cream of the Jewish population in Palestine and unlike the exiles of the 'Lost Ten Tribes', who were deported by the Assyrians earlier, they had not yielded the local gods and sticking to the teaching of the Law became the nucleus of the Jewish Diaspora. The rebuilding of the Jerusalem Temple, however, had to be stopped because the Jews were accused of raising the walls of Jerusalem. In 522 Darius I allowed another group of deportees to return to Judah led by a fabulous Zerubbabel, a descendant from the house of David.

The returned exiles found a different Palestine. Their lands and homes had been either settled by people from neighbouring countries or by the Jews who had been left behind. The latter had begun taking non-Jewish wives and their children spoke Aramaic instead of Hebrew. Both Jerusalem and the countryside were short of food, water and security. Canaanite cults had crept into the life of those who were left behind and these were worshipped together with Yahweh. There is not much information about how Palestine fared during the later part of the Persian rule. The Palestinians lived under religious and civil leaders who were appointed by the Persians. Artaxerxes I (465-423) sent Ezra with a new group of Jews to Judah and charged him with the rehabilitation of the Jewish society according to the teaching of Yahweh. Apart from the construction of the Jerusalem Temple, which was completed about 451 BCE and minor restorations, Persian rule does not seem to have brought any material improvement to Palestine. Ezra's efforts, especially his demand of the Jews who were married to aliens to divorce, were met with opposition. In 445 Artaxerxes appointed his courtier Nehemiah as the governor of Judah. From the political point of view Nehemiah was a tyrant like the ones that the Persians had imposed on the other Greek cities and had the support of the throne. Nehemiah's success enabled Judaism to protect its identity in the coming age. The only news of aggression during the later Persion rule came in 351 BCE when some Jews joined Sidon which had rebelled against Artaxerxes III and were punished by deportation. The Persian rule in Palestine lasted until 332, the conquest of Alexander.

The books of Ezra, Nehemiah, Esther and Daniel, which are known to have been written in the late second or early first centuries BCE, are set in the Persian world of the sixth to fifth century BCE and give us some idea about what happened during the long Persian rule, although often the real events are mixed with fiction and eschatological stories.

JAVAN (GREEKS)

I will set a sign among them; from them I will send fugitives to the nations: to Tarshish, Put and Lud, Mosoch, Tubal and Javan, to the distant coastlands that have never heard of my fame, or seen my glory; and they shall proclaim my glory among the nations (Is 66:19).

Table of the Nations (Gn 10:4; 1 Chr 1:5) shows Javan as a grandson of Noah by Japheth. The word meant Greeks in general and was used by all of the eastern cultures. In the list Javan's sons aptly are Elishah (Crete), Tarshish (Tarsus), Kittim (Cyprus) and Rodanim (Rhodes). If Javan were used for 'Ionians' one would have expected a city like Ephesus or Miletus to be included among his sons. For Isaiah (66:19) Javan is among the coastlands 'that have never heard of' God's fame.

The contact between early Greeks such as the Minoans of Crete and subsequently the Mycenaeans and Anatolia or the Levant had already begun by the middle of the second millennium BCE. Some scholars believe that the immigrants who created the Minoan culture of Crete may have emigrated to the island from Anatolia. Archaeology shows the existence of both Minoan and Mycenaean settlers along the Mediterranean and Aegean coasts in the middle of the second millennium BCE. Although the relations between the Hittites and the Greek world are not yet known, the 'great king of Ahhiyawa' mentioned in the Hittite cuneiform tablets probably referred to the Mycenaean kingdom. The latter's interest in western Anatolia is confirmed by the existence of slaves from coastal cities working in the palaces of the Mycenaean rulers. The base of Mycenaean activity in Anatolia was Miletos (Hittite *Milawata/Millawanda*) which the Hittites were able to subdue only towards the end of their history in the second half of the thirteenth century BCE. It is not yet definitely known if the kingdom of *Wilusa* which was an ally of the Hittites and situated in the Troad or its king *Alaksandus*, both mentioned in Hittite records are '(W)illios' (Ilion) and Alexandros (Paris) of the Homeric epic. *Taruisa*, the Hittite name for the capital of this kingdom also may have later become Troia (Troy).

Shortly after the catastrophe of the Sea Peoples in the 1190s a series of immigrations from Greece and the islands to the coasts of Anatolia began. By the end of the eighth century BCE the Aegean coastline and some pockets on the Mediterranean had been settled. In the course of time the hereditary feudal ideology of these settlements such as Ephesus, Miletus, Priene or Phocaea gave way to a kind of primitive type of democracy of self-governing citizens' communities and each of them became a *polis*. The culture of these cities included various sorts of Anatolian and Eastern elements and is referred to by scholars as 'Ionian' or 'East

Greek'. In addition to characteristic amenities of material culture the Ionian creativity extended to philosophy, astronomy, mathematics or history, activities distinguished from the prototypes in the Greek mainland by a rational and naturalistic outlook. Thales, Anaximander and Hippodamus of Miletus, Pythagoras of Samos, Heraclitus of Ephesus and the 'father of history' Herodotus of Halicarnassus are a few popular names of this prolific culture.[1] When the Ionian cities became large enough to colonize other countries the vacuum in inland Anatolia had been filled by the Lydians and Phrygians and they were compelled to sail to the virgin coasts of the Propontis (Sea of Marmara) and Euxine Pontus (Black Sea) or the western Mediterranean. Although some minor contacts such as the marriage of Midas with a daughter of the king of Cyme or gifts of Midas or Gyges to the temple of Apollo at Delphi are mentioned in ancient literature, except for the alphabet used by the Phrygians the heart of the Anatolian peninsula was hardly touched by the Greek culture. The first entrance of the Greeks into Anatolia proper took place at the end of the fifth century BCE.

Attic crater fragment from Phocaea (Foça). Baked clay. Beginning of the sixth century BCE. İzmir Archaeological Museum. The rim piece is decorated with a scene of symposium. Each couch *(kline)* bears two half-naked men (a young and an older bearded figure) feasting. The convex shoulder fragment shows a combat of foot soldiers armed with swords, spears and shields. They also wear cuirasses, greaves and helmets.

In 401 BCE Cyrus the Younger, the son of Persian king Darius II, marched from Sardis against his elder brother Artaxerxes II who had come to the throne after their father's death. The backbone of his army was the Greek mercenaries who would later come to be known in literature as the Ten Thousand. He followed the Meander river as far as Colossae and Celaenae (Apamea; Dinar). Turning north he travelled by way of Ipsus, Iconium, Laranda, Tyana, the Cilician Gates, Tarsus, Mopsuestia, Issus, and the Syrian Gates (Belen pass) to Syria. Cyrus, however, lost the war at Cunaxa in central Mesopotamia and was killed. The Ten Thousand, refusing to join the Persian forces, marched north and after an adventurous journey through the highlands of eastern Anatolia reached Trapezus (Trabzon). They continued to Cerasus (Giresun) and from Cotyora (Ordu) took ships to Heraclea Pontica (Ereğli) and on to the West. This hurried march through Anatolia, which is related by Xenophon in *Anabasis,* did not leave any trace of Greek culture and its introduction

[1] Some of these persons lived when Anatolia was under Persian rule.

JAVAN (GREEKS)

waited until the conquest of Alexander the Great.

The earliest known direct contact between the Greeks and the Jews took place between the Philistine cities established by the Sea Peoples and the United Monarchy. Although they may have been a mixture of people from the Aegean world and Anatolia's coastlands, scholars agree on the Greek cultural background of these hordes. In the Bible the Philistines are introduced as barbarian invaders from a distant land, a villainous and sinful people worshipping a god called Dagon which they had adopted from the Canaanites. They were brutal soldiers who destroyed the sanctuary at Shiloh and carried off the Ark of the Covenant as booty (1 Sm 4,5). In the course of time they were absorbed ethnically and culturally by the Canaanites and some of them were probably accepted among the Israelites such as the tribes of Dan and Asher (p 43). David's army probably included Cretan mercenaries (Cherethites). The Carian captains and guards participated in putting the seven year old Joash on the throne of Judah in about 840 BCE (2 Kgs 11:4,19). Although it may not have led to cultural exchange the Greek and Jewish mercenaries or slaves in the Egyptian, Assyrian or Persian armies may have also known of each other's existence. Deuteronomy (17:16) warns the future king of the Israelites not to send Jewish people to Egypt to exchange with horses. Joel (4:6) says that the regions of Philistia sold the people of Judah and Jerusalem to the Greeks. While the Israelite slaves had been known in different parts of Mesopotamia since the eighth century BCE the first group of Greeks were moved and settled there after Lydia was captured by Cyrus the Great in 546 BCE.

In the Levant until the conquest of Alexander the trade monopoly between the Western world and the East was in the hands of the Phoenicians. The Greek colonists lived together with the Phoenicians at Al Mina, at the mouth of the Orontes (Asi) river from the mid-ninth to the sixth century, until the arrival of the Persians, and the port became the most important gateway for the material culture of the Near East to the West by which bronze cauldrons, fibulae, vases and other rare products began moving by way of Cyprus, Rhodes and the Aegean islands. Ezekiel (27) in his prophecies against foreign nations says that Javan traded with Tyre articles of wrought iron, cassia and aromatic cane for its goods and other wares.

One of the most important results of the contact between the Greeks and Phoenicians was probably the transmission of a Semitic alphabet to the West. Sometime before Alexander's conquest this alphabet would return, to the surprise of the Phoenicians, with signs representing vowels. The various remarks in the

Horseman figurine from Troy. Baked clay. Hellenistic. Çanakkale Archaeological Museum. He wears a *petasos*, or 'a broad-brimmed hat'. Ancient Persian sources referred to the Greeks of the mainland as *Yuana takabara*, or 'bearing shields' on their heads, or the 'sun-hatted'.

Bible give the impression that for the Israelites, Greeks were traders and one of the insignificant nations of the world. For the Greek philosophers of the Classical period Jews were, like the Egyptians or Hindus, one of the wise but remote nations of the East. The Greeks and Jews also had no language in common. Herodotus who travelled to Egypt through the Levant, except for a brief remark that 'The Syrians of Palestine themselves admit that they adopted the practice [circumcision] from Egypt' does not mention either the Jews or Jerusalem. Although some Israelites were known to have worshipped more than one god, Greek gods are not encountered among these. Scholars believe that some of the similarities encountered between the Greek and Eastern cultures may have been independent developments. To this group may belong the popular motif of the Bronze Age in which a woman is rescued from enemies. As Agamemnon rescues Helen from the Trojans, Abraham twice needs to recover Sarah from her captors in foreign places. The story of Samson and Delilah brings to mind Nisus, king of Megara, whose secret of power is again a lock of hair cut by his daughter Scylla. Samson's fondness of riddles may be associated with that of the Greek hero Mopsus. Joseph's prosperity at Potiphar's house and his fall because of the intrigue of his master's wife, occurs in the story of Bellerophon in the *Iliad* showing that it is common to the repertoire of the east Mediterranean epic. Some myths or motifs such as the Flood, or the disappearance of a god which causes disaster, or the succession of a god by his son encountered in the *Theogony* of Hesiod, the Greek poet who lived in about 700 BCE, are thought to have travelled to the West from the East. In the latter tradition Kronos becomes the ruler of the gods after castrating his father, Uranus, god of heaven, only to be usurped by Zeus, the thunder god. In the Hurrian myth Anu, the god of heaven, is castrated by his son Kumarbi, to be deposed in his turn by the weather god Teshup.

Attic red-figure crater from Palestine. Fifth century BCE. İstanbul Archaeological Museum. A man is paying the fee of a *hetaera* (prostitute). A second man negotiates the price.

TARSHISH (TARSUS) — CILICIA

Solomon also imported horses from Egypt[1] and Cilicia. The king's agents would acquire them by purchase from Cilicia, and would then bring up chariots from Egypt and export them at six hundred silver shekels, with the horses going for a hundred and fifty shekels. At these rates they served as middlemen for all the Hittite and Aramean kings (2 Chr 1:16-17).

The name Cilicia derives from the Aramaic *hlk* (hilakku) and in the past referred to the northern mountain masses and the tribes who lived here. The Cilician plain was watered by the rivers Pyramus (Seyhan) and Sarus (Ceyhan) and known to the Hittites as Adaniya. In the middle of the second millennium BCE it became the home of the Hurrian kingdom of Kizzuwatna, probably with the Tepebağ tumulus in Adana as its capital. A very large part of the Hurrian influence on the Hittite religion penetrated to Hattusa from here especially when Puduhepa of Kizzuwatna, a priestess of the goddess Hepat, married the Hittite king Hattusili III (1289-1265 BCE). The earliest historical event which concerns both Cilicia and Palestine goes back to some two hundred years before Solomon's business transactions which are mentioned in the Old Testament. Excavations at Gözlükule mound, on which the ancient Tarsus (Tarsa) was situated, show that it was destroyed in about 1190 BCE by the Sea Peoples who are known to have continued their devastation towards Syria and Palestine.

Mopsucrene[2] and Mopsuestia[3] situated in the plain are named after Mopsus of Colophon, one of the traditional heroes of ancient Greek migrations. In the latter a building which is thought to have been either a martyrium church or synagogue has revealed mosaics of interesting ecclesiastical nature. The floor of the nave of this building was decorated with a mosaic of Noah's Ark (p 17). The fragments which were recovered from its outer north aisle show that this section was decorated with the Samson cycle. It is, however, impossible to guess if the person who decided the repertoire of the mosaic decoration was familiar with the ancient association of Samson with Mopsus the legendary Greek hero who gave the city his name.

[1] Here Egypt (Mizraim) is thought to be mistakenly used in place of Musri, the less-known region of horse-breeding to the north of the Taurus neighbouring Cilicia.

[2] 'Fountain of Mopsus'.

[3] 'Hearths (or 'home') of Mopsus' (Misis near Adana).

(opposite) Personification of Cilicia. Mosaic from Seleucia Pieria (Çevlik). First half of the second century CE. The Detroit Institute of Art. Detroit. Michigan.

The elaborate inscriptions were from the Greek translation of the Bible (the Septuagint). Apart from a few lines of the inscriptions the fragments of the young attendant who guided the blind hero to the spot so that he 'may touch the columns that support the temple and may rest against them' (Jgs 16:26) have survived.

Scholars speculate on the similarities which bring Samson and Mopsus close to each other. King Azitiwatas (end of eighth century BCE) of Karatepe, in the bilingual inscriptions he left, identifies himself both as the king of the Danuniyim (a Phoenician version of Danuna) and as being from the 'House of Muksas ('Mopsus'). In the Amarna Letters according to a 'letter of Abi-Milki of Tyre, the 'land of Danuna'[4] is placed to the north of Ugarit and the Orontes river and may have been the region of Antakya or Adana. Texts from the time of Tudhaliya IV (1239-1209 BCE) mention a Muksas, the Hittite form of Mopsus, an ally of the Ahhiyawa (Mycenaeans).

Ancient literature informs us that Mopsus of Colophon (near İzmir) joined a group of Greeks returning from Troy and travelled to Pamphylia and Cilicia. In Greek mythology the latter is the son of Apollo and Teiresias' daughter Manto. He beats the famous seer Calchas and causes him to die of chagrin. Later he travels to Cilicia and dies there.

A votive inscription from Misis (Mopsuestia) now at Adana Museum, which dates from the second century CE, invokes Mopsus together with Apollon as a healer-god. After entering into Canaan together with the Philistines the Denyen mysteriously disappear from the records. The exploits of Samson of the Danites recall those of Greek heroes based on physical prowess or erotic ventures, rather than those of other judges and he delights in posing riddles like Mopsus. In a later version he continues to Canaan and raiding the Philistine city of Gaza destroys the temple of their god Dagon. The fifth-century BCE historian Xanthus of Lydia relates that Mopsus after travelling to Canaan cast the local goddess and her son into the pond at the Philistine city of Ashkelon and thus destroyed their cult. His death in Canaan may recall the settlement of the Sea Peoples after their defeat and return from Egypt. In its later history Mopsuestia became famous as the see of bishop Theodore (350-428), a leader of the theological school of Antioch, whose writings as a forerunner of Nestorius (p 196) subsequently became a subject of fierce controversy.

Its location between the Mediterranean and inland Anatolia to which it was connected by the Cilician Gates (Gülek pass) and a second pass by way of Karatepe, enabled Cilicia to recover from the catastrophe created by the Sea Peoples quickly.

Fragment from the Samson mosaic. End of fourth-beginning of fifth centuries CE. Misis Mosaic Museum. It is from Judges (15:4): 'So Samson left and caught three hundred foxes. Turning them tail to tail, he tied between each pair of tails one of the torches he had at hand' (Jgs 15:4).

[4] In Egyptian texts the word is used for the mainland Greece, probably for the Peloponnese.

TARSHISH (TARSUS) — CILICIA

The kingdom of Que which is referred to in Assyrian annals unlike the other kingdoms to its east does not show any Hittite influence and was probably originally established by the Sea Peoples.

The biblical remarks (2 Chr 1:16-17; 1 Kgs 10:28) allude to the economic world of Cilicia and Palestine in the tenth-ninth centuries BCE during which the Phoenicians probably acted as intermediators between the Cilician cities and the United Monarchy. Tyre's network of trading posts on the Gulf of Alexandretta such as Myriandrus to the south of İskenderun enabled it to monopolize the trade in metals and slaves in Cilicia, the Taurus mountains and the upper Euphrates and at the same time to control the sea routes to Cyprus and Crete. Among the regions or cities which contributed to Phoenicia's wealth was Tarshish. The term's usage in the Old Testament covers a span of over four hundred years and its meaning varies according to the period, the author or the translation; most frequently used for 'ocean-going ship'. When it is used as a place name in the Mediterranean (Gn 10:4) it is the son of Javan, Greek in general and placed along with Rhodes, Crete and Cyprus. According to the Bible Tarshish held a monopoly in the metal trade — silver, iron, tin and lead — but it refers to an unspecified territory. From this Mediterranean Tarshish, silver, iron, tin and lead arrived at Tyre. The term is used

A stretch of the Roman road between Tarsus and the Cilician Gates. Second century CE. To the left is a milestone.

in the Old Testament to designate the name of a place only after the sixth-fifth centuries BCE. The city's 'heaped up silver' (Zec 9:2-3) may have come from the Taurus, which were referred to in the Mesopotamian tablets dating from the end of the third millennium BCE as the 'silver mountain' by way of Cilicia or else from Tartessus in the south of Spain.

The Bible gives detailed information about the economic relations between Hiram (I) the Great (970-936 BCE), the king of Tyre and David and Solomon. Hiram is said even to have sent the cedar and fir and labour teams for the construction of the Jerusalem temple. Relations between Phoenicia and Israel were known to have been cemented during the next century by the marriage of Jezebel, the daughter of the king of Tyre, to Ahab of the northern monarchy (Israel) (874-851 BCE). The Phoenician presence in Cilicia is best displayed by the ruins of Azitiwataya (Karatepe). This city was situated at the apex of the Cilician triangle and it controlled a major trade route, second only to the Cilician Gates, from Cilicia to the north towards inland Anatolia.

Here, king Azitiwatas decorated the walls of his palace with reliefs such as Bes figures, palmettes and lotus chains, all taken from the Phoenician decorative repertoire. However the most important discovery was the bilingual inscriptions — in Hittite hieroglyphs and in Phoenician — which also made the decipherment of the Hittite hieroglyphic writing possible in the 1950s. The abundance of Iron Age cities in the mountain heights rather than the marshy plain may point to the unhealthy conditions of the region even at this early date.

The use of Phoenician writing in a popular manner indicates Phoenicia's political and cultural hegemony in the region until the Aramaic language became established at the end of the ninth century BCE. The ascendancy of Aramaic was accompanied by the growing influence of the Aramean and Assyrian art styles. It is not yet known if the Phrygians who occupied the other side of Taurus chain adopted the Phoenician script by way of Cilicia.

Cilicia was within the political periphery of Assyria's interest and became an Assyrian province in the reign of king Shalmaneser III (858-824 BCE). In Assyrian records it was called 'Que' or 'Huwe', a term referring only to the Cilician plain, with 'Tarzi' as its capital and was allowed to be ruled by its native dynasty. Following a revolt against Assyria, king Sennacherib destroyed Tarzi and founded a new city on its present-day site on the plain in about 696 BCE. The city and region would be ruled by the Assyrians until their fall in 612 BCE. After this period and until the Seleucids a local dynasty of Syennesis ruled a semi-autonomous Cilician kingdom. In the Book of Judith the Assyrian general Holofernes marches to Judea through

Relief related to Jonah's adventures from the former church of the Holy Cross at Akdamar island near Van. 915-21 CE. To the left Jonah is being thrown overboard by three sailors and swallowed by the great fish. Next are the fish which has already disgorged Jonah and a smaller fish. Above this Jonah warns the king of Nineveh who is shown seated, and with raised hands in a gesture of dismay, ordering his subjects to turn from their evil ways. The latter are represented by four busts in roundels. In the lower right corner Jonah is 'provided with a gourd plant, that grew up over Jonah's head, giving shade that relieved him of any discomfort' (Jon 4:6). The gourd is depicted as a pomegranate tree bearing fruit.

upper Cilicia (Jdt 1:21) and captures Cilicia (Jdt 2:25) to punish its people who had refused to send him help. Although the region does not lie on the route from Assyria and Palestine the historical route of the Assyrian campaigns frequently included Cilicia before Canaan.

When the God of Israel asked Jonah to go to Nineveh and preach against it the disobedient prophet tried to run away from his divine mission and took a ship 'to Tarshish away from the LORD' (Jon 1:3). Since the Cilician Tarshish (Tarsus) is not located so far away from Palestine as to offer shelter to a runaway the general opinion is that the biblical remark may have referred to other Tarshish (Tartessus), the Phoenician colony in southwestern Spain. A local tradition, however, must have connected Jonah's escape with Tarshish of Cilicia because a Crusader tower at today's Sarıseki — the point of the Amanus where it gets closest to the Mediterranean, somewhere between Issus and İskenderun, in the military zone — later came to be known as 'Pillar of Jonah', the spot where the fish belched out 'Jonah upon the shore' (Jon 2:11).

When the armies of the younger Cyrus and Alexander the Great stopped at Tarsus on their way to the East the city was still ruled by the semi-autonomous Syennesis dynasty. The Seleucids named Tarsus as 'Antioch on the Cydnus'. 2 Maccabees (4:30) informs us that Antiochus Epiphanes (175-164 BCE) included it among the gifts he gave to his mistress Antiochis. In 50 BCE Cicero served as the first Roman governor of the region with his headquarters at Tarsus. In 41 BCE Mark Antony met Cleopatra here. During the Roman period it continued to prosper and attained fame as the home of Paul. The Apostle expressed his pride of being from the city (Acts 21:39; 22:3)'by saying 'I am a Jew of Tarsus in Cilicia, a citizen of no mean city'.

(opposite) Eastern church (sixth century CE) of the Alahan (Apadnas) monastery in rugged Cilicia (Cilicia Tracheia). Fifth century CE.

ALEXANDER THE GREAT

a he-goat with a prominent horn on its forehead suddenly came from the west ... I saw it attack the ram with furious blows when they met, and break both of its horns...trampled upon it; and no one could rescue it from its power (Dn 8:5-7).

In the spring of 334 BCE Alexander, the 'he-goat' of Daniel's vision, crossed the Hellespont and won his first victory against the Persians, the 'ram,' at the battle by the river of Granicus (Kocabaş çayı). After their defeat here, as far as Issus along the Gulf of Alexandretta (İskenderun) there would be no Persian interference. When Alexander began his march the fortune of the Persian empire was already in decline. Darius III was a weak ruler and the Anatolian satrapies, located far away from the capital, were ruled by satraps who acted independently from the central authority.

Alexander's march through western Anatolia followed the coastal route and, with the exception of Miletus and Halicarnassus, the Persian garrisons based at the other cities did not resist him. When he encountered resistance in Caria, Lycia and Pisidia, regions popular for their love of freedom and with limited Greek elements, he did not lose time overcoming these but left it to his officers whom he left behind.

Detail from the Alexander Sarcophagus from Sidon. Marble. 325-311 BCE. İstanbul Archaeological Museum. The scene is thought to represent the battle of Issus (333 BCE) which was followed by Alexander's conquest of Phoenicia and ultimately enabled Abdalonymos, the owner of the sarcophagus, to become king of Sidon. Alexander is represented to the left of the panel; identified by his headgear, the pelt of Nemean lion's head, symbol of Heracles from whom he claimed descent. His raised right hand originally held a metal lance. The sarcophagus originally bore tones of red, blue and purple colours.

From Lycia Alexander travelled into central Anatolia where he sliced the Gordion knot of the mythical Phrygian king Gordias and confirmed the legend which claimed that whoever untied it would rule Asia.[1] His army spent the winter here. In the spring crossing the Taurus chain by the Cilician Gates, which the Crusaders later named 'Gate of Judas', he reached Tarsus. One of the episodes of his stay here was the pneumonia he caught when he took a dive in the river Cydnus (Tarsus suyu), a venture which almost cost him his life.

The battle of Issus, fought with Darius III in 333 BCE, was fateful for the result of his expedition. It ended with Alexander's victory and Darius had to flee from the field leaving all of his belongings and family behind. The victory made Alexander heir to the largest empire of the time. In Phoenicia only Tyre and in Palestine Gaza, which did not open their gates, had to be captured by siege. After spending the winter in Egypt where he founded Alexandria, in the spring Alexander returned by the same route and bypassing Jerusalem once more advanced towards Persia.

Alexander's conquest of Anatolia and *Yehud*, now called Judea by the Greeks, planted the seeds of important social and cultural changes which would become more apparent during the following century. Outside the probably fictitious remark about the encounter of Aristotle and a Jewish philosopher at Assos (p 152) the only information about the existence of Jews in Anatolia until Alexander's conquest is the remark in Obadiah (20), which is thought to have been recorded in the fifth century BCE, about those dwelling in Sepharad (Sardis), a city which had surrendered to Alexander without any fight. As long as they continued to pay the same taxes on land, flocks and persons, etc, which had been levied by the Persian king, to their new master, the replacing of their previous master by a Macedonian one did not introduce any novelty to the life of either the Jews, if there were any others than those at Sardis, or other ethnic groups in Anatolia. Conditions in Palestine were no different. The Jews continued to live following their ancestral laws in accordance with the liberal system established by the Persians. However in their effort to accommodate the Jews in the changing conditions, even though Alexander had not visited Jerusalem, the later Hebrew tradition records him in Jerusalem and has him visiting the Temple, meeting the high priest and sacrificing to the God of the

[1] A complicated knot produced by the legendary Phrygian king when he lashed his cart to a pole, dedicating it to Zeus. Some say that Alexander just pulled the pole out.

Jews. He supposedly was even shown the lines of the Book of Daniel which predicted his victory over the Medes and Persians (Dn 8:20) — although the book would be written about a century and half after Alexander's death. Later Jewish tradition also claimed that their ancestral rights were first granted to them by Alexander, and that it was Alexander who took the first Jews to Alexandria, the city which he was yet to found and also recruited Jewish soldiers in his army as he marched against Persia. A tradition even claims that he carried Jeremiah's bones to his new city to keep snakes and crocodiles out of it.

Alexander's choice of Samaria to settle some of his Macedonians, however, created the greatest schism of Jewish history. The city had been repopulated by the colonists from Mesopotamia after its conquest by Sargon II of Assyria in 721 BCE. The new settlers who had brought with them their own deities, in the course of time gave them up and turning to the Jerusalem Temple began praying to the God of the Jews as the only deity. Their origin, however, made them second-class Jews in the eyes of Jerusalem. When Judean exiles who were released by Cyrus in 538 began to rebuild the Temple they refused the help offered by 'the people of the land'(Ezr 4:1-4), or the Samaritans. But now Samaria, all of a sudden, was defiled by the gods of the Greek pantheon that the Macedonian soldiers brought with them. The Samaritan Jews withdrew to nearby Shechem and built, probably with Alexander's permission, their own temple on Mt Gerizim. The latter, after all, chronologically had greater claim to veneration than Mt Zion as a holy mountain as mentioned in Deuteronomy (11:29; 27:12) and Joshua (8:33). This development caused bitter enmity on the part of Jerusalem and did not end even with the destruction of the temple of the Samaritans in 128 BCE by the Maccabean High Priest and king John Hyrcanus I and the capture of Samaria some twenty years later.[2] Some Samaritans still cling to their sect at Nablus (Shechem).

After his death at Babylon in 323 BCE Alexander's generals shared his empire. Among the several Hellenistic kingdoms which would appear within the following decades the ones which concerned the history of Palestine and Anatolia were the Ptolemies of Egypt and the Seleucids of Syria. The impact of Greek culture on Jews and Judea as well as on the other ethnic groups and countries would begin not with Alexander but his successor monarchs.

[2] In a parable (Lk 10:25-37) Jesus in order to make his point clearer chooses a (good) Samaritan, a member of this group hostile to the Jews.

SELEUCIDS

Antiochus the great, king of Asia, who had fought against them with a hundred and twenty elephants and with cavalry and chariots and a very great army, had been defeated by them...Lycia, Mysia and Lydia from among the best provinces. The Romans took these from him and gave them to King Eumenes (1 Mc 8:6-8).

Coin of Seleucus I Nicator, founder of the Seleucid kingdom. Silver. 321-280 BCE. İstanbul Archaeological Museum; (obverse) Portrait or Seleucus I; (reverse) Zeus holding an eagle and a sceptre; Inscribed *Seleukos Basileos* (king).

By the 290s BCE the major battles had been fought between Alexander's generals and several powerful Hellenistic monarchies were founded. Anatolia, Syria and Alexander's eastern territories as far as India had fallen to the share of the Seleucid kingdom founded by Seleucus I Nicator (321-280 BCE) with its capital at Antioch on the Orontes. Egypt, Palestine, Cyprus, most of the Aegean islands and a few pockets on the Mediterranean seacoast of Anatolia came to be ruled by the Ptolemaic kingdom founded by Ptolemy I Soter (304-285) with Alexandria as its capital.

In order to rule over the vast lands they had inherited the Seleucids founded new cities and fortresses. The veteran Greek and Macedonian[1] soldiers and foreign auxiliaries became the first inhabitants of a chain of cities such as Seleucias, Antiochs or Apameas or smaller settlements such as Thyatira or Philadelphia. In the course of time the limited Greek element of these settlements was to an extent supplemented by new arrivals from Greece. These cities became the mixing point of cultures from the Orient and the Greek world. In the course of time some of the deities which bore similarities became syncretized. By the end of the third century BCE the cult of the divinely favoured Seleucid ruler himself or members of his family had also taken its place with these.

The Seleucids were regarded as just rulers and, in their effort to make themselves more sympathetic than the previous Persian masters, they paid more attention to respecting the customs and religions of the people over whom they ruled. In the Hellenistic cities each large ethnic group had its own quarter with its own administration. The Hellenistic *strategos,* or 'military governor', who replaced the Persian satrap, as was the case with most conquerors, was not interested in the religious life or customs of the ethnic groups who lived under his flag. As long as the taxes were regularly paid and trouble with the other ethnic groups was avoided, subjects could live in the manner they chose. The Seleucids played the most important role in planting the Greek culture in the lands to the east of Greece as far as India. In the Seleucid cities the official language used for cultural life and administration,

[1] Despite the vigour with which they embraced the Hellenistic culture the Macedonians were regarded by Greeks as partly-civilized barbarians who also practised brother-sister marriage.

although it may not have been spoken by all the inhabitants, was Greek. This was Greek vernacular *koine*, 'the common (dialect)', demotic Greek that had developed out of the classical tongue. It was already widely spoken in coastal settlements and to a lesser degree in Lydia, Phrygia and Cappadocia where mostly the ancient local tongues prevailed well into the Christian era (Acts 2:8-10): Lydian, Mysian, Carian, Lycian, Pontic dialects, Persian and Aramaic. In the eastern provinces Syriac, a form of Aramaic, was spoken. By the beginning of Christianity Greek and to a lesser degree Latin had taken their place by Aramaic and Hebrew even in urban Palestine. In the course of time Greek became the common language and even in the remote settlements there were people who could understand a little Greek.

In Anatolia no archaeological evidence has yet come to light about the pre-Hellenistic or Hellenistic Jewish existence. Outside the Jews of Sardis mentioned in Obadiah (20), the earliest Jews mentioned in ancient literature are those at Antioch on the Orontes. These were Palestinians and soldiers who were settled immediately after the foundation of the city by Seleucus I Nicator. Despite their religious prescriptions such as the Sabbath and kosher food, which did not go well with the army service, the Jews claimed that they were popular soldiers in the Persian, Seleucid and Ptolemaic armies. 2 Maccabees (8:20) mentions that in Babylonia eight thousand Jews fought along with four thousand Macedonians against the Galatians and adds that 'when the Macedonians were hard pressed, the eight thousand routed one hundred and twenty thousand.' The Gauls were first brought over into Anatolia by king of Bithynia Nicomedes I in about 279 BCE, as mercenaries to be used against his father Zipoetos and the Seleucid king Antiochus I who supported the latter. They made the central plateau their home and lived mostly on the tribute that they exacted from the neighbouring countries. For the Seleucids, having strong garrisons north of the Taurus chain was imperative for the protection of the prosperous western settlements against raids of the Galatians and revolts of the natives and for keeping communication routes open. These garrisons were in need of reliable people to stand against both the natives and the Galatians. A letter of the Seleucid king Antiochus III, quoted by Josephus, informs us about a major settlement of Jews in western Anatolia:

'King Antiochus to Zeuxis...On learning that people in Lydia and Phrygia are in revolt...I decided to transfer two thousand households of Jews from Mesopotamia and Babylonia together with their possessions into the forts and the most strategic places.'

The king's decree continued that the settlers would be given land for building a house, a piece of land for farming and viticulture and were to be exempted from taxes for ten years and allowed to live by their own customs without being disturbed

Roman copy of the Hellenistic statue of Tyche of Antioch on the Orontes, capital of the Seleucid kingdom. Marble. Vatican Museum. Rome. Its original was in bronze and made by Eutychides (active 296-293 BCE) of Sicyon, a pupil of Lysippus. Tyche (Fortune) wears a turreted crown representing Antioch, holds wheat-ears in her hand and rests her foot on a swimming figure of the god of the Orontes river.

Marble plaque inscribed with the word *Hebrew* in Hebrew from Sardis. Roman period. Manisa Archaeological Museum.

by others. Their long captivity in Mesopotamia[2] had taught them that the best way of survival was to get along with their rulers. The Mesopotamian Jews boasted a tradition of loyalty to the Seleucids and were preferable to the Palestinian Jews who would become part of their empire only in about 200 BCE. While some settlements may have been supplemented by veteran Jewish mercenaries, the Jewish prohibition against the exposure of unwanted children may have helped to increase the population, otherwise preaching of Judaism to others was not an obligation for the Jews and the number of apostates among them was probably higher than the proselytes; resulting from the fear of circumcision which was at that time a dangerous operation. The existence and spread of Jewish communities in Anatolia was very important because some two centuries later during the Apostolic age Christianity would find its first converts among the Jews — mostly hellenized ones — or Gentiles attracted by the Jewish religion, referred to as 'God-worshippers'. Archaeological evidence, which comes from places such as Sardis, Smyrna, Thyatira, Miletus and the cities of the Lycus valley, albeit belonging to several centuries after this period, gives us some idea about the extent of the Seleucid Jewish Diaspora and its later dispersion.

There is no information about how these Jewish communities were administrated by the Seleucids. It is not known if their organization was similar to that of the Antiochene or Alexandrian Jews about which there is some information for this period. We do not know if they had visitors from the Jerusalem Temple or how often they went on pilgrimage. Nevertheless the information which comes from the Roman period shows that they did not lose contact with Jerusalem. These groups, being such a distance from the Holy Land, may have felt the pressure of the central authority less than those in Antioch or Jerusalem or those who lived in Ptolemaic Alexandria and consequently possessed a looser organization. This lack of a compact organization and loose ties with Jerusalem may have been among the reasons why the Anatolian Jews did not later participate in the Jewish uprisings against Rome.

Although the meaning may have varied from one place to the other the Seleucid governors allowed the Jews to follow their ancestral laws. Some places in the Anatolian Diaspora probably had a body of elders (Greek *Gerousia*) in the traditional manner and 'a chief of the synagogue' in charge of basic administration, probably less rigid than its prototypes at Jerusalem. Each Jewish community probably had a *proseuche* (literally 'prayer'), a building with a religious function. The word was used as early as

[2] Deportations of Ten Tribes to northern Mesopotamia and Media by Sargon II, Judeans to Assyria by Sennacherib, captives from conquests of Jerusalem by Nebuchadnezzar II to Babylonia and finally in 350 BCE by Artaxerxes III to northern Persia.

this period and may have referred to any kind of place where the Jews gathered to pray, like the prayer place in Philippi mentioned by Luke (Acts 16:13) as being 'outside the city gate along the river.' A new development of the Hellenistic period for the Jewish world was the introduction of a new type of building which was called *synagogue,* literally 'assembly,' in Greek. The earliest synagogues are thought to have appeared during the Babylonian captivity. They served as the centre of Jewish activities and provided the Jews who were sure of the superiority of their religion with the shelter they needed against the outside world. A synagogue was just a place where the Jewish community met and prayed and heard the Jewish Scriptures. It did not have a priesthood or temple or altar because the Jews could not practise sacrifice outside the Jerusalem Temple.[3] They became the nucleus of the Jewish way of life in the cities and their diffusion all around the Jewish world would play a very important role later in the development of Christianity. Some two centuries later upon entering a town Paul would directly walk into the synagogue and preach the gospel. Some of the synagogues probably had hostels where the itinerant rabbis or Jewish visitors could stay. The existence of the first synagogue building in Anatolia is attested at Antioch on the Orontes in about 150 BCE (p 119) and may indicate the existence of others in the Anatolian Jewish Diaspora before or at this date.

The Jews raised interest among the Greeks in having affinities with them such as indulging in abstract thought and recognizing the supremacy of an abstract ideal. Their having an ancient written literature, like the Greeks themselves, which was translated into Greek in the third century BCE in Alexandria, and their being the 'People of the Book,' was also noted by the Greeks. As long as these peculiar barbarians did not meddle in other people's business they were allowed to keep their peculiar habits such as Sabbath observance, circumcision, ritual baths, the wearing of *tefillin,* or phylacteries and to stay away from Greek religious ceremonies.

Although their religion isolated the Jews from the others it was impossible to shun the world around them completely, especially for those who wanted to take an active role in the Hellenistic city life. The earliest obvious evidence of the Greek influence was found in the field of language. The Jews who were settled in Anatolia could speak Aramaic or Hebrew and probably brought the Torah in Greek with them. The first two languages, however, would be forgotten in the next or following generations, especially by those who taught themselves Greek to move up the levels of the social echelon.

The simple synagogue buildings in the course of time became elegant temples

---

[3] A principle which showed the self-interest of the priests at Jerusalem.

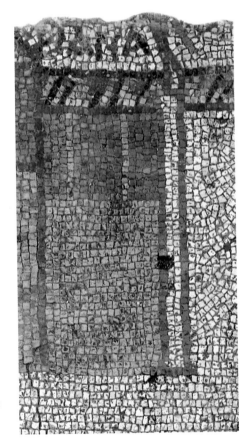

Gate of [*TAU*]*PIANA* (?), or 'at the calf'. Detail from the border of Yakto mosaic found at Daphne (Defne) near Antioch. Mid-fifth century CE. Hatay Archaeological Museum. Antakya. The gate was named after the statue — partly survived on top of the column in the picture — of Antiochus IV Epiphanes taming a bull. Ancient literature informs us that the king received a bronze statute of this kind from the people of Cilicia symbolizing his suppression of some bandits in the Taurus mountains.

Grave stele decorated with an athlete taking oil from a couldron before *agon*, the athletic contests in the gymnasium. Prusa (Bursa). First-second centuries CE. İstanbul Archaeological Museum. Around the figure are his crowns, a bell and an axe.

like the Greek specimens. Their decoration of simple devices such as the elementary Jewish symbols like the seven-branched candelabra *(menorah)*, palm branch *(lulav)*, citrus fruit *(ethrog)*, and blowing horn *(shofar)* and shovel, or Torah ark, David's or Solomon's stars, and rosettes, was later supplemented with twelve zodiac signs and figural scenes accorded symbolic meanings in accordance with biblical stories.[4]

Some Jews, especially members of the upper class, in the course of time became 'hellenized' or began to act like Greeks to varying degrees. The highest point of acting like a Greek was the acquirement of Greek citizenship which was necessary to participate in the administration of a *polis*.

Although the *demos,* or 'citizens body' of the Greek *polis* had lost much of its former freedom and authority under the Hellenistic monarchs the Greek cities still possessed the material amenities of civilized life, provided by the buildings such as an odeon, agora, theatre, library or stadium. The hallmark of a *polis,* however, was the gymnasium because physical training was the foundation of the Greek way of life. Education in the gymnasium was an indispensable part of Greek citizenship; a Jew could only enter the Greek community through the palaestra.

Thus the gymnasium became the focus of the hatred of pragmatic Jews. With its palaestra where men trained nude, pools and baths, and statues of gods and divine kings, each gymnasium represented for Jews the opposite of what their law taught. It was not always possible to cut off the Jewish youth from the outside world and in the course of time as some Greeks were attracted by Judaism a class of Hellenistic Jews appeared. Inscriptions encountered in various parts of western Anatolia, although dating from the Roman period, show that *epheboi* also included local Jewish youths who did not practise circumcision. They are said even to have tried to hide the evidence of circumcision — although it is not known how — in order to be accepted by the Greeks easily. The fact that in 70 CE the Antiochene Jews complained to the Roman governor that their privilege of receiving from gymnasiarchs a rebate for the oil that they used during exercises was withheld shows that some local Jewish youths practised in the gymnasium naked but did not want to use the oil supplied by pagans. Some of the hellenized Jews built for themselves elegant sarcophagi decorated with pagan images accorded new symbolic meanings. The habit of the adoption of Greek personal names, a practice which would accelerate during the Roman era, began in this period.

When the wars between Alexander's generals began, Palestine was caught in the

[4] This practice would last as late as the Iconoclastic period and the Moslem conquest which also banned the use of images.

thick of the fight. Its small and poor land became the battleground of the Macedonian armies which marched back and forth on the Via Maris, 'the Way of the Sea.' After changing hands seven times in two decades Jerusalem was captured by Ptolemy I Soter, ruler of Egypt, who entered Jerusalem on a Sabbath when Jews could not even bear arms and treated its inhabitants harshly. He deported some Jews to Egypt and sold a large number of them as slaves. Nevertheless, in their effort to show the Jews among the docile subjects of their new masters, the Hellenistic kings, later Jewish literature made up stories about how their ancestors accompanied Ptolemy willingly to Egypt and served in his garrisons. They said Ptolemy gave them their ancestral privileges like those enjoyed by the Macedonians. Even if this may not have been true at the beginning, in the course of time the Jews, especially those in Alexandria, established themselves into a community and managed to live as a semi-autonomous group in accordance with their own customs.

Soter's successor Ptolemy II Philadelphus (285-246 BCE) seems to have received the lion's share of this Jewish flattery for he was later credited with the translation of the Torah, or first five books of the Hebrew Bible into Greek, the Pentateuch (Greek Septuagint), for his library at Alexandria. According to the Jewish tradition the king invited seventy-two scholars (six from each of the twelve tribes) to his capital and accommodated them on the island of Pharos where they were even served kosher food during the work, which they finished in seventy-two days. Although the Pentateuch is believed to have been translated in Hellenistic Alexandria and perhaps at a later date, the involvement of a Hellenistic king could not have been as fantastic as told by the later Jewish literature.

The growing contact with Greek literature, legends, and traditions stimulated the production of fictitious stories by the hellenized Jews who were surprised not to find any remark about their ancestors in Greek literature, including Herodotus and tried to accommodate their community more easily in the Hellenistic world. Some scholars believe that stories such as that of the correspondance between the Jews in Judea and Sparta (1 Mac 12) which among many anachronistic peculiarities identifies Abraham as the common ancestor of both nations, or crediting Moses with the invention of the alphabet and writing, are results of this effort. Their strange customs and ceremonies had alienated the Jews from the natives and Gentiles wherever they were settled. The first hostilities against the Jews seem to have begun in Egypt. As early as the third century BCE they were regarded as remnants of a leper colony and accused of invading Egypt in the past together with the Hyksos (rulers of the foreign lands), a Semitic people from Canaan and beyond.

The history of Palestine from about 200 to 70 BCE falls completely into the rule of the Seleucid kingdom. Towards the end of the third century when Egypt gave support to Antiochus III's uncle Achaeus who had rebelled at Sardis the long peace in Palestine came to an end. The Jews like the other people living in the region were caught up in the contest between the two monarchies.

In 200 BCE Antiochus III (223-187 BCE) defeated Ptolemy V of Egypt at the battle of Panion (at the source of the Jordan river) and added Judea as far as Gaza to his lands. Two years later he entered Jerusalem where he was welcomed as a liberator. For the Seleucids this was one more *polis* added to their realm and treated in a similar manner. The *ethnos*, or tribal nation of Jews, were allowed to continue according their own ancestral laws and granted some tax exemptions. The inhabitants who had been sold into slavery were freed. In a decree the Seleucid king prohibited the inner court of the Temple to foreigners. As had been done by the Persian sovereigns of Judea, the king also met the expenses of the Temple and allowed a contribution in kind of corn, salt, oil, wine and suchlike.

In general the Seleucid rule was popular with the Jews. This, however, lasted until the last four years of Antiochus IV Epiphanes (175-164 BCE). The developments in this period are thought to have resulted more from some political misfortunes such as the Roman intervention which snatched Egypt from his grip, or the rivalry between the religious factions in Jerusalem, than from his unstable character. In 167 he plundered the Jerusalem Temple and turned it into a temple for Olympian Zeus. He abolished all kinds of Jewish rituals such as circumcision or the observance of the Sabbath. In 164 having failed to overcome the Maccabean revolt he was persuaded by his ministers to negotiate with Judas Maccabeus and reverting his policy restored to the Jews the rights that had been granted previously. The developments which are described in the books of the Maccabees ultimately led to the birth of the independent Jewish state of the Hasmonaeans. Although the story takes place in the Babylonian world of the sixth century BCE, the Book of Daniel is inspired by the persecutions that this king carried on against the Jewish nation. The stories of the persecution of the Jewish scribe Eleazar who refused to eat pork and of the mother with her sons are thought to have been written in the second half of the first century CE under the influence of the persecutions of Christians and Jews which occurred in Judea, and to have been inserted into biblical literature as in 2 Maccabees (6, 7). Although the conception of martyrdom was at that time absent in Judaism, later Jewish and Christian literature regarded these as the earliest martyrdoms.

The Seleucid capital Antioch on the Orontes opened its gates to the Roman general Pompey in 64 BCE bringing an end to Seleucid history. This was followed by Jerusalem in the next year.

ROMANS, JEWS AND CHRISTIANS

The Romans' role in the history of Anatolia and Palestine is not matched by any other nation who ruled over both countries. The Roman take-over of Anatolia was perhaps made imperative by their fear of Hannibal,[1] who had sheltered the Seleucids, rather than their policy of expansion. Although the battle of Magnesia fought in 190 BCE brought an end to the Seleucid control to the north of the Taurus chain, the official Roman take-over of western Anatolia did not happen until the death of Attalus III of Pergamum without an heir in 133 BCE when he bequeathed his kingdom to Rome. Thus western Anatolia which was until then ruled by a client-kingdom, Pergamum, became *provincia Asia*,[2] with resources unmatched anywhere else in the peninsula, the first and most important Roman province. The example of Attalus III was followed by Nicomedes IV (97-74 BCE) of Bithynia. The Romans allowed the rest of Anatolia to survive as client-kingdoms. However, this did not last long and one after the other Galatia, Lycia, Pontus, Pamphylia and Commagene[3] were annexed to Rome. This development repeated itself in Judea. The Romans allowed the independent kingdom of the Hasmonaeans to survive for a while and incorporated it in 63 BCE in their Roman province of Syria.

Whether it is fictitious propaganda or not, the Bible (1 Mac 8:17-31) informs us that the earliest direct contact between the Romans and the Jews goes back to a treaty made at the time of Judas Maccabeus, about the middle of the second century BCE. Impressed by the power of Rome, Judas sent envoys to Rome and informed them of their wish for an alliance. The Romans are said to have been pleased with the proposal and signing an agreement warned the Seleucid king Demetrius II Nicator (145-138 BCE) against hostilities towards the Jews. This passage also shows that at this time the Jews did not know much about the Romans, or what they knew was wrong. Although there were two consuls as joint heads of the Roman Republic, 1 Maccabees (8:15-16) says that the Romans 'entrusted their government to one man every year' and that there was a senate which met every day. As a result of a renewed alliance, the Romans are said (1 Mac 15:15-22) to have written, this time to the authorities in cities in Greece, Anatolia, Cyprus and Egypt, to inform them about their support and protection of the Jewish population (p 154).

[1] After his death, Septimius Severus (192-211 CE), a Roman emperor African at heart, rebuilt Hannibal's grave at Gebze (Dacibyza) near İzmit (Nicomedia).

[2] Probably from the Hittite *assuwa,* or 'west'.

[3] Except for the first, the boundaries of provinces were frequently changed by the Romans.

Votive monument dedicated 'on behalf of Men Axiottenos and the traces of the gods.' Marble. 184 CE. Manisa Archaeological Museum. The inscription refers to some kind of traces that Men and other gods left on earth after their visit.

The Romans had assimilated the Greek culture, language, customs and religion before conquering Anatolia and Palestine. They had also adopted a Greek ancestry, with the Trojan Aeneas as their eponymous ancestor. Under Roman rule, while the hellenization of the newly captured lands gained momentum, the Latin governing class and their staff, Roman camps, foundation of colonies and recruitment of natives in the Roman army helped Greek and to a lesser extent Latin to reach the remotest corners of the empire. The natives of Lystra for instance first addressed Paul and Barnabas in their native tongue Lycaonian but later did not have any problem in understanding the Greek of the Apostles.

Around the beginning of the Common Era the total number of Jews within the Roman world was probably around five million, one tenth of the population. The Romans had known about the Jews before their eastern conquests because there was a large Jewish community in Rome as early as the second century BCE and they came to Anatolia together with the common judgement against the Jews that they had inherited from the Greeks. The Romans regarded themselves as very religious people and worshipped all deities. For them religion was not a personal private belief but an integral part of the social, political and cultural life. They regarded the Jews as a superstitious group who had peculiar practices which they had already witnessed in Rome. The god of the Jewish people had no images. They avoided sharing meals with natives and did not recognize other deities. They could not sacrifice except at Jerusalem. Their refusal to eat pork, the Sabbath and circumcision were their most distinguishing features for the Romans, and their ritual baths were ridiculed by both Greeks and Romans. In one of his satires the first-century CE Roman poet Juvenal remarks about the Jewish people 'If they ask where to get some water, find out if they're foreskinless' and dedicated the seventh day 'to idleness.' In his *Histories* Tacitus, reflects a similar judgement saying 'Among the Jews all things are profane that we hold sacred; on the other hand, they regard as permissible what seems to us immoral.' For him the Jewish culture was 'perverse and degraded' and the Jews were 'people prone to superstition and the enemy of true religion.' Their history however had taught the Diaspora Jews that the best way of survival was by submitting to their rulers and the Romans did not regard them as a political threat. They even felt it necessary to protect the rights of Jewish communities against the natives. The Jews in general were exempted from military service and permitted to send the annual tax to the Jerusalem Temple. They, after all, were not an upstart group but a nation of antiquity with an ancient written history like themselves and the Greeks and their cult (until 70 CE) had its altar, temple and sacrifices. Those living in Judea were even allowed to mint their own coins without the image of the emperor. When they did not keep to themselves and meddled with their neighbours they were punished as with the cases in139 BCE and 19 CE, when they were expelled from Rome according to Roman writers, in the first case for trying 'to transmit their sacred rites to the Romans' and in the latter for being members of a 'superstitious faith'.

When the Romans annexed Anatolia there were Jewish groups scattered all around the country especially in western, southern and southeastern parts. Most of these had been originally brought from Mesopotamia and settled by Antiochus III towards the end of the third century BCE and by the Roman period may have been supplemented by other Jews who came from Palestine because of wars and poor economic conditions. The literary evidence for the existence of Jews in western Anatolia has been confirmed with archaeological findings from the major cites such as Apamea, Ephesus, Hierapolis, Smyrna and Acmonia. Acts shows that in the first century CE the Jews existed in relatively small towns such as Pisidian Antioch, Iconium and Lystra. The Anatolian Jewish population did not just live in towns but was also scattered through the countryside.

Rome. From *Tabula Peutingeriana* (Peutinger map). Third-fourth centuries CE.

Ancient literature and epigraphic evidence shows that the Gentiles were also not immune to the Jewish manners and some of them were attracted by the latter's monotheistic religion, moral laws and sacred books. Although the number of Gentiles who might have undergone circumcision and become full Jews, or 'proselytes', may have been limited to a few, such as slaves or new family members from mixed marriages, around many synagogues there was a group of Gentiles who were attracted by Judaism, referred to in Greek as *theosebeis*, or 'God-fearers' or 'God-worshipers' (Acts 10:2, 22; 13:16, 26; 16:14; 17:4; 18:7). Lydia of Thyatira whom Paul met and converted at Philippi was such 'a worshiper of God' (Acts 16:14). In addition to ancient literature their existence in cities like Aphrodisias or Miletus is confirmed by archaeological findings. Although their exact standing with Judaism is not known Acts shows that such Gentiles were allowed to enter the synagogue and were influenced by the local Jews to such a degree that they joined them in persecuting Paul and Barnabas at places like Pisidian Antioch, Iconium and Lystra.

In the first century while the Jews in Egypt, Cyprus or Judea revolted against their Gentile neighbours or Rome,[4] the Jews in Anatolia survived as loyal subjects of Rome. They were obviously less nationalistic than their kin in Judea. Only the

---

[4] Palestine Jewish revolt (66-70 CE), Palestine Bar Kochba revolt (132-35 CE) and Cyrene and Egypt (including Cyprus) revolt (115-17 CE).

Antiochene Jews, being so close to the heart of the Jewish reaction, rose and suffered persecutions. The first of these took place in about 40 CE when Gaius Caligula decided to convert the Jerusalem Temple into an Imperial sanctuary and place a colossal statue of himself in it, in the guise of Jupiter (Zeus). The protests of the Antiochene Jews provoked an attack and their synagogue was burned while some of them were exiled. A similar persecution took place in 70 at the end of the Jewish revolt (66-70 CE), following a fire for which they were blamed and punished by deportation.

Despite the legal protection they received from Roman emperors the Jewish communities were harassed by local people and sometimes by the authorities. When they were forced to appear in court on the Sabbath or festivals, deprived of the Temple tax[5] and forced to do military service and civic duties by the authorities, they appealed to the reigning Roman emperor. Josephus, writing in the first century CE, says that in his own day the Jews at Ephesus and throughout Ionia bore citizenship which had been granted them by the Seleucid king who had brought them from the east and settled them there. Although an Ephesian degree from the first century BCE shows that the Romans offered the Ephesian rural population citizenship to secure their support against the Pontus king Mithridates VI, Josephus' remark was probably an exaggeration or it only referred to some basic concessions, such as having their own civil jurisdiction. In the first century Paul and some other Jews are known to have held citizenship, even Roman citizenship, but it is not known how they gained it.

From Cicero we learn that Lucius Valerius Flaccus, proconsul of Asia in 62 BC was accused of directing to Rome gold which had been collected by Jews for the Jerusalem Temple. Jewish funds that the proconsul had confiscated in Apamea, Laodicea on the Lycus, Adramyttium and Pergamum show that such cities had wealthy Jewish groups who did not neglect their responsibilities to the Temple. It is known that in response to the envoy of Hyrcanus II of Jerusalem, the Roman governor Dolabella in 43 BCE exempted the Ephesian Jews from military service and allowed them to keep their customs. He is said to have written to the authorities in Ephesus to warn them that the Jews were not to be forced to appear in court on the Sabbath and not to interfere with the Jewish custom of sending money to the Jerusalem Temple. Local Ionians were known to have objected to the Jews for enjoying the

---

[5] A head tax levied for the upkeep of the Jerusalem Temple on every Jew over twenty years old (Ex 30:13-15) (Mt 17:24). In the Second Temple period it became an annual tax; but voluntary on the diaspora Jews.

benefits of life in their cities without having the same responsibilities as themselves and complained 'if the Jews were to be fellows, they should worship Ionians' gods'. Augustus in 2/3 CE felt it necessary to publish a comprehensive edict outlining Jewish rights.

A new development of the Roman expansion was the evolution of the Imperial cult. The inhabitants of Anatolia and Judea were already familiar with the cult of the deified Ptolemaic or Seleucid kings. However, the Hellenistic ruler cult, especially that of the Seleucid dynasty, was established to strengthen a sense of dynasty, and did not impose on their subjects strict obligations. The Roman Imperial cult was introduced to Anatolia in 29 BCE when Octavian gave permission to Ephesus and Nicaea to set up sanctuaries for the cult of the goddess Roma and his deified father Caesar. Pergamum and Nicomedia were also allowed to establish cult centres for the emperor. Before long about thirty cities in Anatolia had dedicated statues or altars to him under the name of Augustus. In most of these towns a room was spared in one of the already existing sanctuaries to accommodate this new cult which shortly after was extended to the foremost members of the imperial family, dead or alive. The celebration of the Imperial cult turned into the most important social, religious and political event of a Roman city. It became the political symbol of the integrity of the Roman system, its gods, emperor, ruling class, and the peace and wealth of the Roman society as a whole. Sacrifice was the crucial manifestation of this cult and it asserted the loyalty of subjects in the Roman system; an act of homage more than worshipping. The festivals of the Imperial cult were celebrated not just by the officials, priests and members of a particular religious community but also common people. The Jews refused to take part in the ceremonies of the Imperial cult but agreed to offer sacrifices on behalf of the emperor in the Temple at Jerusalem. Their obstinacy in the past and the zeal with which they clung to their ancestral tradition led Rome to allow them a special place among their other subjects.

When Christianity began to spread slowly outside the small world of Judea the Roman annexation of Anatolia was almost complete and the country was a melting pot of various cults and religions. The basic characteristic of the religious atmosphere was tolerance of other people's deities. Even cults such as Isis, Cybele and Attis or Dionysus which practised one or other of the acts such as dancing, self-flagellation or even castration, acts which the Romans mocked and regarded as 'barbarous', were accommodated as long as their members did not force others to join their cult and they sacrificed to the Imperial cult. At the beginning the Christians were seen as the members of a very small, peculiar, antisocial sect within Judaism and

Brick decorated with menorah from the synagogue of Sardis. Roman period. Manisa Archaeological Museum.

did not draw the attention of either the Roman authorities or Roman writers. By the middle of the first century their number may have totalled some fifty thousand people. Some Romans looked on the Christians as members of one of the new social clubs whose members, like those of other clubs, met regularly for a common meal and had their own ritual of initiation and regulations for members, with special speeches, hymns or prayers, and a common chest of contributions. Accordingly as the followers of Heracles were called Heraclists or Dionysus, Dionysiacs they were called *Christiani*, the Christians, followers of *Christus*, a term which was first used in Antioch on the Orontes (Acts 11:26). Some early Christians may have also seen themselves as members of such clubs, because when Paul admonishes the Church at Corinth (1 Cor 11:20-22) he says 'When you meet in one place, then, it is not to eat the Lord's supper, for in eating, each one goes ahead with his own supper, and one goes hungry while another gets drunk. Do you not have houses in which you can eat and drink?'

For some fifty years Christians enjoyed the general tolerance of Rome for Judaism. The protection Paul received from Gallio, the proconsul of Achaia (Acts 18) and from Festus, procurator (financial administrator) of Judea (Acts 25) also shows that the Roman authorities of this period did not yet regard Christianity as a different religion from Judaism and gave shelter to its adherents against the Jews. In fact if Christians had not insisted that there had been no gods on earth until the appearance of theirs and thus insulted other gods and people, their religion might have been accommodated in the Roman polytheism. But, like the Jews before themselves, the Christians denied the existence of other gods. This made them atheists which meant that they refused to believe in the gods that protected the fortunes of the Roman state as evil demons. When the Romans began to distinguish Christians from Jews their attitude changed. They realized that Christianity was born out of the Jewish religion in Judea and looked at it as an apostasy from Judaism, a cult though detested by them at least ancient and venerable. In addition while the preaching of Judaism was not practised by the Jews — nor it was asked for by their religion — the adherents of Christianity were zealous missionaries. They noticed that the Christians were not a race like the Jews but a disorderly group drawn from all levels of society, some with important functions in the civic life of a Roman city. The Christian refusal and abhorrence of civic responsibilities and army life could not be compared with that of the Jews who had been an isolated community since ancient times. Obviously some of the early Christians did not want to follow the advice of the First Letter of Peter (1 Pt 2:12) that they should 'maintain good conduct among the Gentiles', or 'Pay to all their dues, taxes to whom taxes are due...honor to whom honor due' (Rom 13:7). Although a Christian's saying 'God bless you' to a pagan when he sneezed may not have been found strange when he was addressed with 'Jupiter bless you' he felt contaminated by idolatry and was obliged to protest against the divinity of Jupiter.

Since the time of Augustus (27 BCE-14 CE) the Romans punished troublemakers, which included astrologers, magicians, members of foreign cults and philosophers. The Christians bore all the marks of conspiracy and magic and other crimes such groups possessed. They identified themselves as followers of a man who was accused of magic, convicted and executed. Jesus was regarded a magician for his miracles such as healing a man born blind with his spit and clay, or stilling storms or raising the dead. The use of incantations and spells containing Jesus' name caused the Christians to be known as people who used magical formulas. For the Romans magic aimed to destroy established order and law and threatened the hierarchy of the social order. With its irrational power it could kill even emperors. The Christians belonged to an illegal society. Rumour indicated that in their unknown house-churches they committed atrocities such as eating human flesh and drinking human blood — stories derived from the Eucharist — and group sex after blowing out candles. Their preaching of the belief that the immediate end of the world was at hand challenged the security of the Roman system. The Christian refusal of blood and family ties was something unthinkable for the Romans. The Christians avoided the most important social occasions such as weddings or funerals because of fear of staining themselves by idolatry. Being involved in civic life meant that the Christians participated in theatrical performances and watched scenes involving pagan religious ceremonies and sacrifices. These were the ceremonies which protected the people from any kind of divine punishment such as floods, earthquakes, plagues or infertility. Their disgust of social nudity, aversion to public baths and banquets, processions or sacred games such as gladiatorial or athletic contests meant they were shunning the public city life.

An early report of the problems with Christians comes from the reign of the lenient emperor Claudius (41-54 CE). Suetonius writing in the second century in *The Twelve Caesars* says 'Because the Jews at Rome caused continuous disturbances at the instigation of Chrestus,[6] he expelled them from the city.' The information shows that at this time the Romans did not yet distinguish the two religions clearly but punished whoever was involved at the sign of trouble.[7]

[6] Pagans often confused *Christus* with *chrestus* which meant 'good' or 'kind'.

[7] Aquila and his wife Priscilla of Pontus whom Paul met in Corinth and brought with him to Ephesus (Acts 18) were two of the Christians who were expelled from Rome by this incident.

In the same volume in his account of Nero's life Suetonius reports that 'Punishments were also inflicted on the Christians, a sect professing to a new and mischievous religious belief.' Tacitus gives us more detailed information about the Christians in Nero's reign:

'First, then, those of the sect were arrested who confessed; next, on their disclosures, vast numbers were convicted, not so much on the count of arson, as for hatred of the human race. And ridicule accompanied their end: they were covered with wild beasts' skins and torn to death by dogs; or they were fastened on crosses, and, when daylight failed, were burned to serve as torches by night. Nero had offered his gardens for the spectacle...'

The historian describing the execution of the Christians in 64 makes it clear that it was not their incendiarism but their antisocial tendencies obviously also reinforced by the savagery of Nero which led to their execution.

Except for such rare cases there is no evidence of mass persecution of Christians until the third century. In general the local Roman authorities did not want to get involved in religious quarrels among their subjects. The isolated cases which were encountered were affected by the initiation of the local magistrate and the major cause was often the contempt and defiance of the Roman authority, which provided sufficient grounds for punishment. Although at this time no law prohibited conversion to Christianity, any magistrate who heard of a person accused of Christianity was required to investigate. When on a visit to northern coastal cities in 112 CE some local merchants, who probably included butchers and similar professions related to the sale of meat, complained to the younger Pliny, governor of Bithynia-Pontus that although the flesh of sacrificial victims was on sale everywhere there was nobody to buy it. Uncertain about how to treat such cases, Pliny wrote to the emperor Trajan requesting clarification:

'It is my custom, Lord Emperor, to refer to you all questions whereof I am in doubt. I have never participated in investigations of Christians; hence I do not know what is the crime usually punished or investigated, or what allowances are made...Meanwhile, this is the course I have taken with those who were accused before me as Christians. I asked them whether they were Christians, and I asked them a second and third time with threats of punishment. If they kept to it, I ordered them taken off for execution, for I had no doubt that whatever it was they admitted, in any case they deserve to be punished for obstinacy and unbending pertinacity.'

Pliny's letter is important because it is the first account of Christians in Anatolia and it reflects the general ignorance of provincial magistrates about what to do about this mixed multitude. Pliny says that Christianity was illegal but does not know with what offences the Christians could be charged. Trajan replied and approved Pliny's

Sarcophagus decoration from Arycanda in Lycia. Byzantine period. It consists of the first two letters Ch and R, respectively in Greek X and P of Christos. On two sides it has Alpha and Omega.

handling of the matter, adding that 'They are not to be sought out; but if they are accused and convicted, they must be punished.' Large numbers of Christians probably lapsed against Pliny's measures because in the end the meat market recovered. The severity of persecutions against Christians changed according to the emperor or local governor. Despite Trajan's (98-117) persecutions, Ignatius, as he was escorted to Rome to be martyred there, could meet Christian communities on his way, accept their delegations and write letters to them. Some emperors such as Hadrian (117-138) or Antoninus Pius (138-161) even felt it necessary to issue edicts that the clamours against Christians which became widespread after any calamity should not be regarded as legal evidence for convicting them. A Church Father summarised the general atmosphere of the period when he remarked 'If the Tiber floods the city or Nile does not inundate the fields, if there is an eclipse, or earthquake, or famine, or plague, men cry, "Christians to the lion." ' It has been suggested that Ignatius of Antioch was also arrested as a scapegoat for the earthquake of 115 CE. When Polycarp, in the stadium of Smyrna wanted to argue his creed with the governor, the latter said 'Try your arguments on the crowd yonder' and thus showed that it was not his but the people's belief which carried weight.

No matter how few they were, by the middle of the second century there must have been enough persecution cases to lead to the evolution of the concept of 'martyrdom', in western Anatolia from where it spread to the rest of the Roman world. The persecution of Polycarp is the first case where both the 'word' and 'act' of martyrdom are encountered. The martyrdom of Church leaders served as examples to others and seem to have even begun a fashion of voluntary martyrdom. In the late 180s when the Roman governor Arrius Antoninus in western Anatolia was approached by a group of Christians who declared that they refused to sacrifice and asked to be put to death as martyrs, the governor perhaps thought they were out of their minds and said 'You wretches, if you want to die, you have cliffs to leap from and ropes to hang by.' Some governors even gave the accused Christians a chance to leave the city as if they knew what Matthew (10:23) had suggested: 'When they persecute you in one town, flee to another.' The Christian apologists of the later period also tried to distinguish the case of persecutions from voluntary martyrdom and prohibited the latter. The popularity of public spectacles in Anatolia and the need of victims at the arena may have influenced the larger persecutions of this period. As they paid for gladiators and wild beasts which fought in the arena donors began paying for the Christians who were included in the chain of criminals which were sent to the arena to be killed by wild beasts. The Roman emperors Severus and Caracalla permitted Christians to hold city offices but only

(opposite) Parapet piece decorated with the relief of an Eros fighting in the arena. Marble. Third century CE. Theatre of Miletus.

imposed on them those obligations which would not conflict with their beliefs. Septimius Severus (193-211 CE) in order to prevent their number from increasing prohibited the baptism of pagans.[8] The persecution wave which is said to have taken place in the short reign of Maximin (235-38) was probably caused by the severe earthquake of 236. Decius (249-51) was the first emperor who initiated mass persecutions. By the third century the Christians became widespread in the whole empire and all classes, and the emperor in 250 took more drastic measures to win the favour of the gods. He demanded that every citizen in his lands sacrifice to them (though not to the Imperial cult) and obtain a certificate of obedience. The act revealed the Christians who were punished accordingly and also created a profitable market for certificates. The persecutions however lasted until his death. The persecution of the Seven Sleepers of Ephesus, Pionius of Smryna and other cases in Pergamum are assigned to this period. It was after the Decian persecutions that the controversy over whether penance was possible for lapsed Christians began. Decius' successor Valerian thought that by eliminating the leaders and prominent persons he could deal with the problem and in 257 demanded sacrifice only from the higher-class Christians. The persecutions which took place under the Tetrarchs differed. The worst was in the East where Galerius and Diocletian ruled. The latter realized that Christianity had become a state within the state and in 303 began a large scale persecution. He decreed that no Christian could hold Roman citizenship and no Christian slave could be freed. Churches were destroyed and scriptures burned. Diocletian's purge extended to the army which was already penetrated by Christianity. This began the fashion of soldier martyr-saints. In the West where Maximian ruled the edicts of Diocletian did not create anything more than pressure on Christians, without bloodshed. In the Gallic provinces Constantius Chlorus did not see Christians as a threat to the State. The persecutions in the East lasted with intervals until Constantius' son and successor Costantine the Great, following his defeat of Maxentius at the Milvian Bridge (312), issued the Edict of Milan the following year and established the freedom of Christianity and pagans alike. It also established the restoration of all property, whether belonging to individual Christians or to churches. This however did not bring peace to the Church and before long the Christians would themselves begin to persecute the pagans and each other.

[8] The word *paganus*, or 'pagan' meant in a pejorative sense 'peasant' and was not encountered in writing until the reign of the emperor Valentinian I (364-75). For Christians it meant civilians without baptism.

Statues of the four emperors of the Tetrarchy at St Mark's square in Venice. Porphyry. The group was taken there from Constantinople by the Latin soldiers of the Fourth Crusade. Although indistinguishable from each other physically they are thought to represent Diocletian, Galerius, Maximian and Constantius Chlorus.

JOURNEYS OF SAINT PAUL

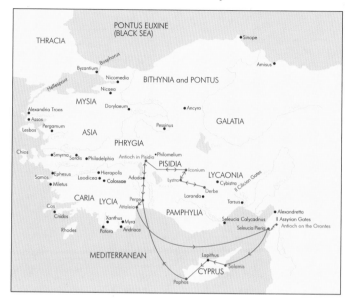

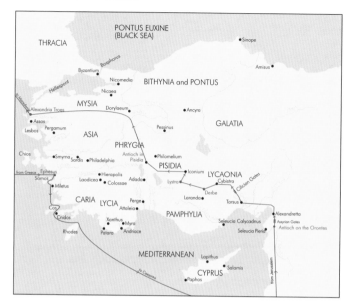

Map of Paul's First Journey.

Map of Paul's Second Journey.

In his first journey Paul was accompanied by Barnabas and the latter's cousin John Mark. They began from Antioch and sailing from Seleucia Pieria arrived at Salamis in Cyprus. The prize of the mission to the island was the conversion of Sergius Paulus, the Roman governor, in Paphos. From here Paul and his friends sailed to Perge and continuing to the northern interior preached the gospel in Pisidian Antioch, Iconium, Lystra and Derbe. In almost all of these towns the Apostles made new converts but also suffered persecution by the Jews and Gentiles who were provoked by the first group. The most important result of the first mission was the foundation of a Church separate from the synagogue at Antioch in Pisidia. They returned by the same way to Perge. Taking a ship from Attaleia they concluded the mission at Antioch. Paul did not forget his difficult experiences of this first journey and later referred to these in his letters.

In his second journey the Apostle, accompanied by Silas, began from Antioch and travelled to southern Galatia. He visited the Christians who had been converted by him during his previous journey at Derbe, Lystra, Iconium and Pisidian Antioch. After he had returned from the first journey to Antioch he heard that some of his converts in Galatia had apostatized under pressure of the local Jews and had written them not to believe the Jews who told them that circumcision was necessary. From here Paul, now with Timothy in the party, travelled first in the direction of Mysia and Bithynia until a vision Paul saw prevented him from going in this direction. He continued to Alexandria Troas where he saw another vision, probably an allusion to his meeting with Luke, who told the Apostle to come to Macedonia. At the end of his missionary work in Greece, on his way to the Holy Land he made a short stop at Ephesus.

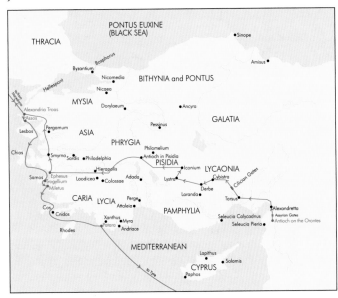

Map of Paul's Third Journey.

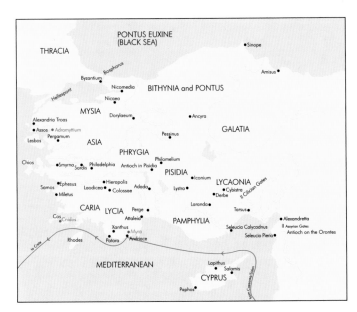

Map of Paul's Journey to Rome.

In his third journey Paul followed the same route as the previous one and visited his Galatian Churches. From here he went to Ephesus and stayed there three years. In Ephesus the Apostle criticized those Christians who were converted by a missionary named Apollo but just by the 'baptism of John' not the 'Holy Spirit' (Acts 19). Much of the evangelization of western Anatolia probably took place during this period when he also wrote most of his letters. He is thought to have made a short round-trip visit to the Church at Corinth. When he was compelled to leave Ephesus because of the silversmiths' riots he went to Alexandria Troas and crossed to Macedonia and Greece. On his return he stayed longer in Alexandria Troas and stopping at Assos and Trogyllium (AV) reached Miletus. Because of his bad memories of this city he avoided Ephesus but called the Ephesian elders to Miletus and addressed them there. In his voyage to the Holy Land his ship made a last stop at Patara in Lycia.

When Paul was in Jerusalem after his third journey he caused a riot of the Jews who, mistakenly, thought that he had taken Gentiles into the prohibited precinct of the Temple. He was arrested and taken to Caesarea where he was kept in prison. When the new governor tried to send him to be judged by the Sanhedrin, Paul, as a Roman citizen, asked to be put on trial at Rome. In the autumn of probably the year 59 Paul, as prisoner 'on appeal' to the Roman emperor, was put on a small vessel at Caesarea which was bound for Adramyttium (Edremit), a coastal town in western Anatolia. After making a short stop at the Phoenician port of Sidon the boat sailed between the Anatolian peninsula and Cyprus and stopped at Myra's port Andriace in Lycia. Here the centurion who was in charge of Paul and the other prisoners found another boat, a freight vessel carrying grain, bound to Italy and revised his route. Before sailing into the open sea the vessel tried to make a last stop at Cnidus but failed because of the contrary winds.

ANTIOCH ON THE ORONTES

The holy spirit said, 'Set apart for me Barnabas and Saul for the work to which I have called them' (Acts 13:2).

The role that Antioch on the Orontes (Antakya) played in the development of Christianity is not rivalled by any other city in Anatolia. In the Bible Antioch is mentioned (Acts 11:19) for the first time along with Phoenicia and Cyprus as one of the places to which the Christians escaped from the persecutions in Judea and began preaching the gospel. The existence of a relatively large Jewish community in the city must have helped the early success of Christianity here. Some of these may have been descendants of those who were settled by Seleucus I Nicator around 300 BCE when he founded the city. The Jews in Antioch were probably organized as a kind of national association similar to that of the other ethnic groups under the Seleucid rule and lived in accordance with their ancestral laws, enjoying certain rights such as carrying out their own judicial system. While some of these early Jewish settlers may have regarded the synagogue as a shelter against the outside Hellenistic world, some, mostly from the wealthier families, may have begun to show different degrees of hellenization even at this early period.

Later Jewish and Christian traditions regard Antioch as the burial place of the mother and her seven sons who were persecuted (2 Mac 7) in the reign of Antiochus IV Epiphanes (175-164 BCE). It is said that in the reign of Demetrius I (162-150 BCE) a shrine was built over their graves. This shrine was known as the synagogue of Kenesheth Hashmunith, after the mother, and said to have possessed relics such as Moses' mantle, the surviving fragments of the law tables and the keys of the Ark. In the Christian era it became a church.

Antioch's suburb, Daphne, was famous for its shrine of Apollo which offered protection to those who sheltered here. It also had a Jewish quarter. This is the reason why in 2 Maccabees (4:33) Onias, the last Zadokite High Priest withdrew 'to the inviolable sanctuary at Daphne, near Antioch'. He was, however, induced to leave the temple and was killed immediately when he came out of it. This temple was built in the grove where Apollo tried to ravish the nymph Daphne, who gave the suburb her name. After their supression of the Jewish revolt in 70 CE Vespasian

Detail from the border of Yakto mosaic from Daphne. Mid-fifth century CE. Hatay Archaeological Museum. Antakya. To the left is a figure wrapped in a mantle with its edge probably raised over his head in an attitude of prayer. The gesture of his hands lifted together in the folds of the mantle suggests the act of adoraton in Christian iconography

and caused the building in front of him to be interpreted as a church, perhaps the Golden Church, the *Domus Aurea,* cathedral of Antioch which was begun by Constantine the Great in 327 and dedicated in 341 by his son Constantius. To the right a house and a man and two donkeys are represented.

and Titus, his son and general came to Antioch where they were received with the rejoicing of the natives. Titus, to the disappointment of Antiochenes, did not accept their request to expel the Jews from the city and cancel their political rights. Titus is said to have set up the 'Cherubim' from the Jerusalem Temple at the gate leading to Daphne next to the Jewish quarter and also built a theatre at Daphne bearing the inscription 'From the Jewish spoils'.

At the time Christianity reached Antioch, the city was the capital of the Roman province of Syria and the base of its military power in the east. Situated at the crossing point of land and sea communication routes Antioch's population was a mixture of races and nationalities, trades and beliefs, various social classes and spoke many tongues. The enthusiasm and interest of Antiochene Jews and Gentiles for the Christian message encouraged the elders at Jerusalem to send Barnabas to the city. It was at this period that the followers of Christ in Antioch were first called Christians (Acts 11:25-26), or the *Christiani* (singular *Christianus*) following the Roman practice of naming the members of a social club after its founder.[1]

After a period of missionary activity at Antioch, Barnabas went to Tarsus and brought back Paul with him to help him there. Although in number they were not as many as those in Rome or Alexandria the Antiochene Jews played an important role in the early development of Christianity. The costly votive offerings that they sent to the Jerusalem Temple give us an idea about their wealth. Their synagogues must have attracted plenty of Gentile 'God-fearers'. Nicolas of Antioch, one of the first deacons (Acts 6:5) chosen to assist the disciples, who later played a part in the Christian Church at Jerusalem, was an Antiochene proselyte. It is however, not known if he is related to the heresy of Nicolaitans referred to by the Apostle John in his letters to the Church at Ephesus (Rv 2:6) or Pergamum (Rv 2:15). The particular heresy is said to have tried to find a compromise between Christianity and dominant social forms, and became the forerunner of the more dangerous Gnostic movement. Nicholas may not have had any relation with the heresy and his name may have been attached to it to win more support.

Antioch served as the base of Paul's missionary activities. In addition to having the liberal atmosphere of a typical Greek *polis,* in which Paul and Barnabas preached the gospel freely, the existence of wealthy members in the Church established here

---

[1] *Ecclesia*, or 'assembly' by which Christians would refer to themselves in Greek or Latin for the Romans meant the political assembly of the people of a city.

who were willing to help Paul's missions may have played a role in this. The first-century Roman world suffered plenty of natural disasters such as earthquakes, plagues and famines, and ancient literature mentions a famine in Judea in 46-48 CE. The relief that the Antiochenes sent to the Christians with Paul and Barnabas was probably related to this event. Although its amount is not mentioned (Acts 11:29) it may have been substantial for Antiochenes were known for their wealth. The gesture was important in showing the solidarity of the Antiochene Jews and Gentile Christians and their disposition towards their other brothers.

Grotto-church of St Peter at Antakya. Situated on the slope of Mt Staurin, the 'Mountain of the Cross', this cave, traditionally, served as a meeting place for early Antiochene Christians. Its present-day façade was added much later. Christian tradition regards Peter as the first bishop of the city.

Dedicatory inscription from the mosaic floor of a church near Antioch on the Orontes. Dumbarton Oaks Collection. Washington. DC. In Greek it reads 'Under the most holy bishop Flavius, the most venerable Eusebius, in charge of the administration of the church, Dorys the priest completed the mosaic of the entire exedra'. The translation and date of the mosaic is established with the help of an identical dedicatory panel from an another room of the same church.

Upon their return to Antioch from their first journey the Apostles saw that some Jews who had come from Judea insisted that unless Gentiles were circumcised they could not be saved. Paul and Barnabas had to go to Jerusalem to discuss the matter with the elders there who had the last word on such matters. Here Paul and Barnabas described their work among the Gentiles during their first missionary journey and on the initiation of Peter and in the Apostolic Council it was decided that circumcision was not necessary for Gentile Christians and the dietary Jewish prescriptions were simplified to a few prohibitions. Paul and Barnabas returned to Antioch and from here Barnabas taking John Mark with him again sailed for Cyprus while Paul taking Silas with him set out for a second missionary journey to Anatolia and Greece.

The Church of Antioch took an active part in the controversies that shook Christianity in its later development. In 325 the city became the seat of the first Church council, where Constantine addressed its participating bishops and the heresy of Arius was condemned. The long and complicated creed drawn up here became the prototype of later creed-making at various synods.

Saint Ignatius

According to the Christian tradition Ignatius (35-110), was the 'second' or 'third' successor of Peter as the bishop of Antioch. He was arrested for his religious convictions and after his trial condemned to death. It has been also suggested that he was chosen and condemned as a scapegoat after the famous earthquake of Antioch in 115 which destroyed the whole city. As he was taken to the Roman capital he is said to have travelled heavily guarded — traditionally by ten brutal soldiers — and in chains. Except for this journey, almost nothing is known about his life. He is said to have been from Syria, a pagan and a persecutor of Christians before his conversion. He may have known a few of the Apostles, such as Paul or John. In the letter that he wrote to the Romans from Smyrna, he tells how he accepted the death sentence with joyful exultation as an opportunity to imitate the passion of Christ, his blood for the wine and his body for the bread of the Eucharist. He also pleads with them not to intervene in his behalf and prevent his anticipated martyrdom by ransoming him even if he should implore them in person.

His route probably started at Antioch, followed by Tarsus, Philomelium (Akşehir), Laodicea on the Lycus (Eskihisar), Philadelphia (Alaşehir), Sardis, Smyrna and by

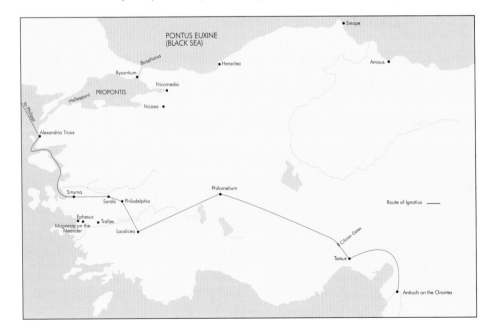

Map of St Ignatius' journey in Anatolia.

boat to Alexandria Troas from where he sailed to Neapolis.[1] After Philippi he would have continued by way of the Via Egnatia through Macedonia to the Adriatic and crossing it, by way of the Via Appia as far as Rome.

During this journey he visited Christian communities on his way and met the representatives they sent to him, opportunities provided by the bribes he paid to his escorts. He also wrote (or dictated) letters to Churches at Ephesus, Magnesia on the Meander (Menderes Manisası), Tralles (Aydın) and Rome from Smyrna and to Philadelphia, Smyrna and to Polycarp from Alexandria Troas. In his letter to the Christians at Smyrna the expression 'catholic Church' is used for the first time in the sense of the 'universal Church'. The subject of his letters with the exception of the one written to the Romans, which deals only with his approaching martyrdom, is the exposition and defence of the Christian gospel against heretical tendencies inspired by Judaism and the widespread early belief that Christ was just divine and could not have lived as a man and died.[2] For Ignatius this was denial of reincarnation. His letters were preserved on Polycarp's initiative and became widely known in the early Church and are regarded as some of the earliest pieces of surviving Christian literature.

In his letters Ignatius emphasizes and repeats the authority of the clergy and gives the impression that this already existed in the Churches of western Anatolia at this early date, a fact also made evident by the letters of the Apostle John to the Seven Churches of Asia. Ignatius says that the hierarchy of the clergy of a Church is the reflection of the divine hierarchy in heaven which consists of a single God, a divine council and the Apostles, mirrored on earth by a single bishop, priests and deacons. The laity can only gain eternal salvation by submitting itself to the clergy. He was martyred by being exposed to wild beasts in the amphitheatre of Flavius (later known as the Colosseum) about the year 110 in the reign of the emperor Trajan (98-117).

[1] His words in his letter to the Romans that he found himself 'in conflict with beasts of prey by land and by sea', if used literally may suggest a sea voyage by ship from Seleucia Pieria to Attaleia from where he may have continued inland.

[2] Greek *dokin*, or 'Docetism', from *dokesis*, or 'semblance'. The Docetes in some forms believed that Jesus was not born of the Virgin but had descended on the Jordan's banks as a perfect man and also miraculously escaped the ignominy of death.

Saint John Chrysostom

John Chrysostom (347-407) is known as one of the most important figures of early Christianity. He was born in Antioch and in his early youth became a hermit in the Syrian desert. After returning to the city he studied rhetoric with the leading pagan orator Libanius and also theology with Diodore, bishop of Tarsus. His oratorical skill at the pulpit made him known as *Chrysostom*, or the 'Honeymouthed'. His attribute, a beehive, inspired a further legend which claims that when the devil upset his inkwell, he dipped his pen in his mouth and it was covered with gold. Outspoken and direct, his sermons remain today the most popular of all discourses among those of the Church Fathers.[1] In 398 he was appointed patriarch of Constantinople. His reformations among the lax clergy of the capital, his open war against unsuitable clerics to one of whom he said that he was no better than a brothel keeper, and his refusal to give financial support for some building projects, made him unpopular. He offended the men in the capital repeatedly proclaiming that a woman had equal right to demand fidelity of her husband. His ascetic refusal to give lavish hospitality offended and disappointed those people who were used to being invited to the lavish dinners at the bishop's house. The malcontents met at Chalcedon (Kadıköy) and when John refused to appear he was deposed.

John's relations with Eudoxia, wife of the emperor Arcadius also turned from good to bad because in a sermon on feminine frailty John had cited the example of the biblical Jezebel, probably to allude to the empress who was a symbol of luxury and sensuality in the capital. The angry emperor exiled him to Bithynia. The day after his departure an earthquake shook the Constantinople and was taken as celestial disfavour. Arcadius and Eudoxia recalled John, and he was reinstated. A few months later there were disturbing festivities at the erection of a silver statue of Eudoxia next to the church of St Sophia. When the noise of the ceremony outside interrupted his sermon John lost control in the pulpit and preached 'Again Herodias raves, again she dances, again she demands John's head on a charger.' The palace decided to get rid of John for sure and a second exile decision was taken. His excited supporters set fire to St Sophia. John Chrysostom was exiled first to Cucusus in eastern Cappadocia. He died three years later at Comana (Tokat) as he was being moved to a remoter spot, Pityus, on the last Roman frontier.

[1] Those writers or teachers from the second century onward whose works are traditionally considered of special weight and worthy of special respect as interpretations of the gospel. John of Damascus (675-749) is generally regarded as the last of them.

Saint Symeon Stylite

Monastery of Symeon Stylite the Elder with the remains of his rock-cut pillar at the centre (Syria).

A development in early Christianity was the appearance of a number of holy men who experienced various forms of asceticism, and also served the laity as priests, healers, seers, or wonderworkers. Although their number was not high, these individuals are belived to have played an important role in the spread of Christianity in Anatolia.

Among these, Symeon the Stylite (390-459) of Antioch is regarded as the initiator of the odd fashion known as the Stylites[1] or the 'Pillar-saints'. It is not known if the pagan tradition of spending a week on phallic cones, probably dedicated to Priapus, which the second-century CE Roman satirist Lucian of Samosata witnessed at nearby Zeugma on the upper Euphrates would have served as a model to Simeon. Known as the elder, he self-inflicted various methods of pain such as living in a disused watertank, spending summers buried up to his chin in the ground or wearing a spiked girdle. When he found that his ascetic life attracted too many invalids who wished to be cured by touching him he placed himself on top of a column from which he administered his blessings and prayers and continued his miracles.[2] His first column was of three blocks representing the Trinity. Over the years he gradually increased the height of the column until it reached 20 m high. It was said that he was able to fly from there like a bird. After his death the column was enshrined in a church, and a monastery known by his name was built by the emperor Zeno in the last quarter of the fifth century.

Daniel the Stylite (409-93), another monk from Constantinople, visited Simeon on his column and when he returned to the capital imitating Symeon erected his column at Anaplous (Kuruçeşme) along the European coast of the Bosphorus, to live on top of it for over thirty years. In later centuries the isolated cones of Cappadocia both offered the seclusion that the stylite saints sought for and saved them from constructing columns.

Symeon Stylite the Younger (d 521) who lived on a column on the *Mons Admirabilis*, the 'Wonder-Filled Mountain', outside Antioch at 'Samandağı', or 'Symeon's Mountain' was another stylite of this period. The surviving ruins show that in the course of time a monastery was built around the saint's column. It is claimed that the work was done by Isaurian stone-masons who worked solely out of gratitude to the saint, in return for the healings that he had bestowed on them.

Monastery of Symeon Stylite the Younger with the remains of his rock-cut pillar at the centre near Antakya.

[1] Greek *stylos*, or 'quill pen'.

[2] His prestige was so great that the assent of the illiterate stylite was required by the government to the Ecumenical Councils of Ephesus (431) and Chalcedon (451).

SELEUCIA PIERIA

Inscription from the tunnel of Titus. In Greek it informs us that this part of work was done under a *nauarchos* (ship-captain).

So they, sent forth by the holy Spirit, went down to Seleucia and from there sailed to Cyprus (Acts 13:4).

Seleucia (on the) Pieria (Çevlik) is mentioned only twice in the Bible. The first instance is found in 1 Maccabees (11:8): 'Plotting evil against Alexander, King Ptolemy took possession of the cities along the seacoast as far as Seleucia-by-the-Sea.' The reference belongs to a tumultuous era in the history of the Levant. Alexander Balas (150-146 BCE), a pretender put forward by Attalus II of Pergamum and also supported by Ptolemy VI Philometer (181-145 BCE) of Egypt had killed Demetrius I Soter and taken the Seleucid throne. His bad rule however made Alexander unpopular with his subjects. Meanwhile Demetrius II Nicator, the eldest son of Demetrius I landed (147 BCE) on the Syrian coast with an army of Cretan mercenaries (1 Mc 10:67). Ptolemy VI Philometer supported Demetrius and campaigning north captured the coastal cities of Phoenicia as far as Seleucia Pieria.

The second reference is more important because here it is shown as the port of Antioch during the Roman era, from which Paul and Barnabas set sail for Cyprus on their first missionary journey (Acts 13:4) accompanied by John Mark. The Apostles may have used the same port to return to Antioch at the end of their journey. The two piers of the outer harbour, until they disappeared into the Mediterranean, bore the names of the two Apostles. The port also may have been used by Ignatius if the beginning of his journey to Rome was by sea.

The city was founded on a promontory of Mt Pieria (Musa dağı) and at the time of Paul had become the most important Roman port in the region for supplying the Roman army based at Antioch. The surviving tunnel was built about a decade after Paul's martyrdom by Vespasian and his son Titus to empty the rain-water which flooded the harbour. The mosaics recovered from the city and the ruins of several churches indicate its importance in this period. One of these large churches was built by the emperor Zeno (479-91) and dedicated to Thecla.

(opposite) Tunnel of Titus. It was cut during the reigns of Vespasian (69-79 CE), Titus (79-81 CE) and Domitian (81-96 CE).

PERGE

After a successful missionary trip to Paphos, Cyprus where the first high-placed Gentile the Roman governor Sergius Paulus, was converted, Paul and Barnabas together with John Mark took a boat to 'Perga' in Pamphylia (Acts 13:13). At the time of Paul's journeys the river Cestrus (Aksu) was navigable as far as the city and the vessel which carried the Apostles was probably bound for Perge's port. Here John Mark left them and returned to Jerusalem. Acts does not explain why he acted like this but the reason may have been Mark's disappointment in Paul's eagerness to preach the gospel to the Gentiles. On their return from Lycaonia Pisidia and before going to Attaleia Paul and Barnabas again stopped at Perge (Acts 14:25). Acts, however, does not say anything more than that they proclaimed the gospel there.

Ruins of Perge. Looking from the city towards the Hellenistic gate with circular towers.

St Paul's church at Antioch in Pisidia. Early Christian period. Looking west towards the exterior of the apse.

ANTIOCH IN PISIDIA

During his first missionary journey Paul, instead of preaching the gospel throughout the cosmopolitan and well-populated coastal cities of Pamphylia, travelled to Pisidian Antioch[1] (Acts 13:14). Here, on the Sabbath, Barnabas and Paul entered the synagogue and after the conclusion of the service the latter got up and spoke. His preaching must have met with interest because they were invited to speak on the next Sabbath as well. Converts from both Jews and Gentiles, who until then had been attracted by Judaism, were made.

Later when he wrote to the Galatians (4:13), a term by which is meant the Christians in Pisidia and Lycaonia, Paul confessed that 'it was because of a physical illness' that he originally took the gospel to this region. He also thanked the Galatians for not having shown any contempt for his illness. It has been suggested that the illness the Apostle spoke of was malaria, which he had probably picked up in the hot and humid Pamphylian plain and this compelled him to move to the healthy climate of the Pisidian heights. Nevertheless, Paul's choice of this particular city among many others in Pisidia is thought to have been the result of the advice he received from Sergius Paulus, his Gentile convert in Paphos, Cyprus. This personage was from the Roman colony of Pisidian Antioch where he had relatives and estates.

At the time of Paul's missionary journeys Antioch (Yalvaç) was a colony, or *colonia* of Rome with many Greek-speaking Romans. The city was called by them Colonia Caesareia Antiocheia. The administrator who pacified the mountain hordes in the region was consul Publius Sulpicius Quirinius who was later transferred to Syria and held the great census at the time Jesus was born (Lk 2:1-7). If it were not for the Jews in the city, Paul's expectations of high-placed Gentile converts might have been fulfilled, because on the following Sabbath a great crowd filled the synagogue. 'The Gentiles were delighted when they heard' the news of Paul, but the Jews

[1] Antioch ad Pisidia = Antioch 'on', 'towards' or 'next to' Pisidia.

'incited the women of prominence who were worshipers' (attracted by Judaism) and the leading men of the city and the Apostles were expelled from the city. Acts informs us that the Apostles visited the city as they returned to the Mediterranean coast.

The Gentile converts that Paul won in these cities seem to have lapsed shortly after his departure with the pressure of Jewish Christians, who claimed that circumcision and other obligations of the Mosaic law were necessary to become a Christian. Paul felt it necessary to write from Antioch on the Orontes and admonish them. In his letter addressing them as 'stupid Galatians' or 'Are you so stupid' (Gal 3:1) he compared them with the Celtic natives of Galatia who were known for their simple-mindedness.

Pisidian Antioch is not mentioned by name in Paul's next two missionary journeys; but is assumed to have been visited.

Colonnaded street leading from Tiberius' square to the temple of Augustus. First century CE. Antioch in Pisidia.

Mountains of St Philip (left) and St Thecla (Takkeli dağ) near Konya. Looking north.

ICONIUM

In Acts (13:51) Paul and Barnabas, having been persecuted and expelled from Pisidian Antioch, travelled to Iconium. Although their preaching was met with the reaction of local Jews the Apostles stayed in Iconium 'for a considerable period' which probably means that they were able to make some converts. Some Gentiles, however, as they had done in Pisidian Antioch, supported the Jews who realized the threat Paul's preaching carried for Judaism, and the Apostles were stoned and forced to flee to Lystra and Derbe and the surrounding countryside. However, after preaching the gospel at Lystra and Derbe, Paul and Barnabas returned to Iconium from where they continued to Pisidian Antioch and the Mediterranean coast.

Iconium (Konya) is not mentioned by name in either Paul's second or third journey. However, Acts (16:4) informs us that during the second journey in Lycaonia, after Lystra 'they travelled from city to city' and 'handed on to the people for observance the decisions reached by the apostles and presbyters in Jerusalem.' The expression that 'the brothers in Lystra and Iconium' spoke highly of Timothy in his second journey may imply that during his stay in Lycaonia the Apostle may have wandered in the region back and forth staying more than once in the same place. Acts (18:23) also says that during his third journey Paul visited the Galatian cities in 'orderly sequence.'

From the story of Thecla in the apocryphal Acts of Paul we learn that in the second century CE, when they are thought to have been recorded, Iconium was one of the fairly large rural settlements where the provincial governor held court during his regular tours and 'commanded Paul to be brought to the judgement seat.'

Saint Thecla's Cave Church

The story of Thecla recorded in the apocryphal Acts of Paul is believed to have contained some truth and to have been inspired by a genuine martyr of the same name in Anatolia. It is thought have been recorded in about 160 CE.

The story is interesting in that it gives us the only physical description of Paul. Ancient literature informs us that the Apostle always sent Titus before him to announce his arrival in a city and in this case Titus described Paul to Onesiphorus of Iconium who went out to meet the Apostle. Thus when Onesiphorus saw 'a man little of stature, thin-haired upon the head, crooked in the legs, of good state of body, with eyebrows joining, and nose somewhat hooked, full of grace: for sometimes he appeared like a man, and sometimes he had a face of an angel' he knew that this was Paul.

St Thecla. Icon. Twentieth century. St Barnabas Museum. North Cyprus.

Paul's preaching at the house of Onesiphorus that the body is the temple of God and should be kept chaste and that virgins who lived in this manner would be rewarded after the Second Coming, which was expected to happen any time during this period with eternal blessing, attracted many women and young girls. Among the latter was Thecla who sat at the window of her house across the street and listened to Paul's sermons, which made her renounce her engagement. Thecla's mother's and her fiancé's complaint brought Paul before the judge and he was condemned to be whipped and expelled from the city for corrupting the women and teaching the maidens not to marry. Thecla was also sentenced to be burned. She was saved by a timely heavy rain and escaped to follow Paul whom she found sheltered with the family of Onesiphorus outside Iconium. The Apostle refused to baptize Thecla for a pretty young girl like her might be tempted in the future. The two travelled to Antioch — which is not mentioned — and here Thecla insulted a rich Antiochene for trying to seduce her. While Paul continued on his journey Thecla was found guilty of sacrilege for removing the wreath (with the image of the emperor) from the man's head and was again sentenced to death. During her persecution a tank of water miraculously appeared in the arena and she was baptized by jumping into it. Meanwhile she had become the protegé of one Tryphaena who had lost her daughter. This was a real personality, the queen Tryphaena,[1] who was a widow of

[1] A dedication by the people of Cyzicus (Erdek) for her generosity to their city has survived. İstanbul Archaeological Museum.

Remains of the apse of the church built above the cave church of St Thecla.

Cotys, king of Thracia, the mother of Polemon II, the last king of Pontus and a great-niece of the emperor Claudius. In the arena various bizarre efforts to kill Thecla gave no result. At the beginning of the last spectacle, when Tryphaena fainted, the governor, afraid of the emperor's wrath, stopped the games and released Thecla. Upon hearing that Paul was at Myra she put on a boy's clothes hoping to be allowed to stay with him in that guise and travelled to Lycia. When they met Paul was still worried if she had been tempted. Thecla told him her receipt of baptism and the rest of her story. From here Thecla went to Seleucia where she lived to an old age. When she was 'ill-treated' by some young men 'she prayed, and the rock opened and she entered it, and it closed after her.'

Thecla's shrine is located a short distance from Silifke (Seleucia on the Calycadnus[2]) at 'Meryemlik' and during the Byzantine period consisted of a cave church and a large basilica built on top of it. The cave where Thecla is said to have spent her last days and descended into the earth alive is thought to be of natural origin. In the third century the grotto was converted into an underground basilica of a nave and aisles with two rows of three Doric columns which were obtained from a Roman building that had stood on the site and was thought to have been a pagan sanctuary. The cave of Thecla became the northern side-chamber of the southern aisle. In the fourth century when a small basilica was built over it the cave began to be used as a crypt.

The cave church seems to have taken its present-day form when a basilica of very large size (the largest in Cilicia), some 81 by 43 metres, was built above it in the second half of the fifth century. Its columns were repositioned to provide support to the columns of the building above. This new basilica had two light wells by which the visitors could see the cave church. Its plan consisted of a portico, a narthex, a nave and wide side aisles. It had a wooden roof. The surviving piece today belongs to the southern section of its apse. In the course of time the space between the southern columns of the cave church had to be filled in for reinforcement. Its interior, also reduced in size is decorated with gold or coloured glass mosaics.

[2] Göksu river in which the German emperor Frederic Barbarossa was accidentally drowned in 1190 during the Third Crusade.

LYSTRA

During the first missionary journey (Acts 14:6) Paul and Barnabas having been persecuted in Iconium travelled to Lystra (Hatunsaray). Here the first person they encountered was a crippled man, 'lame from birth, who had never walked.' When Paul healed the man the local people began crying in their Lycaonian tongue that the gods Zeus and his messenger Hermes had arrived in their city in human form, because the anthromorphic pagan gods, especially Zeus, associated with Hermes had been popularly worshipped in Phrygia (p 18). In front of the city gate stood the temple of Zeus. Since the site has not yet been excavated this is the only thing known about its plan. A second-century CE stone altar which is inscribed in Latin 'Twice fortunate Lystra [Lustra], a Julian colony dedicated [the altar] to the divine Augustus Decreed by the city council' found on the mound helped to identify the location of Lystra. The priest rushed with garlanded sacrificial oxen to honour the visitors. Shocked, the Apostles begged the crowd not to treat them like this but it was useless. At this stage of events 'some Jews from Antioch and Iconium' appeared and changed the opinion of the crowd and St Paul was stoned and thrown out of the city, left for dead. Nevertheless, there must have been some converts here because Acts (14:20) says that 'when the disciples gathered around him' Paul got up and returned to Lystra and stayed there one more night. The family of a grandmother, Lois, mother Eunice, and son, Timothy mentioned in Paul's letter to Timothy (2 Tm 1:5) were probably converted during this journey. The following day however, the Apostles left the city. After their work at Derbe was done the Apostles returned to Lystra and continued on their way back to the Mediterranean coast.

Acts gives a little more information about Paul's activity at Lystra during his second missionary journey. He arrived from Derbe together with Silas and in Lystra 'there was a disciple named Timothy, the son of a Jewish woman was a believer, but his father was a Greek' (Acts 16:1). Paul wanted to take the young boy with him. However, thinking that the Jews to whom he would proclaim the gospel after that might not have heard of the decision of the Jerusalem Council about circumcision or might not accept this, he had Timothy circumcised so as not to offend their feelings.

Although it is not mentioned by name Lystra was probably one of the cities that Paul visited when he left Antioch and 'travelled in orderly sequence through the Galatian country and Phrygia, bringing strength to all his disciples' (Acts 18:23) during his third journey on his way to Ephesus.

DERBE

Acts 14 informs us that during his first missionary journey Paul accompanied by Barnabas travelled to Derbe (Kerti Höyük) after he had recovered from the persecution at Lystra. No detail of Paul's first stay in the city is reported except that they 'made a considerable number of disciples.' During the second journey which Paul had began from Antioch on the Orontes in the company of Silas, Derbe is mentioned by name. Neither Derbe nor any other city in Lycaonia is mentioned by name during Paul's third journey although Acts (18:23) informs us that after staying some time at Antioch at the end of the second journey 'he left and traveled in orderly sequence through the Galatian country and Phrygia, bringing strength to all the disciples' implying that the Apostle visited the people whom he had converted at these places. One of Paul's companions between Greece and Alexandria Troas during the third journey is identified as 'Gaius from Derbe' (Acts 20:4) but this does not explain when and by whom he was converted or when and where he met Paul.

Mound of Derbe. Looking south.

ATTALEIA

On their return from the first missionary journey from Pisidian Antioch Paul and Barnabas came to Attaleia (Antalya) by way of Perge and sailed from here to Antioch on the Orontes (Acts 14:25). No other mention is made of the city in the Bible, nor is there any comment about Paul's missionary work there.

ALEXANDRIA TROAS

Alexandria Troas was founded by Alexander's general Antigonus about 310 BCE, who for a while ruled in Anatolia after Alexander's death and it was named thus to distinguish it from Alexandria ad Issum (İskenderun) and Alexandria in Egypt. During his second missionary journey, accompanied by Silas and Timothy, Paul travelled through the Phrygian and Galatian territory to the north, towards probably Dorylaeum (Eskişehir) where the border of Mysia meets Bithynia, the Roman province to which he wanted to take the message of Christianity. The Holy Spirit, however, did not allow them to continue in this direction and turning westwards they travelled into Mysia and reached Alexandria Troas. Mysia, along with Lycia and Lydia, is mentioned in 1 Maccabees (8:8) as one of the best provinces which were taken from the Seleucids after their defeat at the battle of Magnesia (190 BCE) by the Romans and given to the Pergamene kingdom of Eumenes II. The Mysians are known to have constituted a special detachment in the army of the Seleucid kings. A Mysian commander with the name of Apollonius who was sent to Jerusalem by Antiochus IV Epiphanes and his persecutions are mentioned in the Bible (2 Mac 5:24-26).

In Alexandria Troas Paul saw a vision in which a Macedonian, who is said to have been in reality Luke, stood in front of him and said 'Come over to Macedonia and help us.' Thus, without staying there any longer, they took a boat from the port and sailed to Samothrace and Neapolis and on to Philippi (Acts 16:8-12).

During his second journey Paul had to leave Ephesus in hurry because of the riot of silversmiths and went to Macedonia and Greece. He first travelled to Alexandria Troas by land or sea and crossed the Aegean from there. Referring to this visit in his letter to the Corinthians (2:12-13) he says 'When I went to Troas for the gospel of Christ, although a door was opened to me in the Lord, I had no relief in my spirit because I did not find my brother Titus. So I took leave of them and went on Macedonia.' At the end of their missionary activities there he came to Alexandria Troas and stayed in the city for a week. The famous episode of the restoration of Eutychus to life took place then (Acts 20:7-12). The city is mentioned once more in Acts. In his letter to his disciple Timothy (2 Tim 4:13), writing from Rome, Paul asked him to join him there and not to forget to bring the cloak, 'the papyrus rolls, and especially the parchments' he had left Alexandria Troas.

Alexandria Troas was the last stopover of Ignatius when he was escorted to Rome as a prisoner in the reign of Trajan (98-117). Before crossing to Macedonia he wrote letters to the Churches at Philadelphia (Alaşehir) and Smyrna and a private letter to Polycarp. In his letters in addition to repeating his warnings against Judaizing and Docetism he says that Philo of Cilicia and Rheus Agathopous from Syria caught up with him here and gave him the news that the dispute at the Church of Antioch had come to an end and that they might send delegates to congratulate it.

Ruins of the outer harbour of Alexandria Troas. Beyond the Aegean is Tenedos.

EPHESUS

In addition to the Apostles John and Paul, Ephesus' name is associated with a number of personages of early Christianity. The most popular of these are the Virgin Mary, Luke, Mary Magdalena, Apollos, Timothy, Priscilla and Aquila. Although they may not have been the first Christian visitors to Ephesus, Paul and John are regarded as the planters of Christianity in this city. It is assumed that John came to Ephesus taking the Virgin with him earlier than Paul and began his missionary activity. It is not surprising that when he arrived in western Anatolia Paul found many Churches already established in the region.

The first Christians of Ephesus may have been again found among the Jewish population of the city whose ancestors were probably those who were settled here by the Seleucid kings. In accordance with the Seleucid policy they must have been permitted to live according to the customs of their law. This situation seems to have continued into the Roman period but not without problems. Although decrees issued by several Roman rulers inform us that the Jews in Ephesus were allowed to send the Temple tax to Jerusalem and not to appear in court on the Sabbath the local people complained that they were enjoying the benefits of city life without worshipping Ionian gods.

Paul's second journey which had started from Antioch on the Orontes was directed towards the province of Asia (Acts 16:6) whose capital Ephesus was a large cosmopolitan city where Paul liked to preach the gospel. However, after travelling through Lycaonia and Pisidia he was guided by the Holy Spirit in the direction of Macedonia by way of Alexandria Troas. On his return from Greece he stopped at Ephesus briefly. Acts 18 informs us that taking a boat from Corinth's eastern harbour Cenchreae, accompanied by Priscilla and Aquila, fellow Christians who had become his close friends at Corinth, the Apostle came to Ephesus. Here he had discussions with the Jews at the synagogue. Although he was asked to stay longer it was autumn, the end of the sailing season and he wanted to be in Jerusalem. Thus he left Ephesus by ship for Caesarea.

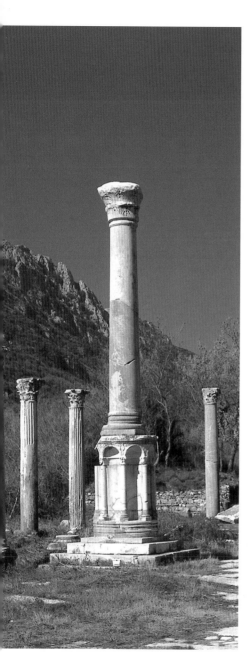

Column which probably bore the statue of John at the tetrapylon on the Arcadian street. Sixth century CE. Ephesus. Its base is decorated with crosses and a bird. The other three columns which carried the statues of the other three Evangelists have not survived.

When he visited Ephesus during his third missionary journey Paul stayed for three years making the city the base of his missionary activities. Acts 19 gives detailed information about this long Ephesus stay. Here Paul preached to the believers who were already baptized but 'With the baptism of John' by another missionary named Apollos, and caused them to be rebaptized. This was a period when more than one form of Christianity existed and many preachers claimed that the Christianity they taught was the true doctrine. After preaching at the synagogue for three months, because of the difference of opinion with some local Jews Paul had to move to the lecture hall of Tyrannus.

The missionary activities of the Apostle during this long stay probably were not confined only to the city but covered the whole region. Ephesus may have been the place from which most of his letters were written. Some information about his activities at Ephesus comes from these letters, such as that Paul seems to have interrupted his Ephesus stay for a round-trip sea journey to Corinth, to strengthen the Church he had founded there in his second journey and to answer their questions. Although in his letter to the Corinthians (2 Cor 1:8) Paul refers to the affliction that he suffered in the province of Asia which put him in despair, he does not give any detail about it. This might be an imprisonment which is mentioned in the apocryphal Acts of Paul. Paul also wrote a letter to the Ephesians when he was in prison there or in Rome.

The most important event which happened during Paul's stay at Ephesus was the riot of the silversmiths. Demetrius, a prosperous member of these craftsmen provoked his colleagues saying that Paul's preaching that 'gods made by hands are not gods at all' (Acts 19:26) was an insult to Artemis and eventually would harm their trade of manufacturing miniature silver shrines to Artemis which were sold to pilgrims who dedicated them to her. The excitement they created in the agora where their shops were spread to other Ephesians and two of Paul's Macedonian companions were seized in the theatre, probably to be lynched. The town clerk had to interfere and calmed the crowd saying that the men they had seized had done nothing to

Re-used marble piece with the word 'ASIARCHS'. Ephesus. In the riot of the silversmiths 'Paul wanted to go before the crowd, but the disciples would not let him, even some of the Asiarchs who were friends of his sent word to him advising him not to venture into the theatre ' (Acts 19:30-31).

insult Artemis and it would be better if Demetrius took his claims to court; if they were charged with rioting, for which obviously there was no cause, the Romans would punish them all. Thus Paul was compelled to leave the city and went to Alexandria Troas from where he visited Macedonia and Greece. On his return trip from Alexandria Troas by boat he did not stop at Ephesus but at Miletus to which he called the Ephesian elders.

In Acts 21 the Jews in Jerusalem who had 'seen Trophimus of Ephesus in the city with him' thought that Paul had brought him into the Temple and began a demonstration which led to Paul's arrest, an event which ultimately resulted in his martyrdom in Rome.

In his letter to the Church at Ephesus John admonishes the Christians there because they 'have lost the love' (Rv 2:4) they had at the beginning but compliments them for hating the works of the Nicolaitans (p 121). It is not certain if the sect was connected with 'Nicholas of Antioch' of Acts 6:5 one of the seven deacons. John does not give any information about his accusation but compliments those who did not succumb to the Nicolaitan teaching. He is more explicit about them in his letter to the Church at Pergamum. The sect, however, was short-lived and there is no trace of it after 200 CE.

So-called St Paul's prison. Ephesus. The westernmost tower of the Hellenistic fortifications built by the city's founder Lysimachus (306-281 BCE).

Saint Paul's Prison

Although Paul in the letters he addressed to the Churches in Greece, Macedonia and Anatolia frequently refers to the persecutions he suffered it is difficult to guess what exactly these persecutions were and where he suffered them. It is not known if his words about 'the affliction that came to us in the province of Asia' (2 Cor 1:8) involves an imprisonment.

According to the apocryphal Acts of Paul however, in Ephesus the furious population 'put Paul's feet into irons, and shut him up in the prison, till he should be exposed as a prey to the lions. But Eubola and Artemilla, wives of eminent men among the Ephesians, being his attached disciples, and visiting him by night, desired the grace of the divine washing. And by God's power, with angels to escort them and enlighten the gloom of night with the excess of the brightness that was in them, Paul, loosed from his iron fetters, went to the sea-shore and initiated them into holy baptism, and returning to his bonds without any of those in care of the prison perceiving it, was reserved as a prey for the lions.' Later Christian tradition, because of its proximity to the Aegean Sea, associated the westernmost tower of the fortifications on Mt Coressus (Bülbül dağı) with this baptism.

House of the Virgin Mary

The house of the Virgin Mary is situated at the top of Mt Solimus (Aladağ) and is known as 'Panaya Kapulu'[1] or 'Meryemana' in Turkish.

The scriptures do not give any information about the latter part of the Virgin's life. However, a popular Christian tradition which goes back at least to the Council of Ephesus (431) maintains that she came with the Apostle John to Ephesus and lived and died there. There is also no information about where John was during the tumultuous period in Palestine between 37 and 48 when Christians fled to Antioch, Phoenicia or Cyprus and it is very probable that he may have taken the Virgin to Ephesus in this period and begun his first missionary activities there. The Bible informs us that at the Crucifixion when Jesus saw his mother and the disciple there whom he loved, he said to his mother, 'Woman, behold, your son.' Then he said to the disciple, 'Behold, your mother.' And from that hour the disciple took her his home (Jn 19:26-27) and eventually to Ephesus.

The late canonical tradition, however, holds that the Virgin died in Jerusalem at the age of 63. The principle evidence is a passage of John of Damascus, written in the eighth century, which relates that in 458 CE the empress Pulcheria, sister of Theodosius II wrote to the bishop of Jerusalem asking him to send the body of the Virgin to the capital. The latter was unable to do so, as according to a reliable tradition she was buried at Gethsemane, and the tomb was found empty three days later, by the Apostles. Since the earlier writers such as Eusebius and Jerome make no mention of a tomb at Gethsemane it is possible that the story may have been an interpolation into John of Damascus' text. The Virgin is also said to have visited the Holy Land several times during her Ephesus sojourn and when she became ill during the last visit the Apostles prepared for her a tomb on Mt Olive. However, she recovered and returned to Ephesus.

Although Christian tradition from the fifth century onwards repeats that the Virgin lived for some time and died at Ephesus it does not give any information about where exactly she lived. The discovery of the location in the middle of the nineteenth century was made owing to a vision of one Catherine Emmerich. This invalid German lady, who for twelve years had not left her bed, and had never in her life been near Ephesus, placed the Virgin's house on a mountain near Ephesus and described it

---

[1] A name partly Greek and partly Turkish, meaning 'Gate', or 'House of *Panagia* (all holy).'

in detail. The search organized in 1891 found the ruins of a building exactly at the spot she had put the house. The building is thought to date from the fifth-sixth centuries but it may have been built on the ruins of an earlier one. It was a place where the Orthodox Greeks of the neighbourhood, and even from a considerable distance, had long been in the habit of assembling to celebrate the Dormition of the Virgin, whom they believed died at that spot. This belief had been inherited through the generations, and might well be very ancient. Shortly after its discovery the archbishop of Smyrna authorized the celebration of the Mass in the building and declared it a place of pilgrimage. Although Catherine Emmerich had also described the location of the Virgin's tomb in the neighbourhood, efforts to find it gave no result.

The Dormition. Icon. Detail. Nineteenth century. Sinop Museum. Tradition has it that when she was at the age of sixty (or seventy-two) the Virgin Mary wanted to be with her son. Upon her wish the Apostles were also brought to her. Behind the bier Christ holds her soul shown as a baby in swaddling bands. St Paul is easily identified at the foot of the bier. Next to him is John. Behind the Virgin's head Peter swings a censer. At the bottom, an angel severs the hands of the Jew Athonios, who, according to an apocryphal story, tried to overturn the bier.

Church of the Virgin Mary

This is known as the first church dedicated to the Virgin Mary. The earliest church was probably built in the mid-fourth century out of the remains of a Roman basilica which probably dated to the time of Hadrian (117-38). The literature about its being the church where the Ecumenical Councils of 431 and 449 CE (p 195) met was confirmed by a sixth-century inscription found here. It addition to condemning Nestorianism the Second Ecumenical Council affirmed that the Virgin Mary was *Theotokos*, or the Mother of God, and spent the last part of her life in Ephesus. The first church on this spot may have been built in the 350s. To the east, an elaborate group of structures, consisting of residential quarters, a bath, and a domed reception room, was built in the fifth century and was the bishop's palace.

The only major building erected after the Persian invasion of 614 CE was a cross-domed church in brick. It was half the size of the previous edifice. When it fell into ruins this was replaced by a smaller basilica with piers which came to be the graveyard church of that part of the city.

In the middle Byzantine era a new church whose ruins have survived to our time was built. Its entrance was through the apse of the former church and thus it is known as the 'Double' church.

Apse of the church of the Virgin Mary at Ephesus. Middle Byzantine period.

Church of Saint John

The apocryphal Acts of John informs us that when Domitian (81-96) heard about John's teaching at Ephesus he sent for him: 'He was brought before Domitian and made to drink poison, which did not hurt him: the dregs of it killed a criminal on whom it was tried: and John revived him; he also raised a girl who was slain by an unclean spirit. Domitian, who was much impressed, banished him to Patmos.' After Domitian's death, under Nerva (96-98), John was released.

The vessel he took was shipwrecked and the Apostle saved himself by swimming on a cork and landed at Miletus. From Miletus where a church was dedicated for him John went to Ephesus. Later tradition has it that John spent the rest of his life there and also wrote the Fourth Gospel known by his name and his epistles. Although he seems to have visited 'the rest of the cities' in the region only Laodicea and Smyrna are mentioned by name. He may have ordained Polycarp as the bishop of Smyrna during his visit there.

When John wanted to be with Jesus he asked his young companions to dig his grave and laying himself in it gave up his spirit. Next morning when grave was dug

Gate of St John's castle. The Ayasuluk hill is thought to have been encircled by fortifications in the seventh century CE against Sassanian and Arab invasions. The gate contained re-used material from the stadium of Ephesus. The pieces which included reliefs showing Achilles dragging the corpse of Hector behind his chariot have not survived. The Trojan hero was thought to have been a Christian martyr and this caused the entrance to be named as the 'Gate of Persecution'.

only his sandals were found and the earth over the grave stirred by John's breathing. This reminded them of Jesus' words to Peter (Jn 21:22-23) ' "What if I want him to remain until I come? What concern is it of yours? You follow me." ' So the word spread among the brothers that that disciple would not die' created the legend that he was not dead, but slept here. Later tradition added that a dust called *manna* rose from the grave and was used to cure sicknesses.

The date of the earliest shrine built on John's tomb is not known. The Ayasuluk hill where he was buried was already in use as a Roman graveyard. The shrine on the barren hill was dedicated to the memory of John as early as the time of Constantine. In the early fifth century this was replaced by a cruciform basilical church and finally in the early sixth century by a magnificent domed basilica built again on a cruciform plan by Justinian. Procopius in *On the Buildings* says that it

John at the temple of Artemis as told by the inscription in French. Manuscript painting. Thirteenth-century French manuscript. The Trinity College. Cambridge. The painting depicts the story in the apocryphal Acts of John in which the Apostle goes to the temple of Artemis and challenges the priests. After his preaching 'the altar of Artemis was parted into many pieces' and half of the temple fell down killing the priests under its beams. The multitude who became Christians destroyed the other half.

was 'most resembling and in every way was rivalling the Temple of the Apostles in the Royal City,' that is the church of the Holy Apostles in Constantinople.

It is possible that its construction began before the reign of Justinian the Great (527-65) and the emperor may have only donated the nave where the columns bear his and Theodora's monograms. It may have taken over 35 years to finish. Research has revealed that in addition to material from the temple of Artemis of the fourth century BCE, other buildings in Ephesus and even pieces from the Hellenistic temple of Apollo at Claros were used in the construction. Its most striking feature was the massive apse attached to the eastern piers of the crossing with a rising semicircle of seats, the *synthronon*. With the construction of an aqueduct to bring water to the hill, the church became the nucleus of a settled community.

Ruins of the church of St John. Looking west. Selçuk. To the right is the place of the altar and the crypt which is said to have held his grave.

Grotto of the Seven Sleepers

A cave to the northern side of Mt Pion is traditionally known as the grotto of the seven young men who took refuge in it from the persecutions of the emperor Decius (249-51). The emperor commanded that all of his subjects sacrifice to the gods and obtain a certificate that they had done thus. The seven boys named Maximianus, Malchus, Marcianus, Dionysius, Johannes, Serapion, and Constantinus, when they refused to do this, were brought before the emperor. The latter gave the boys time until his return to Ephesus to denounce their faith and obey his orders. Upon his return to the city he learned that the boys were by then living in a cave where they had fallen asleep and ordered that the cave should be walled up with stones so that they would die of hunger and thirst. The young men slept about two hundred years until 448, when an earthquake collapsed the wall closing the entrance of their cave and they woke up and sent one of them out to buy bread, but he was arrested and taken before the governor for he had tried to pay for the food with an ancient coin. Thinking that the money had come from a treasure, the governor went with the bishop to the cave, where he found a sealed chest with documents recounting how the seven had been martyred.

When the emperor Theodosius II heard the news he went to Ephesus. Seizing one of the boys he said 'Seeing you thus, it is as if I saw the Lord raising Lazarus from the dead!' Maximianus answered to him: 'Believe us, it is for your sake that God has raised us before the day of the great resurrection, so that you may believe without a shadow of doubt in the resurrection of the dead. We have truly risen and are alive.' The boys then praised God, bowed their heads and died. That night they appeared to the emperor and said that until then 'they had lain in the earth and had risen from the earth, so that he should return them to the earth until the Lord raised them up again. Theodosius ordered the cave to be embellished with gilded stones and decreed that all the bishops who now professed faith in the resurrection should be absolved.'

The story is thought to have been adapted to Christianity in connection with controversy about the resurrection of the body. The cave where they slept and were buried became a shrine which attracted pilgrims and was adorned with a chapel and numerous mortuary installations. The boys themselves were honoured as saints.

Seven Sleepers. Manuscript painting. Late sixteenth century. *Zübdetü't Tevarih,* the 'Legendary Chronicle of the Prophets' Lives'. Museum of Turkish and Islamic Arts. İstanbul. The story is also told in the Koran and its general lines follow the Christian tradition. The major addition in the Islamic tradition is a dog which follows the young men and when they try to get rid of it, tells them in human speech that it is also a believer in God. Also, the Moslem tradition which says that the story took place at the Greek city of 'Efsus' which was named 'Tarsus' after the Moslem conquest has resulted in the creation of another grotto of the Seven Sleepers ('Ashabıkehf') some 15 km to the northwest of this city. A third grotto of Seven Sleepers is situated near Kahramanmaraş.

ASSOS

The city is mentioned in the Bible only once. In Acts (20:12) Luke informs us that at the end of his third missionary journey Paul did not board the ship at Alexandria Troas but preferred to walk some 50 km as far as Assos where he rejoined the party. The reason for this short diversion of the Apostle has not been explained. He may have wanted to clear his head and concentrate on his final destination, Rome. From Assos they sailed to Miletus making stops at Lesbos and Samos.

Strabo informs us that after the Trojan war the Tjekker were settled in Hamaxitus, the home of Smintheus the mouse and disease god, near Assos where the ruins of Hellenistic temple of Apollo Smintheon still stand. The Tjekker were a group of the Sea Peoples who entered Canaan together with the Philistines and settled there. They may have introduced the mouse cult to Canaan. In 1 Samuel (6:4) the five Philistine cities which suffered hemorrhoids and plagues of mice for keeping the Ark decided to send it back to the Israelites. The guilt offering they sent was five golden hemorrhoids and five golden mice. Isaiah (66:17) in his prophecies mentions that the God of Israel will destroy those 'who eat swine's flesh, loathsome things and mice'.

Aristotle is known to have stayed in the city between 347 and 344 BCE as a guest of its tyrant and wrote *On Philosophy* here. An interesting remark related to the philosopher's stay comes from *On Sleep,* one of the essays of Clearchus of Soli (Cyprus) who wrote some two decades after his master. Whether it is fictional or not in this essay Aristotle meets a Jewish sage at Assos and discourses with him. This was the view of the early Greek philosophers and historians who regarded the Jews as priestly sages who could only come from the East. The story may have been inspired by the existence of Jews in the region as there were those who are mentioned in Obadiah (20) dwelling in Sepharad (Sardis).

TROGYLLIUM

This site is only mentioned in the Authorized Version of the Bible. During the third missionary journey the boat carrying Paul and his companions, on her way from Samos to Miletus 'tarried at Trogyllium' (Acts 20:15). At this point the distance between Samos and the promontory which projects from mainland Anatolia is about a kilometre. Ancient maps show Trogyllium at various points of the promontory. In some maps the name is used for the promontory itself. Later pilgrims named an anchorage on the southern coast as 'St Paul's port'.

MILETUS

Inscription related to angel worship from the western wall of the theatre at Miletus. Third century CE or earlier. The identical inscription in each panel reads in Greek 'archangel, protect the city of Miletus and those who live in it' and invokes a planet denoted by a mysterious symbol above it, without mentioning the name of the archangel. The single line below the panels repeats the same formula. The general Sumerian classification of the seven planets were Sun, Saturn, Moon, Mars, Venus, Mercury and Jupiter symbolized in the ancient Hebrew astrology by the angels Uriel, Raphael, Raguel, Michael, Suriel, Gabriel and Yerachmiel.

In Acts (20) Paul made a stop at the city during his third missionary journey on his way from Alexandria Troas to Jerusalem. He called the elders of Ephesus to Miletus and preached to them there. In this farewell speech Paul told his listeners about what awaited him on his return: 'But now I know that none of you to whom I preached the kingdom during my travels will ever see my face again' (Acts 20:25). Although it is not mentioned, Paul may have been to the city during his long Ephesus residence, or the Christians of Miletus may have attended his preachings there. In either case one is expected to believe that Paul was not an unknown personality for Milesian Christians.

The apocryphal Acts of John informs us that on his release the vessel that the Apostle had embarked on from Patmos had an accident and swimming on a cork he landed at Miletus where a church was built in his honour. From here he went to Ephesus.

An inscription carved on a block in the western wall of the theatre shows that the angel worship for which the Colossian Christians were admonished by Paul (p

161) was also practiced in the city. The spot where it was inscribed would obviously have required permission from the authorities and shows the high social status the Jews in the city held. Another evidence of the existence of a Jewish community in Miletus is found at the ancient theatre. Although from the later Roman period, an inscription in Greek left on one of the seat rows reads 'The place of Jews who were also God-worshippers.' Whichever way scholars interpret the inscription it is important in showing that the Jews in Miletus did not shun social entertainment but had the privilege of having reserved front (fifth row) seats which must have been the result of their high official status among the population.

The famous oracle of Miletus may have still been active in the third century CE because early Christian literature relates that at a solemn sacrifice attended by Diocletian and Galerius, the augurs found that they could not discern the usual signs on the livers of the sacrificed animals because some Christians present had crossed themselves. Diocletian consulted the oracle of Apollo at Miletus. The god replied that false oracles were being caused by the Christians. Thus in 303 the Christian cathedral opposite the imperial palace at Nicomedia (İzmit) was demolished and next day an edict was posted declaring that all churches were to be destroyed, all Bibles and liturgical objects confiscated, and all meetings for worship forbidden. A few months later a second edict ordered the arrest of clergy, but the prisons would not accommodate so many and in the autumn an amnesty was granted on condition of sacrifice to pagan gods.

When Ezekiel (27:17) speaks about the trade relations of Tyre with Israel, he says that the latter traded, among other material, in 'Minnith' wheat. It has been suggested that this may have meant wheat from Miletus.

Miletus is the home of Isidorus, one of the two architects who built St Sophia (532-37 CE).

Marble row inscribed 'The place of Jews who were also God-worshippers' at the theatre of Miletus. Late Roman period.

PATARA

When we had taken leave of them we set sail, made a straight run for Cos, and on the next day for Rhodes, and from there to Patara (Acts 21:1).

This is the only place that the city is mentioned. After preaching at Miletus at the end of his third missionary journey, Paul took a ship and came to Patara by way of Cos and Rhodes. Here the Apostle and his companions found a ship bound for Tyre and sailed away.

There is not much information about the beginning of Christianity in this region. The existence of Jewish communities of smaller or larger size is attested to by the letter that the Roman consul sent to the cities under Ptolemaic control in the middle of the second century BCE. In this letter which includes names such as Myndos, Caria, Pamphylia, Lycia, Halicarnassus, Phaselis, Side and Cnidus Rome informs them that the Jews have renewed their earlier alliance of friendship and Rome 'decided to write to various kings and countries, that they are not to harm them [Jews], or wage war against them or their cities or their country, and are not to assist those who fight against them' (1 Mac 15:22-24).

Outside its timber-forests and sheltered harbours Lycia did not have anything to offer its people and urban life was centred at settlements like Patara which enjoyed good harbours. Nevertheless, they were dependent on the commercial sea traffic between the Levant and the Aegean. The popularity of sea transportation made these ports important for Rome, as confirmed by the huge granary built some time after Paul's visit here.

MYRA

In 60 CE Paul, on his way to Rome, changed ships at Myra (Acts 27:5-6), that is at its port Andriace. At the time that the vessel carrying Paul sailed into the harbour, Myra was still on the top of the precipitious hill a few kilometres inland which now rises behind the theatre but already begun to extend to the plain at its foot. This city is now deeply buried and has never been excavated. Some traces of an ancient stepped path have survived. Almost nothing has survived at the top.

The port was founded at the mouth of the river Androcus. Here, the centurion came across a corn-vessel which had come from Alexandria and was bound for Italy and they changed ships.

The apocryphal Acts of Paul also takes the Apostle to Myra before going to Sidon. Here he performs a few miracles and meets Thecla who has followed him from Antioch.[1]

About 300 a Lycian bishop, Methodius, attacked Origen's spiritualizing doctrine of the resurrection. He is known to have been martyred in the last years of persecutions of Diocletian.

[1] Which one is not mentioned.

St Nicholas. Icon. Detail. Nineteenth century. Sinop Museum.

Saint Nicholas

At the west edge of the village of Demre is the church of Nicholas. He is patron saint of Greece and Russia and also of children, sailors, merchants, and scholars. He is still invoked by those unjustly imprisoned, by travellers against the threat of robbers, and by those in peril on the sea.

Nicholas who later reached fame as the bishop of Myra was born at the nearby town of Patara about 300 CE. He is one of the most popular saints in both the Greek and Latin Churches. Not much is known about his life. According to Eudemus of Patara he was imprisoned during persecutions and afterwards released and participated in the First Council of Nicaea (325) where he defended orthodoxy and even punched the nose of Arius so that the latter's bones rattled. Nevertheless, his name is not found in the earliest lists of participants. He is said to have refused his mother's breast every Friday and fast day. When he grew up he distributed the fortune he had inherited to the poor. The most famous of his acts of generosity was his saving of three sisters by supplying them with dowries without which they would have become prostitutes. His symbol is sometimes three bags of gold. His throwing the bags of gold secretly, confirms Matthew's (6:1-4) teaching about almsgiving and have lead to the secret bestowal of presents on children at Christmas.

In another story known as the Pickled Boys he discovered that during a famine an innkeeper had stolen little children, murdered them and cut up their bodies and salted them in a tub to be sold. He restored the children to life. When he is depicted sometimes three children stand in a tub at his side. St George is also attributed with a similar miracle.

One of his attributes is an anchor because he is the patron saint of sailors whom he saved from storms. When he died he was buried in the church where he worked. In 1087 his sarcophagus was broken into and some of his remains are said to have been taken to Bari, Italy. Latin soldiers of the First Crusade and a Russian story claim a similar removal of bones.

CNIDUS

Cnidus was the last landfall mentioned in Anatolia in Paul's journey from Caesarea to Rome. He had been put on an Alexandrian vessel at Andriace, the port of Myra which sailed up the coast to Cnidus; because of the headwinds it took them many days to reach it. They did not anchor there because of the inclement weather which continued and in fact got much worse (Acts 27:7).

The Carians like their neighbours the Lycians seem to have depended on the sea since their earliest history. In the Late Bronze Age they probably constituted a part of the Sea Peoples. It has been suggested that the Philistines referred to as the Pelehites who served in king David's army (2 Sm 15:19) may have been Carians. In 2 Kings 11 'the captains of the Carians' and 'the Carians' were among those who put the seven-year-old Joash, son of king Ahaziah, on the throne of Judah, killing the latter's mother.

ADRAMYTTIUM

Adramyttium (Edremit) is a small coastal town on the Aegean. It is mentioned among those cities which collected gold to be sent to the Jerusalem Temple, though Adramyttium's share was small, inferring a limited Jewish population, in 62 BCE when it was a assize centre. It is mentioned only once in the Bible as the destination of the vessel on which Paul embarked as a prisoner at Caesarea on his journey to Rome, where he would be martyred. In Acts (27:1) Luke relates that together with some other prisoners Paul, under the custody of a centurion named Julius, embarked on a ship which had come from Adramyttium and was returning there. Thus, after making a stop at the Phoenician port of Sidon, where Paul was allowed to see his friends, she sailed north towards the Anatolian peninsula and following the coast of Cilicia and Pamphylia, to Myra in Lycia. The original intention of the centurion may have been to reach Adramyttium and cross to Macedonia from where he would have continued by way of Philippi on the Via Egnatia which ran from Byzantium to Brundisium on the Adriatic.

HIERAPOLIS

Let no one, then, pass judgement on you in matters of food and drink or with regard to a festival or new moon or sabbath (Col 2:16).

Although the Bible distinguishes between Philip the Apostle (Acts 1:13), one of the Twelve and Philip, one of the seven deacons (Acts 6:5), later Christian tradition seems to have regarded them as the same person.

We are informed that (Jn 1:43) Philip the Apostle was from Bethsaida in Galilee. He is referred to several times as the person that certain Greeks applied to when they wanted to see Jesus (Jn 12:20-22). At the Last Supper where Jesus said 'Whoever has seen me has seen the Father' (Jn 14:9) it was he who asked Jesus "Master show us the Father." ' This is where the biblical information about the Apostle comes to an end. Later traditions have him preaching the gospel at Phrygia accompanied by his two virgin daughters, and record that he died at Hierapolis without mentioning a martyrdom.

The apocryphal Acts of Philip mentions that he came to the city of Hierapolis Ophioryme (Snake-street) where probably the Gnostic cult of the Ophites or Ophians who celebrated the Eucharist with snakes was practised. This weird heresy held that the serpent in the Garden of Eden was not the enemy of man but his friend because it gave him the opportunity to free himself from evil by inducing him to eat of the tree of knowledge. Here he fought against the dragon, converted many, was martyred here together with his daughters and a church was built on his grave.

The other Philip is also referred to in Acts 21:8 as 'the evangelist' and again as 'one of the Seven' with whom Paul stayed at Caesarea on his return from the third missionary journey. The Bible describes him evangelizing Samaria. He had 'four virgin daughters gifted with prophecy.'

Recent excavations have brought to light the ruins of a number of churches which show the sanctity the city held during the Christian era. Polycrates of Ephesus informs us that Philip the Apostle spent the latter part of his life in the city and that an inscription refers to a church in the city built in Philip's honour: 'Eugenius the least, archdeacon who is in charge of [the church of] the holy and glorious apostle and theologian Philip.' It has been suggested that the inscription referred to the great basilica in the older part of the necropolis to the west and that it was erected on what was thought to be the location of Philip's tomb. A second candidate for

(opposite) Ruins of the so-called martyrium of St Philip at Hierapolis. Looking south. In the background is Mt Salbacus (Baba dağı, 2308 m)

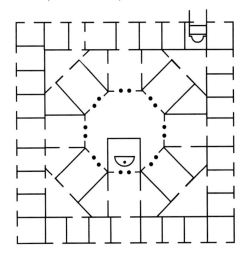

Plan of the martyrium of St Philip. Looking south (after G. Bean).

Philip's martyrium is the octagonal shrine outside the city walls. This was probably built in the fifth century and sometime in the sixth century it was destroyed by fire and never rebuilt; but a small chapel had been built in the west side of the shrine. It consisted of a central octagonal chamber which had a *synthronon*, or semi-circular rows for the clergy, surrounded by rectangular rooms. The latter are thought to have served the pilgrims who came from distant countries.

Inscriptions speak of 'the people of the Jews,' 'the settlement of the Jews who dwell in Hierapolis,' and 'the archives of the Jews'. In the late second or early third century CE one Publius Aelius Glycon on the inscriptions of the tomb which he prepared for himself, his wife and children directed that his sarcophagus should be decorated annually on the feast of Unleavened Bread. For this purpose he had bequeathed a sum of money to the most honourable president of the guild of purple-dyers so that its interest could be used for the wreath. He also left money to the guild of the carpet-weavers so that the grave might be similarly decorated on the festival of Passover. The owner of the grave was a Jew but evidently following a pagan tradition. In the course of time the Jews were absorbed into the Christian Church, an event which made the Talmud say 'The wine of Perugitha [Phrygia] and the waters of Diomsith cut off the Ten Tribes from Israel. Rabbi Eleazar ben Arak visited the place. He was attracted to them and his learning vanished.' Thus when the rabbi returned to Israel he could not read Hebrew anymore and could not write properly.

Keystone decorated with a Christogram from the so-called church of St Philip at the necropolis of Hierapolis.

Main street of Hierapolis. Looking towards Domitian's gate.

COLOSSAE

In his letter to the Colossians written from Ephesus or Rome Paul informs us that the people of this city learned the grace of God from his disciple Epaphras who was a Colossian (Col 1:7; 4:12 Phlm 23). Epaphras also took the Christian message to the other two cities of the Lycus valley, Laodicea (Eskihisar) and Hierapolis (Col 4:12).

The particular sort of heresy which is mentioned in Paul's letter to the Colossians is confirmed by an inscription of the early Christian period on the wall of the theatre at Miletus (p 153). This seems to have consisted of a mixture of Judaism and a cult of angels and some kind of asceticism. The Apostle mentions rules about food and holy days drawn from the Judaistic ceremonies (Col 2:16), reverence to intermediate angelic powers identified with heavenly bodies (Col 1:16; 2:15, 18) and some type of ascetic practices (Col 2:23; 3:5-10), a type of heresy commonly called 'Gnosticism.'[1]

Paul's letter (Phlm 10-22) to Philemon also concerns a Colossian named Onesimus, a slave who had run away from his master, perhaps being guilty of theft. Onesimus was converted by Paul and sent back to his old master not just as a slave but as a brother in Christ. Paul's words 'prepare a guest room for me' show his intention of going there.

In the Byzantine lists the bishop is regularly recorded as of Chonai not of Colossae. The almost indistinguishable ruins of the church of St Michael fall to the north side of the river where the necropolis also is. The town was known as Chonas (Honaz) and situated on the skirts of Mt Cadmus (Honaz dağı, 2570 m). According to the tradition, in order to destroy the church, pagans united the waters of two rivers and diverted them towards the building. The archangel Michael arrived and saved his church by striking with his staff and splitting the rock on which the building rose,

[1] Greek *gnosis*, or 'knowledge.' A generic term used to refer to theosophical adaptations of Christianity of which more than fifty sects existed between about 80 and 150.

whereupon a tunnel or funnel[2] was bored into the rock through which the diverted waters flowed.

In addition to ancient literature the surviving inscriptions show that angel-worship was a form of Anatolian Christianity. The veneration of the archangel was connected with this.

Chonai was known as the birth place of the famous Byzantine statesman and historian Nicetas Choniates (1150-1215) who is known by his *History* in which he gives a detailed and moving account of the capture of Constantinople (1204) by the Latin soldiers of the Fourth Crusade.

[2] Greek *chone*, or 'funnel'.

St Michael of Chonai. Wall painting. Mid-eleventh century. Karanlık (Dark) church. Göreme Outdoor Museum. Cappadocia.

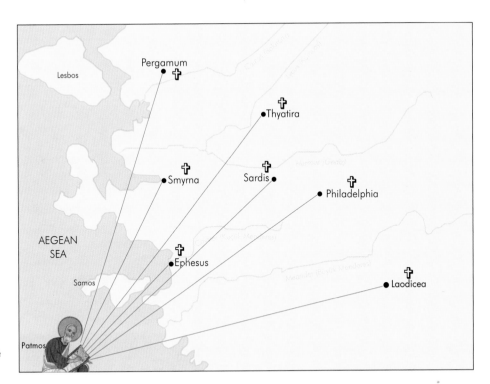

Map of the Seven Churches of the Revelation.

SAINT JOHN AND THE CITIES OF THE SEVEN CHURCHES OF REVELATION

While Christian scholars, basing their studies on syntax and grammar, still discuss the number of persons involved in them, Christian tradition identifies the Fourth Gospel, the Epistles of John and the Book of Revelation all with the single person of John, with the epithets 'apostle', 'divine', 'theologian' or 'evangelist'. He is also referred to as the disciple 'whom Jesus loved' (Jn 19:26, 21:20). He was a Galilean fisherman, the son of Zebedee.

He was exiled to Patmos during the reign of the Roman emperor Domitian (81-96). The apocryphal Acts of John informs us that the emperor Domitian 'heard of John's teaching in Ephesus and sent for him.' In front of Domitian the Apostle was made to drink poison which did not hurt him. He also revived a criminal who was killed by the poison. Much impressed Domitian banished him to Patmos. On Patmos he received the revelations recorded in the Book of Revelation or the *Apocalypse* (from the Greek word for 'unveiling' or 'revelation').

The Revelation falls into the popular category of writings between 200 BCE and 100 CE, revealing the events that will herald the End of the World and offering consolation to those who have retained their faith despite persecution, promising them eternal bliss at the end of time. It was written at a time when the first Apostolic missionary wave had come to an end and Christians who had become tired of waiting for the Second Coming began lapsing. The letters to the 'Seven Churches of Asia,' Ephesus, Smyrna, Pergamum, Thyatira, Sardis, Philadelphia and Laodicea (on the Lycus), constitute the beginning of the book. Seven is chosen as being the perfect number most frequently used in the biblical literature. The choice of cities, however, may have been arbitrary because it has been claimed that the Church at Thyatira was not yet founded at this time, but the Apostle wrote to it in the spirit of prophecy. Otherwise there were other early Churches in the region such as of Miletus or Colossae whose existence was established by then. His seven angels or bishops at this early date show that each of these Churches was organized around a bishop.

Some of the twenty-four elders from the vision of heavenly worship of the Apostle John (Rv 4). Wall painting. End of the ninth century CE. Yılanlı church. Peristrema (Ihlara) valley. Cappadocia.

SMYRNA

In the apocryphal Acts of John, having heard of his works at Ephesus, the people of Smyrna (İzmir) sent the Apostle a message saying that if the God that he preached was not envious and had charged him with impartiality, he should not stay in one place but come to their city so that they might know his God. The traditional appointment of Polycarp as the bishop of Smyrna may have taken place during this visit. However, the words of Polycarp in his letter to Philippi in Macedonia, 'in the time before we ourselves had received the knowledge of Him', tell us that the evangelization of Smyrna was later than that of Philippi and other regions.

Smyrna is the address of one of the letters that John wrote from Patmos to the Seven Churches of Asia. In this letter the Apostle refers to 'the slander of those who claim to be the Jews and are not' and are an 'assembly of Satan' (Rv 2:9). Ignatius is known to have stayed at Smyrna while being taken from Antioch on the Orontes to Rome and he wrote a letter to this city from Alexandria Troas or during the later part of his journey. In his letter he expressed his gratitude for the welcome they had given him and warned them against Docetism, saying the latter would 'become phantoms without substance' as they claimed Christ to be. The letter is also one of the earliest which mentions the religious meals, or the 'love-feasts' that were in practice in the early Church in close relationship to the Eucharist. Ignatius' letter to Smyrna (4:5) also refers to the tension between the Christians and the Jews. Together with his letter, Ignatius sent a personal letter to Polycarp, the city's bishop.

The evidence of the existence of Jews in Smyrna comes from an inscription found here dating from Hadrian's reign (117-38 CE). This is a list of names of those who contributed to public works in Smyrna, which includes a group named as 'the former Judaeans,' probably a group of Jews who came originally from Judea. John's diagnosis about the local Jews is confirmed by the events of the following centuries such as the martyrdom story of Polycarp and Pionius, in which the Jewish residents of Smyrna were among the other people, which meant contact with pagan worship.

In 250 during the Decian persecutions the Christian elder Pionius was martyred in Smyrna's agora, whose ruins have survived to the present in relatively good condition. Except for his arrest and death nothing is known about his life. At his trial Pionius also warned his listeners about the same danger saying 'I understand that the Jews have been inviting some of you to their synagogues. Beware lest you fall into a greater, more deliberate sin...We did not slay our prophets nor did we betray Christ and crucify him.' He was first nailed to a cross and then burned.

Interior of the church of St Polycarp. İzmir.

Saint Polycarp

Apart from his martyrdom little is known about Polycarp's (69-155) life. Early Christian tradition regards him as a disciple of the Apostle John who also appointed him to his post in Smyrna. Polycarp's claim during his martyrdom that he served Christ for 86 years shows that he was probably baptized in infancy. He is said to have visited Rome to consult Pope Anicetus about the date of Easter (the Christian Passover). While the Anatolian tradition followed the custom that is known as Apostolic, celebrating on the 14 Nisan (April) whatever day of the week,[1] Rome followed its own custom, also believed to be Apostolic and celebrated it on the following Sunday. Although the Pope refused to follow the Anatolian calendar he was not against its being followed by Anatolian Churches.

Polycarp is known to have written a letter to the Church at Philippi in Macedonia. In his letter he reminds the Philippians of their duties as Christians and warns them against heresy. Ignatius also met Polycarp when he was taken to Rome and sent him a personal letter from Alexandria Troas.

The account of Polycarp's martyrdom is regarded as the earliest surviving authentic

[1] Quartodecimanism. It has its roots in the Gospel of John; but was condemned by the Western Churches as 'Judaizing.'

account of Christian martyrdom outside the New Testament. It is also the earliest surviving Christian literature in which the words 'martyr,' which in Greek literally meant 'witness,' and 'martyrdom' were used in today's sense. The story of Polycarp's martyrdom is recounted in the form of a letter written from the Church of Smyrna to the Church of Philomelium (Akşehir) to be read to preserve Polycarp's memory throughout the Christian world.

Smyrna was one of the Roman cities where along with common criminals Christians were killed by being thrown to wild animals or burnt. When John wrote to the Church at Smyrna from Patmos and said that the Christians here 'will face an ordeal for ten days' (Rv 2:10) he was perhaps alluding to a spectacle of this kind. At one such spectacle which was held during the Great Sabbath[2] the noble stand of a Christian youth named Germanicus made the pagan and Jewish audience angry and they asked for Polycarp to be brought to the arena and punished. Except for this remark it is not known why Polycarp was arrested.

Although he was reluctant to leave Smyrna his friends moved Polycarp to a farm and later to a more distant one in the countryside. Here, while praying three days before his arrest he had a vision in which flames reduced his pillow to ashes.

One of his household boys, under torture, revealed his whereabouts and Polycarp was arrested and brought to the stadium. The efforts of Herod, the chief of Police and the governor to persuade him to renounce were useless. The audience's demand that he should be thrown to lions could not be fulfilled because on that day the beast-fighting was already over. They wanted him to be burnt alive. When the fire was lighted the flames took 'the shape of a hollow chamber, like a ship's sail when wind fills it.' After a while the spectators realized that Polycarp could not be destroyed by fire and he was stabbed by a dagger-man. When the Jews tried to keep his corpse so that the Christians could not make a cult of it, the centurion burnt it to avoid a quarrel. However, the Christians collected his remains. This is the earliest evidence of the preservation of the relics of martyrs for the celebration of the anniversary of the martyrdom, the 'heavenly birthday' of the saint.

Although the name of the emperor who was reigning is not mentioned the event took place during the reign of Antoninus Pius (138-61), the high priesthood (asiarch) of Philip of Tralles and the proconsulship of Lucius Statius Quadratus in Smyrna.

The story in its inclusion of the attic (upper room) where Polycarp was arrested, his arrival in Smyrna on an ass, the naming of the chief of Police as Herod, Polycarp's prayer before the pyre is ignited, and other similar touches, brings out the parallel between Polycarp's martyrdom and the Crucifixion.

[2] Although it cannot be identified, it was a holiday during which pagans and Jews were free.

PERGAMUM

Pergamum was established as an independent kingdom in the middle of the third century BCE after the wars fought between Alexander's generals. Its support of the Romans in the battle of Magnesia (190 BCE) was rewarded according to 1 Maccabees (8:8) by 'Lycia, Mysia and Lydia' and probably some other Seleucid territories to the north of the Taurus. Although proud of their Greek ancestors and keen to establish the Greek culture in their domain, the Pergamene kings were not interested in royal dynastic ideologies like the Seleucids or Ptolemies. A fanciful story recorded by Josephus informs us about a Jewish mission sent to Rome by the High Priest Hyrcanus I in the second century BCE. The embassy received a senatorial declaration admonishing the Seleucid king of the time against any acts of damage to the Jews. When the Jewish envoys visited Pergamum this was honoured and confirmed by a decree. The Pergamenes also indicated that their good relations with the Jewish people went back to the time of Abraham, 'the father of all Hebrews,' a fact already recorded in the city archives. The existence of Jews in the city comes from a more reliable source. The earliest mention of the Jewish existence is recorded

Marble altar which was probably dedicated to the 'unknown gods' at the temple of Demeter. Roman period. Pergamum (acropolis; middle city). Paul says (Acts 17:23) as he walked in Athens he saw an altar inscribed as 'To the unknown God', probably similar to this one and preached 'What therefore you unknowingly worship, I proclaim to you'. However, for his audience the expression 'unknown god' did not carry a monotheistic sense but a god whose rituals may have been skipped unknowingly. To placate the overlooked deities the pagans set up such altars.

Ruins of the temple of Serapis built in the reign of Hadrian (117-38 CE) at Pergamum (Bergama). A church dedicated to St John was built in it in the fifth or sixth century.

in the 60s BCE when the city is mentioned among several which sent gold to the Jerusalem Temple. However, the limited amount may also imply the small size of the Pergamene Jewish community.

The earliest mention of Pergamum in Christian literature is found in the Revelation of John when he addressed one of the Seven Letters to the Church here. John's mind must have been occupied with the threat of the Imperial cult because at the very beginning of his letter he says 'I know that you live, where Satan's throne is' (Rv 2:13). The reference to the throne may have been an allusion to the centre of authority. If he had a solid thing in mind this would probably have been the statues of the goddess Roma, personification of the power of the Roman empire and Augustus as a god which stood in the centre of the temenos of the Athena temple. If one looks for other candidates to be Satan's throne the city boasted a very rich collection of pagan shrines: the Great Altar[1] whose reliefs were decorated with fighting scenes of the Greek gods with Giants, temples of Athena, Dionysus, Demeter, Hera, Zeus and others on the acropolis and Asclepius down in the plain. John's remark about the teaching of Balaam obviously refers to the pagan practices, in this case the most common was the eating of meat sacrificed to pagan gods. Some of the Pergamene Christians also seem to have succumbed to the teaching of the Nicolaitans, a sect which is thought to have combined pagan elements with Christian teaching (p 121).

[1] Restored and displayed in the Pergamum Museum in Berlin.

Although the name of Pergamum is not mentioned in Acts, as a well-populated Roman city it would not have been outside the field of the missionary activities of Paul. It was very close to Ephesus and connected to it by one of the earliest roads that the Romans built in Anatolia, with a cosmopolitan population which included a substantial Jewish community, typical of the cities where Paul preferred preaching the gospel. Also Pergamene Christians may have visited Paul in Ephesus or at least heard of him especially when he spent three years in Ephesus during his third journey. Acts (20:11) informs us that after the silversmiths' disturbance was over Paul travelled to Macedonia. The most logical path was overland to Alexandria Troas and by boat from there. This trip may have taken Paul through Pergamum.

Galen (130-99 CE), the famous Pergamene physician-philosopher also wrote about Christianity after he moved to Rome and became the private doctor of the emperor Marcus Aurelius' son Commodus. His writings give us an idea of the outlook of the intellectuals of his time about Christianity. Although by this period Christianity had shaken off its Jewish roots, Galen saw the two religions together, regarding Christianity as one of the other philosophical schools whose aim was to direct people towards truth and virtue, and accommodated it in the Greco-Roman world.

Early Christian literature informs us about the three martyrdoms at Pergamum, probably in 250, the same year Pionius was martyred in Smyrna and again by the governor Quintilianus. These three Christians who refused to sacrifice to the gods were sentenced to death by being burned alive at the amphitheatre of the city in the plain: Carpus, a bishop of Thyatira, Papylus, deacon of Thyatira and a woman named Agathonice. The word 'martyr' simply meant 'witness' and was a part of the legal vocabulary of the Greek courts.

Pergamum did not recover from the blow it received from the Goths in the late third century. The only important building activity after this date was the transformation of the temple of Serapis into a Christian basilica. Another church was built at the Asclepium. In the tenth century two small churches of re-used fragments were built over the ruins of the temple of Athena and on the theatre terrace.

THYATIRA

The Church at Thyatira is the address of one of John's letters to the Seven Churches of Asia. Although the ancient history of Thyatira compared to the other cities in western Anatolia was insignificant, the letter of John to the Church here is the longest.[1]

It is not known if John's image of Christ with eyes 'like a fiery flame and whose feet are like polished brass' is used as a biblical cliché or on purpose to allude to the guild of bronzesmiths for which the city was famous. John's letter informs us that the Church at Thyatira tolerated the activities of a woman whom he calls 'Jezebel.' It is not known if this is a real name or not; but the implication is clear. The allegory derives from the Phoenician wife of the biblical king Ahab, who revived the pagan ways in Jerusalem (1 Kgs 16:31; 2 Kgs 9:22; 30-37). The Jezebel of Thyatira obviously led some Christians astray from the path of Christ to relapse and to eat the meat sacrificed to pagan gods and practice fornication. Although she had been warned, Jezebel continued her evil teaching.

In Acts (16:11-15) Paul meets in Philippi 'a woman named Lydia, a dealer in purple cloth, from the city of Thyatira, a worshiper of God' who accepts Christianity and invites the Apostle to stay at her home.

It is known that Thyatira deviated into Montanism at about the beginning of the third century CE. This was an apocalyptic movement which was initiated by one Montanus and two prophetesses at their spiritual centre Pepuza,[2] in Phrygia. The heresy believed in the speedy outpouring of the Holy Spirit on the Church and that the 'new Jerusalem' would descend on Pepuza. The movement spread to North Africa where Tertullian (160-225), the bishop of Carthage became its most famous adherent.

In the persecutions which took place at Pergamum, which was an assize centre, in 250, Carpus, a bishop of Thyatira and Papylus, a deacon from Thyatira were martyred.

Sozon, the bishop of Thyatira, is mentioned among those who participated in the First Council of Nicaea (325).

---

[1] It has been claimed that at this date the Church of Thyatira was not yet founded but the Apostle wrote his letter in the spirit of prophecy.

[2] Not yet identified; probably Dionysopolis (near Denizli).

SARDIS

And the captives of Jerusalem who are in Sepharad shall occupy the cities of the Negeb (Ob 20).

The earliest reference to the existence of Jews in Sardis is found in Obadiah (20) which is thought to have been written in the fifth century BCE. When he mentions the restoration of the kingdom of Jews the prophet includes the exiles from Jerusalem living in 'Sepharad' (Aramaic for Sardis) as the Jewish population which will recover Negeb, which was the semi-desert southern part of the ancient kingdom of Judah. There is no information about how and when these exiles came here.

Some of the 2,000 Jewish families whom the Seleucid king Antiochus III moved from Mesopotamia to Phrygia and Lydia towards the end of the third century BCE may have settled in Sardis. The city was the residence of Zeuxis to whom Antiochus III addressed his letter about this settlement. Although they may not have had citizenship it is known that the Jews of Sardis were a sort of autonomous community of aliens with the right of residence in the city, managing their own judicial and religious affairs. This gave them official standing without losing their identity. By the middle of the first century BCE the Jews possessed a place of assembly in the city which may have been an antecedent of the synagogue later excavated. Sardis was not the only city where relations between the Jews and the natives were strained. In 50 BCE L. Antonius, the governor of Asia, wrote to Sardis to instruct its authorities that the Jews here should be allowed to use their own court to settle disputes. In the reign of Augustus, about 12 BCE, C. Norbanus Flaccus the proconsul of Asia, in accordance with imperial instructions, told the people of Sardis not to prevent the Jews from sending money for religious purposes to Jerusalem.

The synagogue of Sardis is the largest ancient synagogue excavated anywhere and the second earliest known after the synagogue at Masada. At the time it was built, probably along with the ones at Rome or Dura Europus, this synagogue was one of the most important shrines of the Jewish Diaspora. Its size shows that the Jewish residents of Sardis at this time continued to enjoy the privileges given to them by Antiochus III. The Jews in Sardis must have been very powerful people politically to obtain such a building and also rich enough to afford its maintenance. The building is thought to have been originally a basilica which was a part of the gymnasium that was begun to be built after the earthquake of 17 CE, which the younger Pliny calls the worst one in the memory of mankind. It is thought to have been given to the Jewish community in the second half of the second century. Excavation has shown

Courtyard with fountain. Synagogue of Sardis. Looking southwest.

that the synagogue continued to function until Sardis was destroyed by the Sassanians in the early seventh century. The earliest inscriptions from this synagogue are from the later second century CE, the latest from the fourth and fifth centuries.

The synagogue is thought to have taken its present-day form in the first half of the fourth century CE. It begins with a colonnaded hall which opened to one of the colonnaded streets at Sardis. This court was paved with mosaics which included the names of several donors, and had a marble fountain for washing hands at its centre.

Three doors led from this court to a very large rectangular meeting hall which is thought to have been of two floors. Its walls were lavishly decorated with mosaics and coloured marble panels. One of them which stood at the centre of four short pillars reads in Greek 'Samoe, priest and *sophodidaskalos*' (teacher of wisdom) and was probably the spot where this rabbi taught or preached. The end of the hall had a series of circular benches where the elders of the community sat. The ground in front was decorated with a semi-circular mosaic of two peacocks and a vine scroll emerging from a crater with an inscription in Greek about its donors. In front of this stood a table — an unusual feature for a synagogue — from which probably quotations from the Jewish Scriptures were recited. The table's legs were

Artemis temple (third to second century BCE) and church M (fourth century CE) at Sardis. Looking west.

decorated with re-used Roman eagles clutching thunderbolts. Neither the eagles nor the pairs of re-used lion[1] statues which flanked this table were out of place because both animals were among the early adaptations of Jewish art from the Greek repertoire.

In the first century when John addressed one of his Seven Letters to the Church here, Sardis was a prosperous city under the Romans and a judicial seat of the Roman governor.

In his letter John immediately begins chastising the Church at Sardis. There had been back-sliding: 'I know your works that you have the reputation of being alive, but you are dead' (Rv 3:1). To deserve such heavy accusation the Sardian Christians seem to have completely surrendered to the pagan teaching and rituals.

The best known figure of early Christianity in Sardis is Melito, the city's bishop in the latter part of the second century. He wrote many books and treatises and was

[1] The lion, the symbol of tribe of Judah and also associated with the prophet Daniel is the animal which appears most frequently in the Bible.

recorded as the first Christian who travelled to the Holy Land to obtain an exact recorded text of the Old Testament. He was a Quartodeciman (p 166) like the Apostle John and Polycarp. He was one of the earliest Christian writers who attacked the Jews bitterly and held all of them responsible for the death of Christ. He may have died around 185 CE.

Excavations have brought to light several church ruins. The oldest of these is probably the one (church M) which is situated in a corner of the Artemis temple built in the second half of the fourth century. The objective of choosing this particular spot was probably both to consecrate a pagan site and the existence of a nearby cemetery.

Crosses and words in Greek from the south jamb of the main (east) door of the Artemis temple at Sardis. Fourth to fifth century CE. The words, which are carefully scratched on the marble surface, read *fos*, or 'light' (top) and *zoe*, or 'life' (bottom). The popularity of doorways for inscribing such words praising the Lord and purifying the place is thought to have become a tradition from the literal interpretation of Deuteronomy (6:9) or (11:20) where the Hebrews are advised — among other places — to 'write them on the doorposts of your houses and on your gates'. Crosses may imply the zeal of the local Christians to commemorate the pagan temples, a practice which began fashionable after the edict of Theodosius I (378-95) which prohibited the pagan worship.

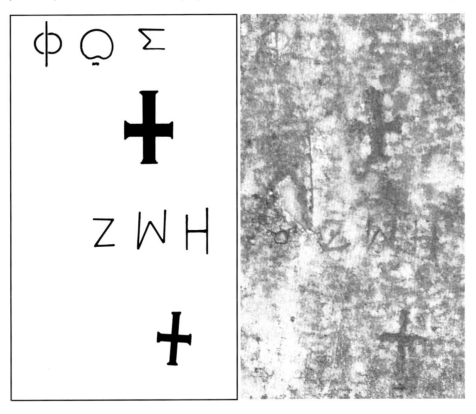

PHILADELPHIA

The Apostle John addressed one of his Seven Letters to the Church at Philadelphia. In his letter he praises the Philadelphian Christians despite their 'limited strength' for keeping up their uncompromising faith and not denying Christ's name and not relapsing under the pressure of the Roman authorities. John accuses the Jews of the city as being the assembly of Satan and says that they will, in the end, recognise Christ. He also warns the faithful that Christ's Second Coming is at hand and that those who follow Christ's example will be rewarded.

Although situated close to Ephesus where Paul spent three years on his third journey Philadelphia is not mentioned in Acts. However, the Christians there may have attended the preaching of the Apostle and have been familiar with him.

The city was visited by Ignatius on his way to Smyrna as he was taken as a prisoner to Rome. In a letter that he wrote to them from Alexandria Troas Ignatius tries to controvert their errors and warns them against the dangers of the tension caused between the circumcised Jewish Christians and the Gentile Christians. He urges unity and obedience to the bishop as the most efficacious remedy. He says that the persecutions in Antioch in Syria (on the Orontes) have ended and suggests the Philadelphians follow the example of other Churches and send a deacon to congratulate the Church there.

The letter of Polycarp's martyrdom to the Church at Philomelium (Akşehir) also mentions the city as one of those where Christians were persecuted by saying 'Including those from Philadelphia, he was the twelfth to meet a martyr's death in Smyrna.'

LAODICEA

The fact that when the Roman proconsul Lucius Valerius Flaccus seized the gold collected there for the Jerusalem Temple in 62 BCE he found that it amounted to more than 200 pounds[1] in weight, shows the existence of Jews in the city at this early date and their wealth. After a few years the local people wrote to Gaiucus Robinus, the proconsul of Asia at the time, that in accordance with his command

---

[1] The story is told in *Pro Flacco* of Cicero who defended the governor as his lawyer when the latter was persecuted in Rome.

they would allow the Jews to follow their customs and regard them as friends. The city was probably an active banking centre, for Cicero informs us that he planned to cash drafts here when he travelled through the region in 51 BCE and administered justice in the city.

Although it is not clear if Paul passed through the region as he travelled 'through the Phrygian and Galatian territory' (Acts 16:6) on his way to Bithynia on his second journey, there is a good chance that he walked through the Lycus (Çürük su) valley on the third journey. Acts (18:23) speaks of his travelling 'through Galatian country and Phrygia,' and 19:1 of his going 'through the interior of the country for reaching Ephesus.' This should very probably be interpreted as a route by way of Apamea (Dinar), Colossae and Laodicea on the Lycus (Eskihisar) to the Aegean coast. Although his words 'and for those in Laodicea and all who have not seen me face to face' (Col 2:1) make it clear that the Colossians had not seen him in the flesh. He may have passed through their cities on one of the journeys or visited during his long stay in Ephesus on the third journey. Paul's words in his letter to the Colossians (Col 4:16) show that this was a circular letter addressed to the Laodiceans as well.

The city is the destination of one of the letters of the Apostle John to the Seven Churches. In this letter John reproves it saying the Church here was neither cold nor hot, but lukewarm; it boasted that it was rich and in need of nothing, not

Sarcophagus from Laodicea. Marble. Second century CE. İzmir Archaeological Museum. Its face bears the busts of its owners in a garland of oak-leaves borne by Nikai and an Eros.

knowing that it was poor, blind and naked; therefore let it buy gold of the risen Christ refined by fire, white garments and salve for the blind eyes (Rv 3:14-22). The letter bears local allusions: Laodicea was rich, famous for its garments. It is not known if the colour of the famous black wool of the region came from dyes or a kind of black sheep. It was woven directly into the shape of garments of the period such as *paragaudae* with purple borders, *chalmydes* or short cloaks, and the *paenulae* (2 Tim 4:13). The last kind was a type of seamless coat only with a hole for the head, woven to resist rain. It would eventually become the ecclesiastical chasuble. The remark that the Church here was to 'buy ointment to smear on your eyes so that you may see' may have been inspired by the famous 'Phrygian powder' for diseases of the eyes which was compounded here. Its water may have been literally lukewarm. The surviving water tower and remains of an aqueduct contain baked clay pipes choked by lime deposits. The water came from the south, first by an aqueduct and then, nearer the city, through stone barrel pipes. It may have come from hot springs and have been cooled down to lukewarmness; but even if it was originally cold, the heat of the sun no doubt warmed it until it was flat and unpalatable.

Eusebius tells of a paschal controversy in Laodicea about 164-66 and about this time its bishop Sagaris, who bore a Phrygian name, was martyred. The synod held in the city in 367, though only a regional council, is highly significant for the history of the New Testament canon and for the development of Church law generally. The council's stringent measures against Montanist (p 171) and Quartodeciman Christians (p 166), and its rules for worship, exhibit the final triumph of orthodox uniformity over local Phrygian peculiarities.

In 380 Laodicea became the meeting place of another Church council. Although it was not ecumenical this council is interesting in the fact that it shows that Judaism was still attractive for Gentile Christians. The canons drawn at the council forbade the observance of the Sabbath and other Jewish practices such as the use of phylacteries and the worship of angels. The last had nothing to do with Judaism but was a Gnostic peculiarity of the region (p 161). It may not be by accident that the Book of Revelation, despite the immense part that angels play in it, contains a similar warning: when John falls down before the angel to worship him, the latter forbids it, saying: 'I am a fellow servant of yours. Worship God' (Rv 22:8-9).

MAGNESIA ON THE MEANDER

Magnesia on the Meander (Menderes Manisası) was named thus to be distinguished from its namesake on the skirts of Mt Sipylus (Manisa dağı, 1517 m) to the north, Magnesia on the Sipylus (Manisa) and a third one in Thessaly. It was famous with its temple of Artemis *Leucophryene,* or 'Whitebrow', who was said to have made herself visible during its construction. The information about the existence of Jews here comes from Josephus. The historian informs us that when the proconsul of Asia, Gaius Rabirius, asked the population of Laodicea, Tralles and Magnesia on the Meander to allow the Jews to keep their own rituals and the Sabbath in the second half of the first century BCE the request was refused by the last two cities.

Like the Church at Ephesus the Magnesian Christians sent a delegation to meet Ignatius at Smyrna, led by their bishop, Damas. In the letter he wrote to the Church at Magnesia from Smyrna Ignatius cautioned them against taking 'advantage of' their bishop's 'lack of years' and inexperience, and stressed the need for ensuring unity by complete obedience to the bishop's authority. Relations between the Jews and Christians of the city may have been strained because in his letter he warns the Christians about the danger of relapse into Judaism. Emphasizing the latter problem he says 'If we are still living in the practice of Judaism, it is an admission that we have failed to receive the gift of grace' and 'To profess Jesus Christ while continuing to follow Jewish customs is an absurdity. The Christian faith does not look to Judaism, but Judaism looks, to Christianity.'[1]

It should be remembered that Judaism and Christianity were not yet completely distinct religions. Many people must still have had a 'dual membership' as late as the time of the Fourth Gospel, when believers in Christ were being excommunicated from the synagogues (Jn 9:22, 34; 16:2).

TRALLES

Ancient literature informs us that the relations between the local people of Tralles and the Jews were not friendly in the first century BCE. Although it is not mentioned in Acts or anywhere else in the early biblical writings, being situated on the main road from central and southern Anatolia to the western coast, Tralles (Aydın) must

[1]The earliest known appearance of the word as a noun in literature.

have had an early Christian community and been familiar to both Paul and John. A tradition even regards Philip the Apostle as the city's first bishop. The inscriptions from Tralles mention one Capitolina, a God-worshipper in the Jewish community who belonged to the highest levels of society.

The Church at Tralles had heard that Ignatius would be passing through Smyrna, and sent its bishop Polybius to greet him. From Smyrna in response to this visit Ignatius sent a letter to the Church at Tralles. In the letter he expressed his customary recommendation that they should respect their bishop as they would Jesus Christ and concentrate on the danger from the adherents of Docetism which claimed that the appearance was an optical illusion and mere semblance.

The story of Polycarp's martyrdom informs us that the high priest (asiarch) of the time was one Philip of Tralles.

Although it does not have anything to do with the development of Christianity, a citizen of Tralles, the architect Anthemius, by building the church of St Sophia (532-7) contributed to a different aspect of the new religion.

Sarcophagus fragment decorated with sacrificial bulls-heads. Marble. Roman period. Aydın Museum.

EDESSA

Although archaeology has shown that the history of Edessa (Urfa), 'the blessed city' does not extend beyond the Seleucid foundation in about 300 BCE, early Christian writers, probably jealous of Haran, so small and insignificant when compared with their city but so often mentioned in the Bible, interpolated some of the biblical stories to the history of their own city. One of the most popular of these has it that Nimrod 'built Edessa, a city of Mesopotamia, after he had migrated from Babylon, and ruled in it, which aforetime had been named Erech' which is Orhay (Edessa). 'Orhay' or its Greek from 'Orrhoe' may have derived from *hurru*, or the cave-dwellers (*Orro*, Greek *Osrhoene*) of the region who constituted the strongest ethnic element in the region in mid-second millennium.

In later Jewish, Moslem and Eastern Christian traditions Nimrod is regarded as an enemy of Abraham and thus once the hero was associated with Edessa it led to the tradition that Abraham also had lived here. Jacob, Jethro, Elijah and Jonah

The pool of 'Halil-ür Rahman', or of the 'Beloved of God' with the sacred carp. The epithet is used by Moslems for Abraham in Edessa (Urfa).

are among the biblical personages who are popularly associated with the city and its environs.

Edessa is known as the first kingdom (about a century before the time of Constantine) that adopted Christianity as its official religion. Early Christian literature mentions the exchange of letters between Jesus and Abgar V Uchama, or 'the Black', king of Edessa (Urfa). The letters which were published in Syriac and in Greek later became talismans. In one version of the story Jesus sent to the king a napkin on which his image was impressed by which Abgar was cured of his sickness. The Apostle Thomas sent Thaddeus (Syriac *Addai*), 'one of the Seventy [-two]' referred to in Luke (10:1), to Edessa where he lodged in the house of Tobias the Jew. According to the tradition Thaddeus was a Jew from Galilee, born at Caesarea Philippi (Paneas) 'where the river Jordan comes out.' Abgar was assured in a dream that this person was the disciple promised by Jesus. Thus Thaddeus cured the king and converting plenty of Abgar's subjects founded the first Church in Edessa. Later Thaddeus was identified with the Apostle Thaddeus (Mt 10:3; Mk 3:18) who is also mentioned in Luke (6:16) as Judas the son of James, one of the Twelve Apostles, because the latter also preached in the East, to the Parthians, Persians and others.

Thaddeus. Wall painting. Mid-tenth century. Karanlık (Dark) church. Göreme Outdoor Museum. Cappadocia.

A form of East Aramaic, known as Syriac, originally the dialect of Edessa, was used for Christian literature between the third and thirteenth century and played a part in the transmission of classical learning to the Arabs. It is still spoken by communities, mainly Christian, in southeastern Anatolia. The Bible may have been translated into this language at Edessa.

The most important personality of Edessa in the fourth century was St Ephraim. He spent his last years in Edessa. Tradition relates that he lived in a cave and earned his living as a bath attendant refusing all offers of positions. He may have taught at the famous school of Edessa and written against heresies of Bardaisan, Marcion, and Mani. He is also credited with the founding of one of the first Christian hospitals in the East. When he died he asked to be buried not with the bishops and the rich, but with the poor.

Edessa also found itself among the religious quarrels which began in the fourth century. The Arians in the city seem to have flourished after Constantine's death.

In the course of time as Edessa grew it usurped the prosperity of Haran. After Haran's sack by the Mongols in 1259 it took the opportunity to tap its water and sealed for ever the fate of its rival downstream.

Abraham in flames. Manuscript painting. Late sixteenth century. *Zübdetü't Tevarih,* the 'Legendary Chronicle of the Prophets' Lives'. Museum of Turkish and Islamic Arts. İstanbul. Outside the flames are Nimrod, a guard, the devil and the catapult used to throw Abraham from the castle. The Moslem tradition has it that when the latter refused to worship idols he was sentenced to death in a fiery furnace. However, this was so hot that no one could approach it. The devil — shown black in the picture — taught Nimrod how this could be achieved and thus Abraham was seated inside a catapult and cast into the fire. Where he fell, unharmed, appeared a pool and the firebrands were turned into sacred carp. The two columns which have survived and are claimed to be those to which the patriarch was tied bear Corinthian capitals.

Holy Cloth. Icon. Eighteenth century. Ayasofya Museum. İstanbul. Christian tradition has it that the first icon was created by Christ himself. This was a portrait which was said to have come into existence without human involvement (*acheiropoietos*) and it cured king Abgar of Edessa from his disease. After a short while the king placed the image above one of the city gates. His great grandson, who was a pagan, wanted to destroy the holy image. However, the bishop of the time made a niche in which it was placed and which was then walled up with a burning lamp inside. The holy image and the still-burning lamp were discovered in the middle of the sixth century CE when Chosroes I, king of Persia, besieged Edessa. The image was intact and it had been imprinted on the inner side of the tile which concealed it. Thus the first icons — on cloth and on tile — were created. The icons of the Holy Cloth commemorate this event, showing the face of Christ represented respectively on a piece of cloth or imprinted on the tile. Tradition has it that the icon was bought in Edessa by Constantine VII Porphyrogenitus (913-59) and Romanus I (920-44) and brought to Constantinople and placed in the church of the Virgin of Pharos in the Great Palace. After the sack of the city by the Latin soldiers of the Fourth Crusade in 1204 the icon was lost. The design on the piece of cloth came to be known in Greek as the *mandylion*, or holy cloth. Sometimes two angels standing on either side of the face and holding the white cloth are added.

The Benediction of the Apostles. Wall painting. Tenth century CE. Tokalı church. Göreme Outdoor Museum. Cappadocia.

CAPPADOCIA

'Are not all the people who are speaking Galileans? Then how does each of us hear them in his own native language? We are Parthians, Medes, and Elamites, inhabitants of Mesopotamia, Judea and Cappadocia, Pontus and Asia, Phrygia and Pamphylia...but we hear them speaking in our own tongues' (Acts 2:7-12).

The quotation from Acts shows that although by the first century CE Greek had become the common language in Anatolia the Cappadocians and other people still spoke their local languages which were not known in Palestine. It also shows that the Anatolian Diaspora Jews including Cappadocian Jews went on pilgrimage to Jerusalem. In the Bible Cappadocia is also mentioned among the five provinces of Anatolia to which Peter's first letter is addressed (1 Pt 1:1). A part of Cappadocia was included in the Roman province of Galatia and in the past some scholars believed that Paul might have thus visited Cappadocia and that when he addressed the Galatians in his letter he also meant Cappadocian Christians. The recent and general opinion is that Paul visited only southern Galatia and his letter concerns just the Christians in this region.

The name of this region is said by some to have derived from the word 'Katpatuka' which was first encountered in the list of the countries who paid tribute to the Persians during the reign of Darius I (522-486 BCE) and is said to have meant 'the Land of Beautiful Horses'. The elder Pliny, however, in his *Natural History* shows the river Cappadox (Delice), a tributary of the Halys (Kızılırmak), as the origin of the name. Ancient literary sources refer to the inhabitants of the region as Syrians and sometimes as White Syrians, *Leukosyriai,* to distinguish them from those who live to the south of the Taurus chain.

The origin of Christianity in the region is not known. Although according to the tradition the 'Apostle of Armenia', Gregory the Illuminator (240-326), was brought up a Christian while an exile in Cappadocia and on his return to Armenia succeeded in converting king Tiridates (238-314), Cappadocia is not mentioned in early Christian writings and there is no archaeological evidence related to Christianity

Basil the Great. Wall painting. 1315-21.
Kariye Museum (former church of the
monastery of St Saviour in Chora).
İstanbul.

going back this far. Research has shown that most of the known churches of the
region rose as rural martyriums where the martyr's anniversary of execution would
have been celebrated mostly during the Decian persecutions in 250 and after.

Cappadocia, which until then produced just horses and slaves, became the home
of some prominent bishops who carried the flag of the Nicene Creed and played
a very important role in the formation of today's Christianity. These are Basil the
Great, Gregory of Nyssa[1] and Gregory of Nazianzus[2] known as the Cappadocian
Fathers. Their social and educational background made them leaders of the time
and they organized the monastic movement in Cappadocia.

Saint Basil the Great

Basil (330-79) and Gregory (340-94), brothers, were born into a wealthy and
influential Christian family from the Pontic region. Basil was educated at Caesarea
in Cappadocia, Constantinople and Athens both in pagan and Christian culture.
He chose the ascetic life and began to live as a hermit by the river Iris (Yeşilırmak)
near Neocaesarea (Niksar) and devoted himself to according to the austere Rule
which he drew up, founding a monastic community. In his Rule he tried to stop the
orthodox monks from becoming indifferent to the calls of secular society and
civilization by the ascetic life which they led, as disapproved of by the synod of
Gangra (Çankırı) in 340 CE, saying 'If you always live alone, whose feet will you
wash?' In 364 at the behest of his bishop Eusebius of Caesarea (Palestine) he left
his retirement to defend Orthodoxy against Arianism. In 370 he was elected the
bishop of Caesarea (Kayseri) and held this office for the rest of his life. Shortly after
taking his seat he was visited by the Arian emperor Valens who unsuccessfully tried
to force him to support Arianism. His ecclesiastical career was largely devoted to
the defence of the Christian creed as formulated at the Council of Nicaea (325)
against the Arian heresy which formally came to an end at the Council of
Constantinople in 381, shortly after Basil's death. In addition to his missionary and literary

[1] Thought to have been located somewhere between Archelais (Aksaray) and Tyana
(Kemerhisar).

[2] Nenezi village near Aksaray.

(previous page) The Call of the First
Disciples. Simon (Peter) and Andrew and
James and John. Tenth century CE. Tokalı
church. Göreme Outdoor Museum.
Cappadocia.

Gregory of Nazianzus. Wall painting.
1315-21. Kariye Museum (former church
of the monastery of St Saviour in Chora).
İstanbul.

works he is known to have established hospitals and hostels for the poor. Among
his works *Longer and Shorter Rules* written for the conduct of monastic life still
constitutes the basis of the Rule followed in the Eastern Church. Although strict,
Basil's Rule avoided the extreme austerities of the hermits of the deserts and regarded
asceticism as a means to the perfect service of God, to be achieved in community
life under obedience.

Saint Gregory of Nyssa

Gregory (340-394) was the brother of Basil the Great and the bishop of Nyssa.
Little is known about his life. In 371 he was consecrated bishop of Nyssa by his
brother. Their father was converted by a group of bishops who were travelling
through the region to attend the Council of Nicaea (325). After a few years the
father became the first bishop of Nyssa. Gregory was one of the key figures at the
First Council of Constantinople (381) and known as an eloquent preacher on state
occasions in the capital. He was however more of a scholar than a man of action.
Some of his works have survived.

Saint Gregory of Nazianzus

Gregory of Nazianzus (330-389) was educated in Caesarea in Palestine,
Alexandria and Athens where he became a friend of Basil the Great. He preferred
the seclusion of a monastery in Isauria to the bishopric nominated to him. After the
death of the emperor Valens, who had favoured the Arians, Gregory became the
champion of the Nicene Creed and took his place at the First Council of
Constantinople (381). He is known to have spent the rest of his life in rural retirement
with study. He is recognized as one of the foremost interpreters of the theology of
the Trinity as it had first been formulated at the Council of Nicaea in 325. In his
writings he mentions a visit to the pilgrimage site of St Thecla near Seleucia on the
Calycadnus (Silifke).

ECUMENICAL COUNCILS

Christianity, which began as an obscure sect in Judea, survived and shaking off its Judaistic roots developed in the cosmopolitan world of Greco-Roman pagan cults. As it followed its natural path various sorts of local Christianity factions such as Donatists, Novatians, Paulinists, Marcionites, Docetists, Montanists, Meletians and Arians and many others emerged. While some of these disappeared without becoming widespread heresies some shook Christianity at its roots. The dissensions which were part of the latter group rose from the concept of worshipping a being who was also a man, a concept which had become more complex by the addition of the third divine element, the Holy Spirit.

By the reign of Constantine the Great (324-37, sole ruler) it had become possible to summon general councils which were called ecumenical[1] to find answers to such questions. It was believed that if all the bishops came together the Holy Spirit would descend and guide their decisions. The number and sort of participants and the decisions of these meetings, however, would often be decided by the politics of the period, being manipulated by the emperor.

There were seven such councils before the disagreements between Latin (Western) and Greek (Eastern) Christians prevented the holding of any more councils recognized by the whole Church. Except the last one which dealt with Iconoclasm the main topic of the councils was to answer the questions about the Person of Jesus or the Holy Spirit or to reassert the already defined dogma against heretical views such as Arianism, Monophysitism, and alike. However, in addition to such major questions, regulations about Church discipline were also made. Apart from these councils there were some which the Roman Church regards as ecumenical, because the Roman Church believes itself to be the one legitimate Christian communion in the whole world; but these later councils were not attended by the representatives of the Greek Orthodox Churches, and are not regarded by those Churches, nor by the Anglican Church, as having been really ecumenical.

[1] Greek *oekumene*, or 'inhabited world'.

Gravestone installed in the wall of the caravanserai of Kadınhan on the ancient road from near Laodicea Catacecaumene (Ladik) to Iconium (Konya). It belongs to Abras, priest of Novatians. The Novatians were against the swift re-admittance of the apostatized Christians into the Church. In a particular edict, Constantine the Great exempted the Novatians from the penalties of heresy.

First Council of Nicaea (325)

The doctrine about the Person of Jesus had troubled both the common believer and the theologian from the very beginning of Christianity but had not surfaced until the time of Constantine. A quarrel which began between a Libyan priest called Arius and Alexander, bishop of Alexandria, about the true doctrine of the Person of Jesus turned into a sharp dissension and split the clergy into two major antagonistic parties. Arius claimed that there was only one Person, God the Father, not three distinct, equal and co-eternal Persons in God. The Son was not exactly of the same nature as the Father and therefore was not equal with the Father and had to be subordinate. Jesus was the Son in that he was the highest of created things, a sort of demigod created for the salvation of the world. He had a human body but not a human nature. Nevertheless his unhuman nature was not equal to God. Arius' opponents, however, held that God and the Son were 'of the same substance,' or *homoousios.*

For Constantine to hear news of such dissension at the time he saw the new faith as a weapon to achieve unity in his empire was frustrating. This was not the first time that the peace of his empire was suffering from a heresy because it had already been disturbed by the Donatists[1] of North Africa as early as 313. However, that was a regional heresy and it did concern Egypt which was the major grain supplier of Byzantium, or New Rome (Nova Roma). He was also unable to comprehend why the Christians argued about something which is not mentioned in the Gospels and which happened in the past. The news from Egypt was so disturbing that while he was on his way there he cancelled the rest of his trip at Antioch on the Orontes and returned to Nicomedia. He decided to call a council of all bishops at Ancyra (Ankara) because it could be reached by the two halves of his empire easily, after Easter 325. However, later he decided to transfer the council to Nicaea (İznik), where he could attend in person and control the proceedings.

The Council of Nicaea was regarded as the First Ecumenical Council because of the large number of representatives who attended it. To achieve this the participants' expenses were met by the State and they made use of the State transportation service freely. However, with the exception of a few bishops who had come from the Latin West, all of the participants were Greek bishops and mostly from the Churches from the eastern half of the empire. Gregory of Nyssa and Jacob (James) of Nisibis (Nusaybin) were two of the participants. Later Christian tradition added some important bishops, such us Nicholas of Myra, to the list.

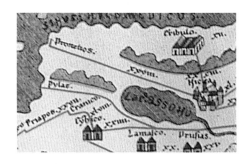

Nicaea and the lake Ascania. From *Tabula Peutingeriana* (Peutinger map). Third-fourth centuries CE.

[1] An uncompromising Christian sect which rejected the authority of Rome. Constantine, being unable to settle the heresy, abandoned the Donatists to God's judgement.

Underground tomb chamber near İznik. Fourth century CE. Originally a flower basket stood between the peacocks, the bird which in antiquity symbolized immortality because its flesh is thought not to decay. The disc bore a christogram.

The meetings began at the imperial palace by lake Ascania (İznik) on 20 May 325 with Constantine's opening address urging the bishops to achieve unity and peace. The victory over the Arian heresy was achieved by the intervention of Constantine. The creed agreed upon by the emperor and important bishops and proposed for adoption at the council was sharply anti-Arian; affirming that the Son is 'of the same substance' with the Father. Its wording, however, could be interpreted by the Arians in their way. Although the number of participants may have been between 220 and 250, traditionally 318[2] out of 320 bishops signed the creed.

[2] In early Christianity the symbolic 318 fathers who participated in the council were frequently invoked. The number, being the total of prime numbers from 7 to 7^2 is thought to have gained a special significance in history from the fact that in Genesis (14:14) Abraham 'mustered three hundred and eighteen of his retainers' to rescue Lot. The number may have had a wider use in the ancient Near East; for example when Taduhepa, the daughter of Tusratta, king of Mitanni journeys to Egypt to marry Amenophis III (1390-1352 BCE) she is accompanied by 317 maids (plus herself).

The opposition came from the two Libyan bishops who were concerned not with the main issue but with a canon which subjected them to the control of Alexandria. Nevertheless, they were condemned and exiled like Arius who was present as an observer at the council. This was the first time that Christians persecuted one another for differences in faith. The meetings ended with a brilliant banquet. During the sessions and afterwards, until his death in 373, the flag of the Nicene cause would be carried by Athanasius who had left his desert hermitage to fight for the cause of orthodoxy, who accompanied bishop Alexander at the council as a deacon and stood by him. It would, however, take several centuries for Arianism to disappear completely. Arius is claimed by his enemies to have died in a lavatory in Constantinople where his bowels burst — thought to be caused by poison — but an end that his enemies regarded as the revenge of God.

The council also discussed some matters of discipline in the Church. Until then while the West and Alexandria held Easter on a Sunday, the other Churches in the East calculated it according to the Jewish calendar. It was decided that Easter should be celebrated always on a Sunday and never on the same day as a Jewish festival. The council also confirmed the special authority of the bishop of Antioch over Syria and that of Alexandria over all of Egypt. The Churches of Antioch and Alexandria, by virtue of the Apostolic foundation that they could claim, were to be allowed to exercise greater rights than other Churches.

The First Ecumenical Council did not achieve unity in the Church but prevented problems from being voiced openly, at least until the death of Constantine. Despite all the efforts of Constantine the results of the First Ecumenical Council of 325 disappointed him. Gregory of Nyssa (340-94) summarized the situation in the capital as follows:

'If you ask a man for change, he will give you a piece of philosophy concerning the Begotten and the Unbegotten; if you enquire the price of a loaf, he replies: 'The Father is greater and the Son inferior'; or if you ask whether the bath is ready, the answer you receive is that the Son was made out of nothing.'

The problems surfaced immediately during the reign of his successor. The pro-Arian sentiments and policy of Constantine's son and successor Constantius I (337-61) alienated the Orthodox Christians and by the 60s a new (semi-Arian) formula, which asserted that the Son's essence is 'like' the Father's, or *homoiousios*, was developed in Antioch and seemed to bear the closest resemblance to the Nicene

Creed. The emperor decided that the Nicene Creed was the major cause of disputes and the vague formula of 'likeness' was more suitable to achieve a compromise, a hope which proved to be too optimistic.

His successor Julian (the Apostate) (361-63) tried to revive paganism and hoped that the different factions in Christianity would continue to fight and consume one another. He regarded Christianity as apostasy from Judaism and planned to rebuild the Jerusalem Temple which was destroyed by Titus in 70 CE. Christians regarded the end of sacrificial worship and fall of Jerusalem as the end of Judaism. During his Persian expedition, Julian decided to build the Temple at his own expense and from Antioch sent his friend Alypius to supervise the rebuilding. The work, however, was interrupted and abandoned. Ancient literature mentions disasters such as balls of fire bursting from underneath the foundation or fire falling from heaven on the construction and the workers.

While some of the emperors after Julian were pro-Arian or Arian, some were opposed. Christians suffered severe persecutions during the reign of rulers of the opposing belief. At the end if the Orthodox cause won this battle it was more because of the fact that Christians had been worshipping Christ as God since the beginning of Christianity, rather than the efforts of Orthodox clergy or emperors.

Orthodox Christians escaping from the Arians during the reign of the Arian successor of Constantine the Great. Manuscript illumination. The Homilies of St Gregory of Nazianzus. 880-86. Bibliothèque Nationale. Paris.

Theodosius I, the Great, who brought an end to the heresies, greets St Gregory of Nazianzus, the leader of the triumphant orthodox cause. Manuscript illumination. The Homilies of St Gregory of Nazianzus. 880-86. Bibliothèque Nationale. Paris.

First Council of Constantinople (381)

Although the First Council of Nicaea had condemned the Arian belief and reasserted the dogma that the Father and the Son were of the same substance, some theologians believed that the Holy Spirit, the third Person of the Trinity, differed in substance from the other two Persons, being a kind of 'creature' of the second Person. This heresy was called Macedonianism.

In May 381 a second ecumenical council was summoned by Theodosius I (378-95) to meet in Constantinople in the church of St Irene to define the nature of the Holy Spirit. He had recognized Christianity as the official religion of his empire a year before. The emperor had done his homework carefully and already instructed the Churches that the object of the council would be the reconfirmation of the Nicene Creed. This time no representatives came from Rome. The council reaffirmed the Nicene faith in the sense that it reasserted the keywords 'of the same substance', or *homoousios* and that the Holy Spirit was of the same substance with the Father and the Son. This council brought an end to Arianism, which had already been split into smaller dissensions, within the empire. It continued on among the Goths,

Cyril of Alexandria. Wall painting. 1315-21. Kariye Museum (former church of the monastery of St Saviour in Chora). İstanbul.

who were converted among many other Arian missionaries by Ulfila (311-83), translator of the Gothic Bible, and among Vandals and Lombards.

The most important decision which concerned the Church hierarchy was that — to the vexation of Alexandria— 'the bishop of Constantinople should have rank after the bishop of Rome because it is New Rome.' Thus Constantinople replaced Alexandria which until then had held the second place after Rome and also moved above Antioch and Jerusalem.

Council of Ephesus (431)

Another question which disturbed the Church during the last quarter of the fourth century concerned the interpretation of the relation between the divine and human natures of Christ. The First Council of Nicaea (325) had declared that 'Christ is truly God' against Arius and everybody had agreed with this statement. In the First Council of Constantinople (381) while this clause was repeated, an already accepted dogma that 'Christ is truly man' was added on behalf of Anatolia and Syria and it bore an emphasis on the humanity of Christ.

By the beginning of the fifth century the definition that Christ was both God and man or 'wholly God and wholly man' began to raise some questions. Did Christ have a split personality or if not, was he two persons? This question became the seed of a bitter quarrel between Alexandria and Antioch. Although none of these theological schools opposed Christ's oneness, in accordance with the religious background of their theological school, they were indispensably compelled to weaken one nature of Christ for the benefit of the other.

The Alexandrian school, led by the patriarch Cyril, with its deep belief in the redemption, emphasized Christ's divine nature. The school of Antioch, without dispossessing Christ's redemptive power, saw him as the ideal human and Christian model of man and thus stressed his human nature. The founder of Antiochene theology was Theodore of Mopsuestia (Misis near Adana). Nevertheless when events took a irreversible turn his flag was held by Nestorius. The latter was born in Germanicia (Maraş) and except that he was a monk and a frequent speaker at Antioch's cathedral, not much is known about his life. In 428 Nestorius was appointed patriarch of Constantinople.

Nestorius believed and preached that Christ had two distinct natures, one human and the other divine. Otherwise one could not speak of God as 'a baby two or three months old.' Also by the third century the application of the epithet 'Mother of God', or *Theotokos* to the Virgin had become common especially in the eastern lands of the empire and spread to Constantinople and the West. In Antioch the epithet was not used popularly and for a member of the Antiochene theological school, which defended the complete humanity of Jesus, it suggested that the divine nature was born of a woman, which was disturbing. In the capital Nestorius bringing together those who called the Virgin Mary 'Mother of God'[1] or 'Mother of man' suggested that she should be called 'Mother of Christ,'[2] a term which represented both God and man, as used in the Gospels. Shortly after these sermons Nestorius found himself accused of heresy by Cyril of Alexandria.

The dispute over theology however had also deep political undertones because Cyril was convinced of the superiority of his Apostolic see of Alexandria over the Church of Constantinople, which was the most recent among the major sees. To this the long-standing theological rivalry between Antioch and Alexandria must be added. In 429 Cyril denounced Nestorius for heresy and accused him of denying the deity of Christ and thus appealed to the emotions of the orthodox Christians. In 431 Thedosius II had to summon a council in Ephesus to find a solution to this problem.

The meeting began at the church of the Virgin Mary whose ruins have survived to the present. Cyril assumed the presidency and accused Nestorius of teaching that Christ was merely an inspired man. Cyril's agents had spread the news that the reason why Nestorius disliked the title 'Mother of God' was that he did not believe that Jesus was God. Cyril and his party, without waiting for the arrival of John the patriarch of Antioch, who sided with Nestorius, declared the latter a heretic and excommunicated him. Rome supported the decision. The patriarch of Antioch upon arriving at Ephesus held another council and excommunicated Cyril. Theodosius II, although favouring Nestorius, was compelled to depose both leaders. Cyril, however, bribing his way out of prison with his Church's money returned to

---

[1] Greek *Theotokos*, or 'Godbearing'.

[2] Greek *Chrestotokos*, or 'Christbearing'.

Alexandria. Nestorius was exiled to his monastery near Antioch, then in 435 to Petra and a few years later to the Libyan desert where he died in 450.

After a short while the Alexandrians began to be called Monophysites.[3] The followers of Nestorius were identified first with the word Duophysites[4] and later Nestorians. The moderate theologians and politicians of the period attempted to bring together the Alexandrian and Antiochene schools. Cyril of Alexandria and John, patriarch of Antioch, under pressure from the capital established a pretentious truce. This peace did not last long but fell apart as soon as new bishops took the place of the old ones; for John died in 442 and Cyril in 444. In order to establish a peace between the Churches of Antioch and Alexandria only two years after the council Cyril had declared a formula of re-union which also agreed with the Antiochene theology. Not to offend his previous supporters he accepted the phrase 'union of two natures', which became 'one nature after the union.' For a time each party had to seem to consent to the situation even if under strain. In 449 Theodosius II was compelled to call another meeting at Ephesus. This time it ended up with the confirmation of the Monophysite cause. This meeting was referred to by Pope Leo I, the Great, as a 'den of robbers,' *latrocinium*, and thus was known as the 'Council of Robbers.'

Nestorianism, nevertheless, found fertile soil outside the empire. As early as the sixth century there were 'Syrian Christians' or 'Assyrians' in lands as far apart as India, central Asia and China. The Church of the East was popularly called the Nestorian Church even though its teaching has never been Nestorianism. They established a theological school at Nisibis (Nusaybin) and a patriarchate at Seleucia-Ctesiphon on the Tigris. They were protected by the Persian kings who were the enemy of the Byzantines. In the course of time while some of them turned to the Roman Church some turned to the Monophysite doctrine which was the opposite of Nestorianism. At present a limited number of Nestorian Christians live in Iraq and neighbouring lands.

By the end of the fourth century Christianity was divided into three main Churches: the Church of the West (Rome and Constantinople), the Church of the East (Persia) and the Church of Africa (Egypt and Ethiopia).

[3] Greek *mono*, 'one' and *physis*, 'nature'.

[4] Greek *duo*, 'two', and *physis*, 'nature'.

Council of Chalcedon (451)

Although Pope Leo I, the Great, asked Theodosius II to summon a council for the definition of the orthodox doctrine once more, to bring an end to the ecclesiastical chaos, his request was refused. Shortly after Theodosius' death his sister Pulcheria, marrying a senator and veteran soldier Marcian (450-57), became empress and in accordance with the Pope's wish summoned a great council at the church of St Euphemia[1] in Chalcedon. The participancy of some six hundred bishops at this council shows the extent of the displeasure that the Robbers Council had created in the eastern provinces. This was the greatest of the seven ecumenical councils, and in importance second to only the First Council of Nicaea. The council reconfirmed that Christ was a single person with two natures, one divine and one human. However, it was unable to define the relationship between the two natures which was the cause of the controversy. Thus both Nestorianism, which overstressed the human element in Christ, and Monophysitism, which overemphasized the divine at the expense of the human nature of Christ, were condemned. The result did not satisfy either Alexandria or Antioch.

Among the other decisions taken at the council — when the Roman delegates were absent — was the elevation of Constantinople to the level of Rome: 'The See of Constantinople shall enjoy equal privileges with the See of Old Rome.' This left Rome nothing but titular supremacy. In other words while the bishop of Rome might enjoy a primacy of honour in the Church universal, the bishop of Constantinople, the evident capital of what was left of the Roman empire, became his equal in authority. This canon known as 'Canon Twenty-Eight' was strongly objected to by Rome and became one of the steps which ultimately led to the separation of the Churches of the East and West in 1054. The new position given to the church of Constantinople, combined with national and political factors, also alienated Egypt, Syria and Palestine from the empire.

Shortly after the council the Egyptian Monophysites elected their own patriarch in Alexandria, separate from the one assigned to the port by the capital, and took the first step for the foundation of the Egyptian Church which would be known as the Coptic[2] Church. When the Moslem armies who believed in the single Person of Allah arrived in the seventh century, the Coptic Church readily submitted to them.

Constantinople and Chalcedon. From *Tabula Peutingeriana* (Peutinger map). Third-fourth centuries CE. The city is identified with the Column of Constantine ('Çemberlitaş') carrying his statute and the statue of Zeus of Olympia, one of the Seven Wonders of the World which he had brought to his capital. Across the Bosphorus is Chalcedon.

[1] Named after a virgin who was martyred in 303.

[2] Greek *coptic*, or 'Egyptian'.

Second Council of Constantinople (553)

During the following period while some Christian theologians sought new formulas to bring the Monophysite East (Egypt, Syria and Palestine) into the body of the Church, the quarrels and fights between the Chalcedonians and the Monophysites continued. Until Justinian came to the throne in 527 most of the Byzantine emperors were tolerant to the Monophysites and this alienated the Western Church.

The reign of Justinian (527-65) was marked with conquests both in the east and west. In the capital he had built the church of St Sophia which is still one of the oldest and greatest edifices of the Christian world. Nor could the teaching of pagan Greek philosophy be tolerated, except in Christian institutions. In 529 he commanded that the Platonic Academy in Athens be closed forever. He wanted to recover the West for which the acceptance of the Chalcedon cause was indispensable. As a Christian Roman emperor and vice-regent of God on earth he felt duty bound to enforce uniformity of belief on his subjects and to unite Church and State firmly under his control. Heresy, especially that of the Monophysites was to be stamped out. However, dealing harshly with Egypt would harm the corn traffic to his capital.

The Monophysites were not happy with the previous Council of Chalcedon (451) because of the fact that although it had reaffirmed the orthodox definition it had acquitted the three major Nestorians of the time whose works were most objectionable to the Monophysites. They asked for another council which, as it would reassert the Chalcedonian definition, would condemn the propositions or 'chapters'[1] written by these three theologians: Theodore of Mopsuestia (Misis), Theodoret of Cyrrhus (in Syria) and Ibas of Edessa (Urfa). The council summoned in Constantinople met in the church of St Sophia. Justinian stayed away from the meeting. The letters he sent to the participants however (only two dozen of 168 participants were from the West or Africa) told them what he hoped to hear. The meeting ended with the expected decision and acknowledged the errors in the writings of these three theologians and said that it was not proper to anathematize the dead. The result failed to placate the Monophysites.

This result did not add anything new to the problems between the Chalcedonians and Monophysites. The latter created an underground episcopate which has lasted to the present day among the Syrian Jacobites, Copts and Ethiopians who reject Chalcedon.

[1] After which the problem was named the 'three chapters controversy'.

The emperor Heraclius carrying the True Cross. Manuscript painting. Detail. Fifteenth-century CE copy of William of Tyre's *History of the Crusades*. British Library. London. He is said to have carried it along the *Via Dolorosa* to the church of the Holy Sepulchre which he had restored.

Third Council of Constantinople (680-1)

Heraclius[1] (610-41) took over an empire which had been losing ground against its enemies in the north (the Avars and Slavs) and in the east (the Sassanians who would soon be supplanted by the Saracens). He worried that the Monophysite Christians who were isolated from the Western Church might join the eastern enemies of the Byzantine empire and to find a solution to the disputes between the antagonistic groups he summoned the Sixth Ecumenical Council. The previous compromise formulas defining the nature of Christ were condemned and the doctrines of the Council of Chalcedon (451) were accepted as truth. To bring peace to the Church, a new formula which skirted the question of natures by claiming that while Christ had 'two natures,' as confirmed at Chalcedon he had only a 'single will', was proposed by the efforts of the emperor Heraclius shortly before his death. Although this proposal was accepted by the East, Rome opposed it and consequently it did not achieve the unity that Heraclius had expected.

However, the claim was found inconsistent with the reality of Jesus' human nature and to settle the 'Monothelete' doctrine, also called Monotheleotism[2] Constantine IV (668-85) summoned the Third Council of Constantinople. The meetings were held in the *Trullos*, or the 'Domed Hall' of the Great Palace and at the end the doctrine of the 'single will' was condemned and the Chalcedonian faith affirmed.

[1] His most famous feat was the defeat of the Sassanians and the replacing of the Holy Cross in the church of the Holy Sepulchre at Jerusalem in 630. It was carried away by the Sassanians in 614.

[2] Greek *mono*, 'one', *thelein*, 'to will.'

Second Council of Nicaea (787)

The Second Council of Nicaea was prompted not by a doctrine about the nature of Jesus but by the iconoclastic controversy. It is the seventh and the last of the councils which were recognized by both the Catholic and Orthodox Churches.

This controversy began in the eighth century and gained strength in the eastern lands of the empire. Was it right to make painted or sculptured representations of Jesus and the saints, and direct homage to such images? The defenders of image-worship claimed that if Jesus was really a man, it was logical that he could be representad in visible form. When the Jews had been forbidden to make images of God, the reason given (Dt 4:12) had been that they 'saw no form ' of God. In Jesus, however, God had shown Himself in visible form, and therefore if the making of images was wrong, this was denying the Incarnation. The Monophysite East thought that the humanity of Christ was inseparable from his divinity and the effort to represent the *aleptos,* or incomprehensible, was useless. The drawing of Jesus' image was trying to separate his humanity from the divinity.

Ayasofya Museum (former church of St Sophia). İznik. The church was the site of the Second Council of Nicaea. The ruin in the picture dates from about 750.

The conflict over images remained as a doctrinal argument until in 726 Leo III (717-41), known as the 'Isaurian' (from Germanicia, Maraş) enforced Iconoclasm. The reason for his attack on images is not clear. He may have wanted to insure the support of his army which was mostly recruited from Anatolia where iconoclastic belief was strong, influenced by Judaism and Islam. His edict enforced the removal of all the icons from churches. The controversy which he began lasted for over a hundred years and contributed to the alienation of the Byzantine Church from that of Rome. The iconoclastic policy of the State continued through the reigns of his successors Constantine V (741-45) and Leo IV (775-80).

The destruction of images, *eikons,* lasted until the succession of Irene (780-97) upon her husband's death, as regent for her infant son Constantine VI. Irene was a zealous iconodule and wanted to restore the holy images. However, much of the army was still iconoclast and she moved with caution. She decided to summon a second council in Nicaea. It was held in the church of St Sophia, whose restored ruins still survive. Among other things this council declared that icons deserved reverence (Greek *proskynesis*) but not adoration (Greek *latreia*) which was due to God alone and condemned the iconoclasts. This statement was confirmed by Pope Adrian I, but partly because of an incompetent translation it was not acceptable generally in the West. For instance, the two words, *proskynesis* and *latreia*, were equated in translation so it appeared that the council ordered Christians to worship icons in the same way they worshipped God. With this council the division between Rome and Constantinople, which had been stimulated by the Fourth Ecumenical Council in Chalcedon (451) became complete, the Roman Catholic Church and the Eastern Orthodox Church each going its own way.

The political and economic failures of Irene and her successors caused a reaction in favour of iconoclasm again from 814 until 843. The iconophile cause was meanwhile being maintained by the monks of the monastery of Studios at Constantinople under their abbot Theodore (759-826). The empress Theodora, who ruled as regent for Michael III, after the death of her iconoclast husband Theophilos (829-42) summoned a council in Constantinople, which reaffirmed the rulings of the Seventh Ecumenical Council of 787 and on the first Sunday in Lent 843 restored the icons for the last time with a procession in St Sophia that has come to be known as 'the Triumph of Orthodoxy.' Although not popular with the multitude the iconoclast emperors were successful soldiers and without them the life of the Byzantine empire might have been shorter.

Abbreviations of the books of the Bible used in this volume

Acts	Acts of the Apostles	Is	Isaiah	Na	Nahum
Am	Amos	Jdt	Judith	Nhm	Nehemia
1 Chr	1 Chronicles	Jer	Jeremiah	Nm	Numbers
2 Chr	2 Chronicles	Jgs	Judges	Ob	Obadiah
Col	Colossians	Jl	Joel	1 Sm	1 Samuel
1 Cor	1 Corinthians	Jn	John	2 Sm	2 Samuel
2 Cor	2 Corinthians	Jon	Jonah	Phlm	Philemon
Dn	Daniel	Jos	Joshua	Ps	Psalms
Dt	Deuteronomy	1 Kgs	1 Kings	1 Pt	1 Peter
Est	Esther	2 Kgs	2 Kings	Rom	Romans
Ez	Ezekiel	Lk	Luke	Rv	Revelation
Ezr	Ezra	Lv	Leviticus	Sg	Songs
Ex	Exodus	1 Mac	1 Maccabees	Tb	Tobit
Gal	Galatians	2 Mac	2 Maccabees	Ti	Titus
Gn	Genesis	Mi	Micah	2 Tm	2 Timothy
Heb	Hebrews	Mt	Matthew	Zec	Zechariah

Other abbreviations

AV	Authorised Version (King James' Bible)	d	death
BCE	Before Common Era (the equivalent of Before Christ, BC)	p	page
CE	Common Era (the equivalent of anno Domini, AD)	St	Saint

All biblical spellings and quotations are from the New American Bible,
1987 Nashville, USA. The spelling and reigns of the Near Eastern rulers are from
'Who's Who in the Ancient Near East', 1999, New York. The dates of rulers such as Solomon
(961-920 BCE), indicate their reigns. When there is no danger of confusion the suffix BCE or CE is omitted.

Marble cross from the baptistry of
the church of the Virgin Mary at Ephesus.